CRAFTED BY
GOD

Examining the
DIVINE DESIGN *of the* BIBLE
as a LIVING BOOK

DAN HAYDEN

A WORD FROM THE WORD
Orlando, Florida

Dedicated to
HOWARD HENDRICKS, beloved "Prof"

With great appreciation for your profound influence
on my life and ministry:

As a *teacher*, you instilled in me
a passion to learn.

As a *motivator*, you encouraged me
to go beyond my perceived limitations.

As a *communicator*, you enthralled and inspired me
with the wonders of God's Word.

As a *creative thinker*, you taught me
how to observe beyond the obvious.

As a *spiritual leader* and man of God
the example of your life became the
the aspiration of my heart.

To a large extent, you are the human inspiration
behind what is written in this book.

Along with hundreds of your other students
I praise God for you with a deep sense of gratitude.

CONTENTS

PART 1
THE BODY OF ESSENTIAL TRUTH

PART 2
REACHING THE WORLD

ACKNOWLEDGMENTS

J udy Van Kampen and Scott Pierre — I can only begin to express my deep appreciation for believing in me and supporting this endeavor. The book could have never been realized without your gracious investment of interest and resources. I am greatly indebted to you both.

Evelyn Bence — Looking for an editor was easy. It had to be Evelyn (at least, that was my hope), editor of my earlier book Did God Write the Bible? (Crossway Books, 2007). When you agreed to edit this book as well, I was overjoyed. Your technical ability, in conjunction with your perceptive analysis of subject-flow, has made this book so much better than it would have been. My most sincere thanks!

Artist, Michael Rogers — A special thanks to my friend, artist Tom Allen, for introducing me to Michael Rogers, the gifted artist of this book who took my complex ideas and turned them into magnificent picture-illustrations. Thank you, Michael, for clarifying the physical analogies in this book. You both have blessed my life.

Graphic Artist, Beth Thomas — Your creative designs have graced the covers of countless CD and DVD albums on my web site, www.awordfrom theword.org. Superlative accolades are insufficient to express my appreciation for your talent. I could not be more pleased with your inspired work. Thank you especially for this cover design for Crafted by God.

Somersault Group — These days finding a publisher can certainly be a challenge. My heartfelt thanks to the Somersault Group (Grand Rapids, MI), for your willingness to engage this project in spite of my relative anonymity. A special thanks to John Topliff for your expert guidance and to Beth Shagene for your amazing abilities in interior design. Thanks to all of Somersault Group — consummate professionals in the publishing world. It has been a pleasure to work with you.

And finally, to my beloved wife, Karilee, goes the exclamation point of my gratitude. For many years we have shared the dream of presenting this study to the people of God. This book has literally been a team effort: your encouragement and partnership have been invaluable. Your executive and production skills have made me look better than I am. God has used your inspirational love to propel me beyond myself. With all of my heart—thank you, Hon!

My deepest appreciation must go to *Jesus Christ, my Lord and Savior.* This work is about Your Word—not mine. As the moon reflects the light of the sun, I can only hope that *Crafted by God* reflects the glory of who You are and what You have done.

CHAPTER ONE

A SURPRISING MOSAIC

I thought they were going to string me up by my toes. A beautiful picture of interlocking pieces lay on the table as the puzzle neared completion. But one piece was missing, and it was not to be found anywhere ... under the table ... tucked in the chair cushion ... blending in with the color of the rug. The search was in vain.

My dramatic moment had arrived. As my family had started the puzzle, dumping the pieces out of the box, I had stealthily slipped one into my pocket so that I could triumphantly produce the final piece and press it into place. (It wasn't the smartest thing I ever did.) Whew! The reaction of the family could be compared to a tornado ... (or maybe a third-world political revolution).

In the end, the final mosaic of the puzzle pieces looked great. But I learned my lesson, and I've never done that again. I don't ever want to encourage another family near-lynching.

GRASPING THE CONCEPT OF DESIGN

Working a puzzle can be fun. The objective is to get each piece into its right place so that the final picture can be enjoyed. Mosaics are like that.

Each piece in the system may have striking coloration and form, but only when it is in concert with the full spectrum of other pieces does it prompt a "wow." A holistic view of the completed picture is even more spectacular than an atomistic examination of individual parts.

As an analogy, this describes the book we call the Bible. Sixty-six separate books are masterfully interlocked into an artistic mosaic that is truly profound. True, each book is a wonder to behold. But when observed in its natural groupings, such as the Pentateuch or the Gospels, each book in turn contributes to a much larger picture of divine truth.

Think, for instance, how intelligent design in the universe has taken the scientific world by surprise. Evolutionists thought origins came by random chance. But the more they have delved into the wonders of God's creation, the more their discoveries have backed them into a corner of reluctant admission. In the complex systems of the universe, whether macroastronomy or microbiology, everything fits. Design is everywhere.

Such is the wonder of God's Word—and it takes us by surprise. Nothing emerges by random chance. From Genesis to Revelation, Old and New Testaments alike, intelligent design is an inescapable conclusion. Considering its forty different authors with life spans covering more than fifteen hundred years, writing from diverse cultural backgrounds in three languages, the harmony and unity woven into the biblical text is astounding. Marvelous symmetry and design are everywhere, producing a powerful argument that the Bible is indeed a divine book.

PURSUING THE DISCOVERY

I was in my first year of ministry before I discovered the incredible balance and symmetry woven into the fabric of biblical structure. My seminary training concentrated on the details of the text rather than the broad stroke of synthetic design. I knew the historical context of every book in the Bible and could unravel the intricate grammar of verses and chapters. But getting the big picture came later and through the influence of an English preacher —J. Sidlow Baxter.

Baxter's classic *Explore the Book* opened a whole new realm of Bible study by exposing me to the intriguing wonder of holistic vision. Seeing whole books instead of mere verses and paragraphs brought an expanded understanding of the biblical authors' purposes. Getting a bird's-eye view of major divisions of books (Pentateuch, Major Prophets, Gospels, Pastorals, etc.) set me on an adventurous course for discovering the divine intent of Scripture. J. Sidlow Baxter had captured my interest and peaked my curiosity, prompting a lifelong passion for biblical overview and design.

The initial perspective of symmetry and design outlined in this chapter is based on Baxter's work. I stared, amazed, when I first grasped what God had done in the design of His Book. I didn't realize this discovery of masterful symmetry would seed a later personal insight that would prompt me to write this book. But I'm getting ahead of myself. For now, let's briefly look at the traditional divisions of the biblical text.

Our Bible consists of sixty-six component parts. These are divided into two distinctive major collections, the Old Covenant Scriptures and the New Covenant Scriptures; or, as we commonly name them, the Old Testament and New Testament. But each of these two testaments, the one consisting of thirty-nine books, the other of twenty-seven, is found to be arranged in certain clearly homogeneous groups; and in this connection careful investigation reveals the presence of a marvelous Divine design running through the whole.

—J. SIDLOW BAXTER[1]

OLD TESTAMENT

The Pentateuch

The Bible begins with five books that are foundational to the entirety of Scripture: Genesis, Exodus, Leviticus, Numbers, and Deuteronomy. Called the Torah by the Jews, the books later received the designation Pentateuch by the Greek-speaking translators of the Septuagint. Authored by one man, Moses, these books describe the beginnings of God's dealings with humanity and are historical in nature.

Historical Books

Following the Pentateuch, twelve additional books of history reveal the sequence of Israel's national existence. The books of Joshua, Judges, and Ruth form a natural bridge from Moses' beginnings to the establishing of Israel's monarchy. Then the double books of Samuel, Kings, and Chronicles lead us step by step through the period of the kings: from the positive strength of a united kingdom to the tragic civil war that divided the nation and on to the ultimate demise of the monarchy. Three concluding historical books unfold the subsequent history of Judah's restoration to the land of Israel after the Babylonian captivity: Ezra, Nehemiah, and Esther. These twelve books are also historical in nature, dividing into nine pre-exile (before the Babylonian captivity) and three postexile.

So consider what we have so far with the seventeen historical books of the Law. Five books of Moses provide the foundation for the national perspective of Israel, followed by twelve books of continuing history, divided into segments of nine and three.

Major Prophets

Setting aside the books of poetry for a moment, let's notice a second major division of Old Testament Scripture: the Prophets. Here again we discover seventeen books paralleling the structure of the historical (or Law) section.

The Major Prophets come first: Isaiah, Jeremiah, Lamentations, Ezekiel, and Daniel. Notice the number is five, as with the Pentateuch. The Major Prophets form the foundation of the prophetic section outlining the entire scope of biblical prophecy.

In addition to being major in importance, these books are major in size. The only small book in the Major Prophets is Lamentations, written by Jeremiah, one of the major prophets. Lamentations also serves a major function by providing the connection between the last prophets of the monarchy (Isaiah and Jeremiah) and the prophets of the captivity (Ezekiel and Daniel).

Minor Prophets

The prophetic sequence continues with the twelve books of the Minor Prophets: Hosea, Joel, Amos, Obadiah, Jonah, Micah, Nahum, Habakkuk, Zephaniah, Haggai, Zechariah, and Malachi. Considered one book in the Hebrew tradition, the section was divided into separate identities by the Septuagint translators. The authors give us short gems of prophetic truth that complete the Old Testament scenario of prophecy.

As with the Historical Books after the Pentateuch, the Minor Prophets (minor because they are shorter) share the exact same sequential division into nine pre-exile prophets (Hosea–Zephaniah) and three postexile (Haggai, Zechariah, and Malachi). In other words, the first group of nine minor prophets prophesied during the historical period of the kings of Israel. Haggai, Zechariah, and Malachi, on the other hand, were prophets of the restoration as Israel came back from captivity under Ezra and Nehemiah.

Surveying the seventeen books of the Law (historical section) and the seventeen books of the Prophets (prophetic section), we discover an amazingly beautiful symmetry. Both pillars begin with five foundational books (the Pentateuch and the Major Prophets) and continue with twelve books each, divided proportionally into nine pre-exile and three postexile books. This picture of balance speaks loudly of intentional design.

The Poetical Writings

Let's return to the five poetical books placed strategically in the center of the Old Testament: Job, Psalms, Proverbs, Ecclesiastes, and Song of Solomon. These central books go together as a unit of poetical writings that probe the personal experiences of life in contrast to the Law and the Prophets (books of prose) that share perspectives on Israel's national life. Here again we find an interesting phenomenon of balance and focus. Between the seventeen books of history and the seventeen books of prophecy, we find at the heart of the Old Testament five very personal books that express the heart of God for the individual. The Old Testament is indeed a masterful work of divine symmetry.

Is this accident or design? Think of it: over thirty writers contributed to the Old Testament, spaced out over twelve hundred years, writing in different places, to different parties, for different purposes, and little dreaming that their writings, besides being preserved through generations, were eventually to be compiled into that systematic plurality in unity which we now find in the Old Testament. When one reflects on this, surely one

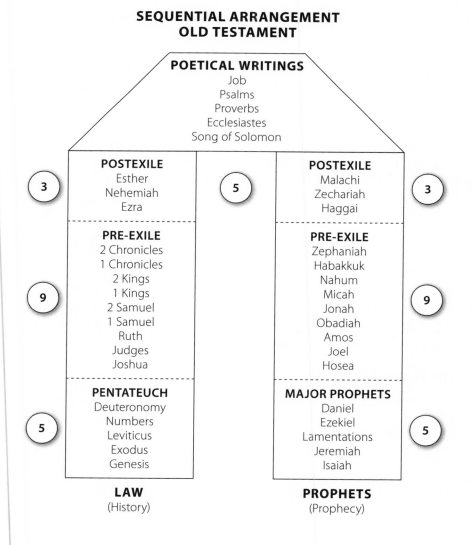

SEQUENTIAL ARRANGEMENT
OLD TESTAMENT

POETICAL WRITINGS
Job
Psalms
Proverbs
Ecclesiastes
Song of Solomon

POSTEXILE Esther Nehemiah Ezra	3 / 5	**POSTEXILE** Malachi Zechariah Haggai / 3
PRE-EXILE 2 Chronicles 1 Chronicles 2 Kings 1 Kings 2 Samuel 1 Samuel Ruth Judges Joshua	9	**PRE-EXILE** Zephaniah Habakkuk Nahum Micah Jonah Obadiah Amos Joel Hosea / 9
PENTATEUCH Deuteronomy Numbers Leviticus Exodus Genesis	5	**MAJOR PROPHETS** Daniel Ezekiel Lamentations Jeremiah Isaiah / 5

LAW
(History)

PROPHETS
(Prophecy)

cannot be charged with fancifulness for thinking that behind the human writers there must have been a controlling divine design.

—J. SIDLOW BAXTER[2]

NEW TESTAMENT

Like moving from one exquisitely decorated room to another, we step from the Old Testament into the equally fascinating New Testament. Designed differently, it is no less intriguing in its harmonious arrangement.

The Gospels

Opening the New Testament we are immediately introduced to the long-awaited Messiah. Anticipated by the prophets and longed for by the people of faith, Jesus Christ emerges in the gospel record as the Savior of mankind. Four gospel portraits emphasize unique characteristics of His life and work: Matthew, Mark, Luke, and John. The Gospels are not only the foundation of the New Testament; they also claim to be the fulfillment of Old Testament hope.

This is how the New Testament begins.

Book of Acts

Continuing the history of the gospel record, the book of Acts recounts the formation of the church. Beginning with Jesus' ascent into heaven, the text records the Holy Spirit empowering the followers of Christ to establish His church (later referred to as the body of Christ) throughout the Mediterranean world. James the brother of Jesus, Peter, and John stand out as the leadership team of the Jewish church in Jerusalem at the epicenter of the Christian movement. All three eventually write epistles (or letters) to be included in the New Testament Scripture. Next, the apostle Paul travels around the Roman Empire introducing Gentiles (non-Jews) to the Christian message and writing to churches in strategic cities; these epistles also became Scripture. So, Acts is a historical book connecting the Gospels with the rest of the New Testament and laying the historical foundation for the Epistles.

Paul's Epistles

The first group of church epistles comes from the pen of the apostle Paul: Romans, 1 & 2 Corinthians, Galatians, Ephesians, Philippians, Colossians, and 1 & 2 Thessalonians. Written to congregations of believers in Gentile cities, these epistles address the full scope of salvation in Christ. The masterful treatise of Romans appears first to establish the foundational truths of salvation, and this Pauline section concludes with the wonderful hope of the second coming of Christ in the Thessalonian epistles. Sometimes referred to as the Gentile Christian Epistles, these nine Pauline letters are doctrinal in nature.

The Pastoral Epistles

Paul also wrote four additional epistles to individuals: 1 & 2 Timothy, Titus, and Philemon. Unlike the church epistles written to congregational groups, these letters exhibit a pastoral emphasis and are therefore called the Pastorals. Timothy pastored in Ephesus, Titus in Crete, and Philemon's house was the location for the church in Colossae. The interesting thing about the Pastorals is that they are positioned between the Gentile Christian Epistles (Romans–2 Thessalonians) and the General Epistles (Hebrews–Revelation), much as the Poetical Writings of the Old Testament come between the Law and the Prophets. Focusing on the individual, the Pastorals are at the heart of the New Testament epistles.

General Epistles

The last group of epistles is Jewish in nature and written largely by the apostolic leaders of the Jerusalem church: James, Peter, and John (see Galatians 2:9). The nine books are Hebrews (author unknown), James, 1 & 2 Peter, 1, 2, & 3 John, Jude (written by the brother of James), and Revelation (written by John).

Hebrews is obviously written to a Jewish audience, James to the "twelve tribes scattered abroad," Peter to the Jews of the Dispersion, and John contrasts his audience to Gentiles in 3 John. Like the Gentile Christian Epistles, these Jewish Christian Epistles are doctrinal in nature, stressing the need to be faithful to Christ, as well as the brethren, in times of persecution and difficulty. Nine in number, they begin with the great doctrinal book of Hebrews and conclude with the prophetic books of Jude and Revelation. The Jewish Christian Epistles are a parallel image of the Gentile Christian Epistles, each comprising nine books arranged in a symmetrical pattern.

As a whole, the New Testament has its own peculiar design. Yet an observable pattern of symmetry and balance graces this portion of the Bible, just as it did in the Old Testament.

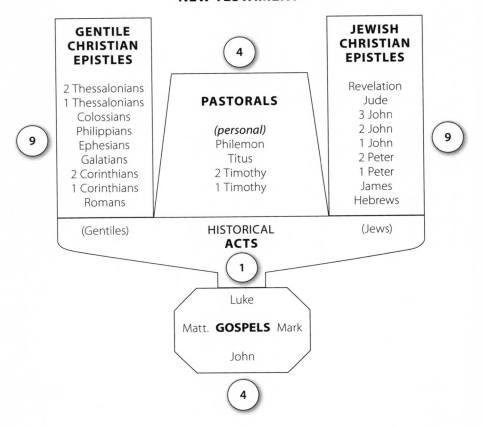

SEQUENTIAL ARRANGEMENT
NEW TESTAMENT

GENTILE CHRISTIAN EPISTLES

2 Thessalonians
1 Thessalonians
Colossians
Philippians
Ephesians
Galatians
2 Corinthians
1 Corinthians
Romans

(Gentiles)

PASTORALS

(personal)
Philemon
Titus
2 Timothy
1 Timothy

JEWISH CHRISTIAN EPISTLES

Revelation
Jude
3 John
2 John
1 John
2 Peter
1 Peter
James
Hebrews

(Jews)

HISTORICAL ACTS

Luke

Matt. **GOSPELS** Mark

John

A EUREKA MOMENT

Driving alone late at night can provide ample opportunity for reflection. Such was the case as I headed home from an all-day conference I had taught on the Song of Solomon. Autumn was giving way to winter, but the early snows of Wisconsin had not yet compromised the roads. Traffic was light on Interstate 90, so I had a little over an hour to do nothing but think. The small crowd had responded well, and I thanked the Lord for a good day. Soon I was mulling over the amazing symmetry and balance of Scripture (as outlined above).

Suddenly a light went on—not in the car, but in my head. Have you ever had one of those eureka! moments, where God seemed to shine light on something you'd never seen before? I was stunned.

"Put the head on top, dummy," my mind quipped as I envisioned the image swirling into place. There it was! I could hardly believe what my mind saw: the form of a man, clear as could be!

A EUREKA MOMENT

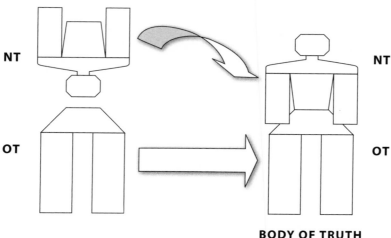

BODY OF TRUTH

Several places in the New Testament, Jesus Christ is said to be the Head of the church (e.g., Eph. 1:22; Col. 1:18; 2:19). And the Gospels give us detailed record of the One who is the Head. To put the head on top, our schematic of the New Testament simply needed to be inverted. Then, when the New Testament arrangement was placed onto the Old Testament, lo and behold, a full body with head, torso, two arms, and two legs appeared.

Consider further that the book of Acts is connected to the Gospels by common authorship; Luke wrote both the Gospel bearing his name and Acts — the book that reveals the formation of the body of Christ (the church) and provides the historical background for how the Jew and Gentile were brought together to form that one body (see Eph. 2:14 – 16). This is exactly what the neck and shoulders do for the human body. The neck connects the head to the body, and the shoulders unite both sides of the body into one body function.

Next in line is the central portion of the body, the torso. The two parts of the torso — the chest and abdomen — comprise the main part of who we are. In like fashion, a central part of the New Testament epistles (the Pastorals) and a middle grouping of books between the Law and the Prophets (the Poetical Writings) express God's concern for the individual. The arrangement of these two sets of books, as they fall into the central portions of both testaments, fits well with this developing form of a human.

Then come the appendages. Two symmetrical arms engage the world around us, just as the Jewish Christian Epistles and the Gentile Christian Epistles reach out to everyone in the world. Both flow out of the book of Acts, as the two arms of a man extend from the shoulders. Finally, two legs are the foundational support of the body. Even so, the Law and the Prophets emerge as two pillars upon which all Scripture stands.

That night in the darkness as I traveled alone, I saw for the first time that the Bible, seen holistically, presents to us the picture of a man. Sixty-six books in their natural arrangement[3] form a mosaic of a human body. I knew of course who the man was. Only *one* man saturates the pages of Scripture —anticipated in the Old Testament and reflected upon in the New Testament—and that is the person of Jesus Christ! He alone is the Word, having become flesh.

PERFECTION

For us, perfection is only a dream. For God, it is a lifestyle. Perfection flows out of His wisdom and unlimited ability, so that whatever He does is exact and precise. Exquisite design and perfect order can be seen in all His handiwork.

When God chose to reveal Himself by special means through His Word

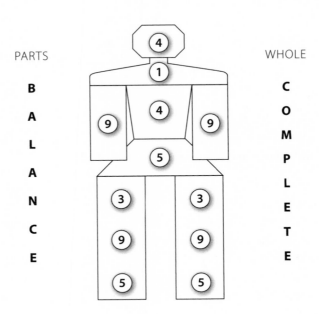

written (the Bible) and His Word *living* (Jesus Christ), each was conceived in perfection. Jesus was not only sinless (Heb. 4:15); He was flawless (1 Pet. 1:19–20). As for the Bible, it is both inerrant (without error in the original manuscripts) and complete. This is evident in the perfect symmetry and balance we have observed in the orderly arrangement of books.

BEHOLD, THE MAN

Riding the monorail through the center of the Contemporary Resort on your way to the Magic Kingdom at Disney World, through the window on the right you can see a striking tile mosaic. Each tile piece is colored with its own design, but, seen from a distance, all the individual pieces blend together to reveal a magnificent picture on the hotel wall. Mosaics are works of art—and this mosaic is a masterpiece of artistic design.

The Bible is like that. Traveling through the landscape of biblical revelation, we view one book after another observing its unique, colorful design. Each piece radiates its own beauty, and we are captivated by the truth it contains. Yet we can easily become content with examining individual pieces and miss a discovery of the broader picture.

Referring to a different art form with a similar effect, A. B. Simpson, founder of the Christian and Missionary Alliance, applied this ability to see the larger picture to our understanding of Scripture.

> I once saw a copy of the Constitution of the United States, very skillfully engraved in copper plate, so that when you looked at it closely it was nothing more than a piece of writing, but when you looked at it from a distance, it was the face of George Washington. The face shone out in the shading of the letters at a little distance, and I saw the person, not the words, nor the ideas. I thought, "That is the way to look at the Scriptures and understand the thoughts of God, to see them in the face of love, shining through and through; not ideas, nor doctrines, but Jesus Himself as the Life and Source and sustaining Presence of all our life.[4]

Simpson was not commenting on the artistic arrangement of books as I have unfolded it in the previous pages. He was describing the Christ-centered emphasis permeating the Word of God. Yet how much more powerful is this analogy when the mosaic design of Scripture is understood!

Jesus Christ is the essence of Scripture; He is not only found in its content, but also visible in its structural form. The sixty-six books of the Bible blend together as a sixty-six-piece mosaic of the Man who *is* the Word. Marvelously designed by God, this literary mosaic of Jesus Christ is a wonder to behold and a treasure to contemplate.

This discovery led me to a question: What would happen if I examined each grouping of books in the light of their respective anatomical areas? Would I find a correspondence between the anatomy and physiology of the body with the Bible books that fall into the various sections of the body mosaic? Like an arrow, this possibility pierced and lodged in my mind. I immediately embraced the challenge as a passion of my life.

In the pages that follow, I invite you to travel with me through the twists and turns of this intriguing discovery. I trust that you, like me, will respond with wide-eyed wonder and experience rushes of enthusiasm as we uncover one treasure after another.

The
WORD *became* FLESH
The BIBLE = a Mosaic of Christ

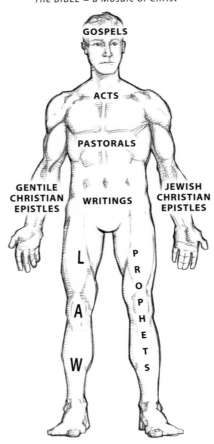

CHAPTER TWO

THE LIVING WORD

Before we plunge into the study of biblical sequence and form to see if the anatomical analogy is a legitimate representation of the structure of Scripture, let's pause to consider what all this means. Perhaps we should ask a few basic questions.

For instance, what is the significance of understanding that the Bible and the person of Christ are intimate reflections of each other? Should we expect a close affinity between them? If so, how surprised should we be to discover that this affinity extends to the form in which each is presented to the world? Are we straining at a novel idea or observing a natural correlation?

LIKE NO OTHER BOOK

The Word of God is alive and powerful! It throbs with divine life and penetrates into the secret chambers of the human heart. "For the word of God is *living* and *active* ... discerning the thoughts and intentions of the heart" (Heb. 4:12, emphasis mine). What other book in the history of humankind can boast this claim?

In this thematic overview of Scripture, which emphasizes the Christ-centered (or Christocentric) nature of the Word of God, we discover a living dynamic with all the pulsating reality of a living person. God does nothing apart from purpose and design, so it should not surprise us to see an amazing correlation between the inspired Word (the Bible) and the incarnate Word (Jesus Christ).

When the Word became flesh and lived among us, Jesus' body was crafted in the same manner as ours today—with functioning systems working in intricate harmony (e.g., skeletal, muscular, nervous, circulatory, endocrine). I have discovered that the "body" of divine literature we call the Bible reflects this same creative genius. The groupings of biblical books outlined in chapter

1 are blended together in systemic fashion. Nothing is redundant. Everything is crucial. Each part has a specific function and everything fits.

And that is what this study is about.

Crafted by God is a unique study that will take us into a new and exciting depth of appreciation for the Word of God. As we compare the Bible (the Written Word) and Jesus Christ (the incarnate Word) mirroring each other, we'll see them as one—not just in content and thought, but also in form and function. Together they are the Living Word crafted by God!

SPECIAL REVELATION

Certain things can be known about God from His creative handiwork. The fingerprint of God can be seen on everything He made. Even evolutionists are beginning to concede an intelligent design in the universe.[1] Any logical, unbiased perusal of the scientific world points to that conclusion. And where there is intelligent design, there must be an intelligent Designer.

GOD ⇐ ▫ ▫ ▫ ▫ Creation
Intelligent Designer   Intelligent design

Psalm 19:1: The heavens declare the glory of God, and the sky above proclaims his handiwork.

Romans 1:20: For his invisible attributes, namely, his eternal power and divine nature, have been clearly perceived, ever since the creation of the world, in the things that have been made.

Yet this general revelation is limited in what it can tell us about God. We can know that He must be there somewhere (His "divine nature"), and it is quite evident that He is incredibly powerful (His "eternal power"). Beyond that, it's a guessing game—unless God decides to be more specific in what He reveals to us concerning Himself. And that is exactly what He did!

The Bible claims to be the self-disclosure of God—who He is, what He is like, and what He does. Throughout the first part of the Bible (the Old Testament), God additionally promised to make a personal visit to planet Earth to resolve the dilemma of mankind's sin and alienation from God. A Messiah is anticipated. Then in the second part (the New Testament), Jesus Christ is presented as that Messiah. He is God, having come to earth to be our Savior.

God went beyond general revelation (creation) to give us special revelation, more detailed and specific. And He did it in two ways. First, He gave us a Book—the Bible. Second, He came in person—Jesus Christ. He gave us an up-close-and-personal look at Himself through a Book and a Person. Obviously we can know a whole lot more about God now.

Both the Book and the Person are said to be "the Word of God." The Bible is the Word (Heb. 4:12), and Jesus Christ is the Word (John 1:1–2, 14). In the Bible we have the *Word written* and in Jesus Christ we have the *Word living.* Furthermore, there is a close affinity between these two special revelations of God. They are *inseparable* and they are *intertwined.*

A CLOSE RELATIONSHIP

Anyone who understands who Jesus Christ is as the Son of God and what the Bible says about Him knows that the Bible and Jesus are closely connected. Consider the following observations.

The Bible — A Revelation of Jesus Christ

The entire Bible explains how mankind, which is dead in trespasses and sin (Eph. 2:1), can receive and experience the life of God. Bottom line: eternal life can be obtained only by receiving Jesus Christ (the Son of God) as Savior (John 1:12; 1 John 5:11–12). Jesus Himself taught that life is not in the Scripture, but in Him (John 5:39–40). Since the whole Bible is devoted to explaining how fallen men and women can be restored to life with God, the Bible is thoroughly Christ-centered.

This is obvious in the New Testament, but it is also true for the Old Testament. Notice what Jesus said in two scriptural studies after His resurrection.

Luke 24:27: And beginning with Moses and all the Prophets, he interpreted to them in all the Scriptures the things concerning himself.

Luke 24:44–45: Then he said to them, "These are my words that I spoke to you while I was still with you, that everything written about me in the Law of Moses and the Prophets and the Psalms must be fulfilled." Then he opened their minds to understand the Scriptures.

Here's the point: they did not understand the Scriptures until they could see Jesus Christ in all areas of the Old Testament (the Law of Moses, the Prophets, and the Poetical Writings). The central theme of the Bible wraps tightly around the person of Jesus Christ.

Jesus Christ — Devoted to the Bible

Not only is the Bible a revelation of Jesus Christ; Jesus was totally committed to the Scriptures as the truth for life. As a child, Jesus was very familiar with the Hebrew Bible. By the time He was twelve, He knew the Scriptures so well that all the teachers were amazed at His understanding (Luke 2:46–47). Later, as an adult, Jesus entered the synagogue in Nazareth and read from the Scriptures "as was his custom" (Luke 4:16). The Scriptures were an integral part of His life.

Furthermore, Jesus relied on Scripture as the final authority when resisting Satan's temptations. In each of the three attempts by Satan to derail Jesus from His messianic mission, Jesus quoted verses from Deuteronomy (the Law of Moses) to deflect the devil's advances. The Bible was Jesus' "sword of the Spirit" (Eph. 6:17).

Then, too, Jesus devoted His life to fulfilling the Scriptures. As He began to teach the Sermon on the Mount, He said, "Do not think that I have come to abolish the Law or the Prophets; I have not come to abolish them but to fulfill them" (Matt. 5:17). Jesus repeatedly insisted that He was fulfilling the Scriptures by the things that He said and did (e.g., Luke 4:21, 24:44).

Jesus Christ immersed Himself in the Scriptures to the point where it could be said that the Living Word was consumed with the Written Word.

Common Characteristics

It is interesting to observe that both Jesus Christ and the Bible have the same unique nature. The undergirding essence of Christ is a union of two natures (divine and human) in one person. The Bible also exhibits this same nature, as it is divine and human in one book.

Consider how both the Written Word (the Book) and the Living Word (the Person) were introduced into our world.

The process for the writing of the Bible is described in 2 Peter 1:21: "men spoke from God as they were carried along by the Holy Spirit" (who was the divine agent). The instrument He used was men (who were human), and the product of this process was the divine-human Book (the Bible).

In the case of Jesus' birth, we see an identical process, as the angel explained it to Mary. "The Holy Spirit will come upon you ... therefore the child to be born will be called holy—the Son of God" (Luke 1:35). Notice that the Holy Spirit (who is divine) was the agent to impregnate Mary (who was human) as the instrument, so the product was the divine-human Person, Jesus Christ.

So grasp the significance of this. A divine agent (the Holy Spirit) working on human instruments (men and Mary) combined to bring both the Written Word (the Bible) and the Living Word (Jesus Christ) into the world as a unique Book and a unique Person. They each have similar conceptions, with identical natures.

They also exhibit similar qualities. Both the Bible and Jesus are *holy* (Rom. 1:2; Luke 1:35); they are both *eternal* (1 Pet. 1:25; Mic. 5:2); and each is the embodiment of *truth* (John 17:17; 14:6). They both reflect the qualities of God.

Furthermore, they are both called the same thing; they both have the same name. Each is the "Logos" (the Word): the Bible (Heb. 4:12) and Jesus Christ (John 1:1–2, 14).

Putting it all together, we see that the Bible and Jesus Christ are identical in nature (a union of the divine and human); each exhibits the same qualities of deity (holy, eternal, and truth); and both are called the "Logos" (the Word of God). The Bible is indeed a mirror image of the person of Christ.

COMMUNICATING WITH WORDS

In the Genesis record, man was created in the image and likeness of God (1:26–27) with the elements of personality—intellect, emotion, and will. That means that men and women have a much higher status in the world than any other element of God's creation.

We are also told that God's intention from the beginning was to develop a pattern of communication with His human counterparts so that a bond of friendship would occur. So in the Garden of Eden, God and man talked together and enjoyed one another. God was not aloof and distant. He was intimate and near.

This is what is meant when John the apostle tells us that God was the Word and the Word was God (John 1:1–2). By using the word *Word* as a descriptive designation of God, John is emphasizing the fact that the true God of heaven and earth is a communicating God. Mankind experiences God when God communicates with words.

God and man were alike—not exactly, but in significant ways that made fellowship and communication possible—and what they said to one another was a reflection of who they were. Their words were not disembodied thoughts hanging in the air. As they talked, it was as though a piece of each of their minds connected in the inner sanctum of the other. Not only was man communicating with God, but God was making Himself known to humankind.

I'm saying that "being" and thoughts are connected. Words spoken by God were flowers emerging from the seedbed of life. Thoughts blossomed with energy because they were indeed alive with the pulsating life of the Communicator. Words laden with ideas of the divine mind were transplanted through space into the minds of the man and the woman.

God is a communicating God. The communication itself throbs with God's very life and pulsates with the energy of His being. This is what the writer of the book of Hebrews meant when he wrote, "For the word of God is living and active, sharper than any two-edged sword, piercing to the division of soul and of spirit, of joints and of marrow, and discerning the thoughts and intentions of the heart" (4:12).

Actually, the original Greek text of this verse begins with the word *living*: "Living is the Word of God . . ." A clear emphasis is placed on the Bible's living quality. Other writings may be laden with the ideas of men and women, but much more is being claimed for the Word of God. The Holy Scriptures are said to flow with divine life. They are living expressions of God Himself flowing through the printed page into the private chambers of the human heart.

That's why this text also says that the Word of God is "active." This Greek word is *energes*, from which we get our word *energy*. In other words, the Word of God is energetic—throbbing with the omnipotent life of almighty God! It does incredible things, like piercing down into the secret recesses of the heart, laying bare the hidden things of life. The Holy Scriptures are a living, energetic extension of God Himself.

According to 1 Corinthians 2:9–16, this communication of God's Word was accomplished by the Holy Spirit because "no one comprehends the thoughts of God except the Spirit of God" (v. 11). The Spirit translated divine thought into words that articulated those thoughts, so that God's Word was imparted to us "in words not taught by human wisdom but taught by the Spirit" of God (v. 13). In other words, the Bible was verbally inspired by the Spirit of God.

It is interesting to note how this text summarizes this inspiration process. Paul concludes by saying, "But we have the mind of Christ" (v. 16), indicating that the verbally inspired Word of God is actually the thoughts of Christ's mind.

Some editions of the Bible reflect the words of Jesus found in the Gospels in red letters to distinguish them from the general text. In 1 Corinthians 2:16, Paul seems to be saying that the entire Bible should be in red letters! Jesus Christ is the storyteller from the first words of Genesis to the final exclamations of the Revelation. Christ is talking with us through the Scriptures, so that what is in His mind is being transferred to our minds by the words of the text. In the final analysis, when we have the Bible, we have the mind of Christ.

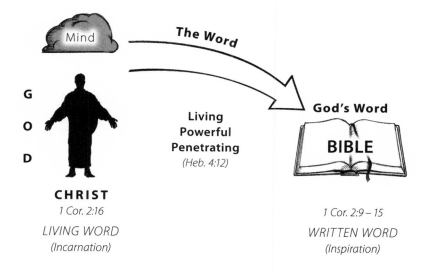

The Word Became Flesh

And then the unthinkable happened! The Word became flesh and lived among us (John 1:14). God materialized in space and time, and for the first time in history, human eyes gazed upon a visible manifestation of the Word of God in human form. Just as mankind had been created in the image and likeness of God, so in reciprocal fashion the Word was made in the image and likeness of man.

When God stepped out of eternity to become a man on the earth, He revolutionized the concept of deity. No other religion or philosophical system had ever entertained such an idea. Men had often aspired to be gods and mythical gods often looked like men, but the notion that God would join the ranks of humanity was as outlandish as man becoming an insect. That sort of thing just never happened. But, according to the Bible, it *did* happen.

The Word (or God) had been a Person from eternity past; but in a moment of time spirit morphed into flesh as God adorned Himself with a human body. It was just like the body He had crafted for Adam. *Or was it the other way around?* (You know, like "which came first—the chicken or the egg?"). Here the question is, which came first in God's planning process, the body of the Son of God incarnate or the body of Adam in creation?

Actually there is reason to believe that the human form of Jesus was in the mind of God long before He molded the frame of Adam from the dust of the ground. Consider Peter's words in his first epistle: "Knowing that you were ransomed ... with the precious blood of Christ, like that of a lamb without blemish or spot. He was foreknown before the foundation of the world but was made manifest in the last times for the sake of you" (1:18–20).

What an amazing thought! Peter states that God had foreknowledge of the "lamb" (Jesus Christ, the Son of God—the Word having become flesh) dying for the sins of humanity before He ever created the first human beings. That certainly must mean that God knew exactly what His Son would look like as a man long before He created Adam and Eve. So it is conceivable that an incarnation prototype existed, serving as a model for the assembly line of human reproduction.

I am suggesting the possibility that humans look like they do because Jesus looked like He did—not vice versa. The fact that Adam was made in the image of God may mean more than mankind bearing the stamp of personality. When "the Word became flesh" (a clear reference to Jesus), He had a torso, two legs, two arms, and a head. So that's how God also crafted Adam and Eve.

In our next chapter on the Gospels, we will look more carefully at the vision Ezekiel had of God as he began his prophetic writing. Here I simply want to point out that at the core of Ezekiel's vision of God was the appearance of a man. "And from the midst of it came the likeness of four living creatures. And this was their appearance: they had a human likeness" (1:5). In the conclusion of his vision, Ezekiel said, "and seated above the likeness of a throne was a likeness with a human appearance" (1:26). Ezekiel was stunned that in the midst of his vision of God, God looked like a man.

Could it be that Jesus, in His incarnation, was given a head, a torso, two arms, and two legs because that is the best physical representation of who God is? The human form is what God looked like when "the Word became flesh" (John 1:14). This is what Adam and Eve looked like when they were made "in the image of God" (Gen. 1:27). It seems that when the Word takes on a visible form, it takes the shape of a human.

So why does the Word look like a human being? Think of it this way—God has total control over all that He thinks and does (a head); He feels with the emotions of His viscera and heart (a torso); He accomplishes wonderful deeds (arms); and He comes and goes with great mobility (legs). The human body seems to be a graphic image of who God is. Whatever the explanation, when the Word of God took on visible form, it had the appearance of a man.

Such thinking, in part, led me to further investigate the possibility that the form of the Written Word (the Bible) and the form of the Living Word (Jesus Christ) are by design the same.

God Himself crafted the form of each, and mankind was created to reflect the same form. The inspiration of God's thoughts in a *book* and the incarnation of God's Person in a *body* are as inseparable from each other as thoughts and the mind from which those thoughts are generated. They are indeed mirror images of each other. And we, in turn, are made in that same image.

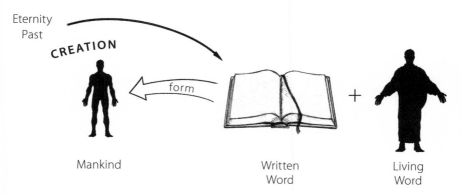

Eternity Past

CREATION

form

Mankind

Written Word

+

Living Word

READY TO PROCEED

If what I have been saying about the close and intimate connection between the Written Word and the Living Word is true (and it seems to be), then the possibility that they both exist in a similar form should not surprise us. It is obvious that in His incarnation Jesus Christ (the Living Word) had a body. As the body of Truth, the Scriptures may actually reflect the body of Christ.

At this point, this is theoretical thinking that begs to be investigated. Yet it has been important for us to establish the principle that the two special revelations of God are true reflections of each other. This extensive study is built upon that premise.

So let's begin. And let's begin at the top. In the mosaic design, the Gospels emerged as the head. We begin, therefore, with the Gospels.

PART 1

THE BODY OF
ESSENTIAL TRUTH

CHAPTER THREE

FACIAL PORTRAITS

The Gospels

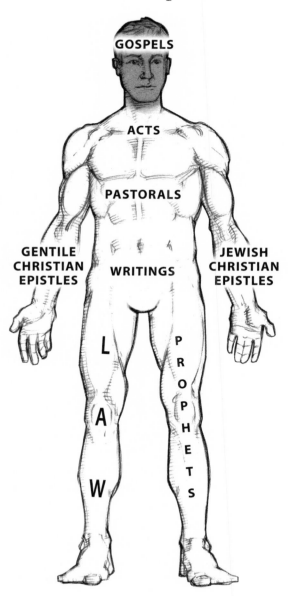

GOSPELS

ACTS

PASTORALS

GENTILE CHRISTIAN EPISTLES

WRITINGS

JEWISH CHRISTIAN EPISTLES

L A W

P R O P H E T S

THE GOSPELS

The life of Jesus Christ has been called the greatest story ever told because it chronicles the greatest life ever lived. From the accounts of Jesus' miraculous conception and virgin birth to the spectacular events of His death, burial, resurrection, and ascension into heaven, the Gospels shine as radiant luminaries among the literary masterpieces of the world. As Ralph Waldo Emerson once observed, the name of Jesus is not so much written as plowed into the history of the world.

Of all the biographies of famous people, none has received the acclaim and notoriety of the story of Jesus. For almost two millennia, the accounts of Jesus' phenomenal miracles and His life-changing gospel have been passed on from generation to generation. Translated into all the major languages, the four portraits of Christ's life have penetrated into nearly every culture of the world. Each time the story is told, it seems to have a new and fresh appeal as it grips hearts with wonder and elicits responses of faith. The life of Jesus is indeed the most enthralling story in the history of mankind.

Why are there four gospels—all apparently telling the same story? Is the Bible engaging in redundant storytelling for a reason? Are the gospel accounts just ancient biographies—or is something more being communicated as each author tells the story? And, in light of the body analogy, how are the four Gospels similar in form and function to the human head?

Such questions capture our attention as we begin our study of the biblical mosaic of Christ. It is fitting that we start with the head (the Gospels) rather than with the feet (Genesis and the Pentateuch), because the head is in the supreme position of the human anatomy. The exaltation of Christ as the head of the body is the crux of the matter in any study of Scripture.

Right up front we need to establish our method of approach. Above all, the text of Scripture must take precedence over any application of the body analogy. Thus we must first analyze the nature of the Gospels themselves and their God-intended meaning. Only then can we legitimately observe whether or not the Gospels resemble God's design of the human head.

So let's first address the question, why are there four gospels instead of one grand telling of the story of Jesus? The prophet Ezekiel gives us our first clue.

THE FACE OF GOD

Ezekiel's prophetic writing begins with a spectacular vision. Taken captive by the Babylonians in the second deportation (597 BC), Ezekiel was sitting on the bank of a Mesopotamian river in the vicinity of the other captives. Suddenly a whirlwind disturbed the tranquil air and a fireball, engulfed in a cloud, dropped out of heaven. In the words of Ezekiel, "The heavens were opened, and I saw visions of God" (1:1). The glory of God had descended upon him as though he were in the Sanctuary of the Temple in Jerusalem.

Then Ezekiel saw an amazing sight: four living creatures in the core of this fiery presence of God, collectively giving the appearance of a single man (1:5). As a Levitical priest, Ezekiel knew from the writings of Moses that man had been made in the image and likeness of God (Gen. 1:26–27). But here it was reversed. God Himself was appearing as a man. Furthermore, it took four living creatures to portray the full expression of this deified Man. Ezekiel said, "They [plural] had the likeness of a man [singular]" (KJV).

As the vision unfolds, Ezekiel is struck by the faces of the four living creatures. The distinguishing feature of each creature was its face. The face of a *man* is mentioned first. Then the face of a *lion*, the face of an *ox*, and finally the face of an *eagle* (1:10). God was presenting Himself as a man, with four likenesses.

These four living creatures appear again in the book of Revelation, with the exact same faces, in a slightly different order. The lion comes first, followed by the ox, the man, and the eagle (4:7). Actually the order is the same, except that the face of a man goes from first place in Ezekiel to third position in Revelation. It appears that Ezekiel may have been stunned by the human aspect of God's glory. Twice he mentions that he saw the *form of a man* in his vision of God (1:5, 26), and so he lays stress upon the human face of the creatures by mentioning it first (1:10). This evidently was a unique thought to Ezekiel.

John (the author of Revelation), on the other hand, had known Jesus Christ and witnessed firsthand the human incarnation of God. What had impressed John was the fact that the incarnate Christ was also the King of the universe — with the authority to open the seals and judge the world. So for John the lion is mentioned first. Later he will refer to Jesus as "the Lion of the tribe of Judah" (Rev. 5:5).

In Ezekiel's vision all four of the faces blend together to present a solitary man at the core of this fiery image of God. He also describes a throne upon which the man with four faces is sitting (1:26). This is similar to John's description in Revelation, where he sees the four living creatures hovering "in the center and around the throne" (4:6 NASB). Can there be any doubt but that the divine man in Ezekiel with four likenesses in his face is the same person as the one described in Revelation where he is surrounded by the identical four likenesses? I think not. This royal man in the visions is none other than Jesus Christ, the one and only God-man.

THE SYMBOLS EXPLAINED

Let's consider the use of symbolism in these two visions. The mention of animals as symbolic representations is as common today as it was in the ancient world. Athletic teams call themselves the Lions or the Bears or the Seahawks, and cars are labeled Cougars or Mustangs. In using these terms, the owners or producers are saying that the team or product reflects the characteristics of the symbol. The name represents who the person is or what the product is all about.

While in high school, my son was given the nickname Weasel by his friends. I assumed they were referring to him as an excellent athlete. He was fast and smart and very tenacious—just like a weasel. Then one day I asked the friend who had given him the label if those were his motivating thoughts. His response deflated my lofty expectation. "Well," he answered, "as you know, Rob has asthma—and he wheezes. So we call him Wheez-el."

That's the idea behind the symbols in the visions of Ezekiel and John. The man in each vision is obviously divine, and the four living creatures reflect four major characteristics of that man. In some ways, he is like a lion. In others, he is more like an ox. Then again, he has the qualities of a man, balanced by the intriguing characteristics of an eagle. He is all of those things blended together in a single Person.

Using John's order in Revelation 4:7, let's begin by looking at the lion.

In Scripture the lion is often a descriptive likeness of kingship. After all, everyone knows that the lion is the "king of the beasts." When speaking of things that go about in a majestic fashion, Proverbs 30:30–31 makes a comparison by using an inverted parallel (the first and last things mentioned are being compared). In this way, the proverb brings the lion and the king together by saying, "a lion which is strongest among beasts, and turn[s] not away for any … and a king, against whom there is no rising up" (KJV). The lion and the king are thought of in the same way. Also the royal line of Israel came through the tribe of Judah, whose insignia was the lion. This is why Jesus is called "the Lion of the tribe of Judah" (Rev. 5:5). The face of a lion is the face of a king.

The second animal mentioned in Revelation 4 is the ox (the King James Version translates it "the calf" or ox calf). Used as a beast of burden, the ox was the strong servant animal of ancient Israel. Harnessed together in yokes, oxen pulled plows and wagons in service to their owners.

Writing to Timothy, Paul instructed him as to why certain teaching elders ought to be paid by those who receive the teaching. Quoting Deuteronomy he says, "You shall not muzzle an ox when it treads out the grain" (1 Tim. 5:18). In other words, just like the ox that eats fallen grain while it is working, so the person who serves the Lord by teaching the Word of God should be able to live by what he does. The face of an ox is the face of a servant.

Think for a moment about what we have so far. The divine-man in the visions is a lionlike king. At the same time, He is an oxlike servant. That's a paradox, for sure. Kings usually are not servants; and servants can only wish they were kings. But here they are blended together in a harmonious unit. The man is a king, and at the same time He is a servant.

Third, John saw the face of a man (the first face in Ezekiel). Man is the highest creation of God. In Psalm 8:4–5 we read,

> What is man that you are mindful of him,
>   and the son of man that you care for him?
> Yet you have made him a little lower than the heavenly beings
>   and crowned him with glory and honor.

Mankind is the only creature made in the image and likeness of God and therefore is the only created being who can have fellowship with God. The face of a man is that which is uniquely human.

Last in both visions appears the face of an eagle. Chosen to be the symbol of the United States of America, an eagle is the most glorious of the majestic birds. With binoculars I have watched eagles soar out of range into the upper reaches of the sky, as if to enter the very presence of God. Perhaps that is why the Scriptures use the eagle as a symbol for Deity. Isaiah 40:31 tells us,

> But they who wait for the LORD shall renew their strength;
>   they shall mount up with wings like eagles;
> they shall run and not be weary;
>   they shall walk and not faint.

Undiminished strength while walking or running is suprahuman. It is, in fact, to be "Godlike." The face of an eagle is the face of God Himself.

Again, we are presented with a paradox. Man is not God, and until Ezekiel saw his vision, it was inconceivable to think of God as a man. Yet the man on the throne in these visions is *both* a man and God. That is truly intriguing.

So consider what Ezekiel and John saw in their visions of God. They saw a radiant man at the core of God's being, represented by four living creatures: a lion (king), balanced by an ox (servant); and a man (human) who is also an eagle (divine).

According to John in the Revelation, this is the holy One who is worthy to open the seven seals of the scroll held in the hand of God (5:1 – 5) — who is also said to be the Lamb that was slain (5:6 – 8). This is obviously a symbolic description of Jesus Christ. Here are the four faces of the Messiah who is God incarnate, the Savior of the world.

THE FOURFOLD CHRIST

Perhaps we can now begin to understand why the Bible contains four gospels. Each gospel is a unique portrait of Jesus Christ in one of his fourfold dimensions. All contain some similar biographical information about Jesus. Yet each has specific inclusions and exclusions concerning Him, because each emphasizes a particular aspect of His character. The Gospels are not, strictly speaking, biographies. Each is a special portrait of Christ that describes one of the four faces of who He is: the Lion, the Ox, the Man, and the Eagle.

Matthew — Jesus the Lion

If you were trying to prove that someone was the rightful heir to the throne, how would you do it? First, you would need to establish the blood line. Is this person a legitimate heir? This is exactly how Matthew begins his portrait of Christ. He traces Christ's lineage back to King David, as well as to Abraham, the original recipient of God's unconditional Covenant. Matthew is the only gospel writer who does this.

Then Matthew gives us additional unique information. The annunciation of the angel to Joseph, through whom the kingly line has come, completes chapter 1. Royal Magi from the East come to worship the newborn King in chapter 2, and King Herod is jealous because a rival king has been born. Mark, Luke, and John give us none of this. But it is all germane to Matthew's purpose of painting a portrait of Christ as the King of Kings.

Kingly credentials are well established in Matthew, as he carefully delin-
eates the miracles and authoritative teaching of the King. Kingdom discourses are methodically recorded in fuller detail than the other gospels: the
Sermon on the Mount (chaps. 5–7), Parables of the Kingdom (chap. 13), and
the Olivet Discourse (chaps. 24–25). Finally Matthew ends with our Lord's
great declaration, "All authority in heaven and on earth has been given to me"
(28:18). Christ is, indeed, the Lion of the tribe of Judah, the rightful heir to
the throne of David.

Mark — Jesus the Ox

Mark is altogether a different portrait of Jesus. Mark gives us no genealogy
and no account of Jesus' birth. Why? Because genealogies and birth circumstances are not important for servants. All that matters is: can they work?
So in Mark, Jesus is busy working as the gospel begins. One act of service
after another crowds the sequence of Mark's portrait. The key verse for Mark
seems to be "For even the Son of Man came not to be served but to serve, and
to give his life as a ransom for many" (10:45).

There is only a brief temptation reference in Mark, because temptations
are not out of the ordinary to a servant's work. Discourses are limited in
Mark's portrait; teaching is secondary to the work of serving in the role of a
servant. In fact, Mark is the shortest gospel, specifically for this reason. If you
shortened the discourses of Christ in the other gospels to what we have in
Mark, Mark's portrait would be longer than all the others, because he tells us
more than the others of what Christ did. Christ is a servant in Mark's portrait
and fulfills in precise detail the picture of an ox.

Luke — Jesus the Man

Who is best suited to render an opinion as to whether someone is truly
human, rather than being an extraterrestrial masking as a person? A physician. And apparently that is what God thought as He tapped Dr. Luke for
the job of writing the gospel portrait of Christ as a man. Luke "the beloved
physician" (Col. 4:14) put the stethoscope on Jesus' life and in effect said,
"Yep. He's a real man."

Luke is the only gospel besides Matthew that includes a genealogy of
Jesus. But Luke presses the lineage all the way back to Adam, the first man
(3:38). Why? Because he is interested in demonstrating that Jesus is a true
son of Adam and is, therefore, a genuine human being.

Luke, unlike any of the other writers, begins his gospel with the story
of the birth of John the Baptist. John was the forerunner of the Messiah,

commissioned by God to introduce Jesus Christ to the world. Dr. Luke tells us of John's fetal response to the new life in Mary's womb (1:39–45). This meeting of two pregnant women, Elizabeth and Mary, and the surprise response of John to the presence of Jesus is of great interest to the physician writing the story. Unborn human life was acknowledging the unique human life within Mary.

Luke records the annunciation of the angel to Mary—not Joseph, as in Matthew's account. Since Mary as a virgin conceived the Christ child, it was through Mary that Jesus received His humanity. A virgin conception was absolutely enthralling to the medical mind of Dr. Luke. Furthermore, as Luke tells the story, shepherds visited the manger. No mention of kings as in Matthew. Luke is the only one who mentions that the common working man came to worship the Savior in Bethlehem.

All the way through his portrait of Christ, Dr. Luke reveals the inner passion and pathos of the man Jesus, more than any other gospel. Even at the end, Luke treats us to the very human encounter of Jesus with two of His discouraged followers on their way home to Emmaus. The other three Evangelists leave that poignant story for Luke to tell. Luke doesn't diminish the Lion or the Ox, but as a physician he is particularly taken with the man.

John — Jesus the Eagle

John's gospel, on the other hand, is the most unusual of the four. Not only does John include otherwise unrecorded material about Jesus' life, but his purpose transcends the other writers. Without question Jesus is *the* King, *the* Servant, and *the* Man. But John raises the level of observation above human perspectives to convince us that Jesus is also the everlasting, omnipotent God. So that we will not miss the point, he concludes his gospel by saying, "These are written so that you may believe that Jesus is the Christ, the Son of God" (20:31).

Wasting no time establishing the theme of his portrait, John begins, "In the beginning was the Word ... and the Word was God ... And the Word became flesh and dwelt among us" (1:1, 14). John has no genealogy of Christ. Think about it. Who are the parents of God? Christmas is reduced to one verse: "And the Word became flesh" (1:14). The reason of course is that Deity was never born; it was "given" (Isa. 9:6). Shepherds don't appear in John, and kings are glossed over. Instead of Bethlehem, we are transported into heavenly places to view the divine purpose of the Incarnation. Neither is Jesus tempted in John, for as James informs us, "God cannot be tempted with evil" (James 1:13). Other omissions and inclusions in John are just as impressive.

Seven miracles are woven together around significant discourses in the Gospel of John to create the indelible impression that Jesus is indeed God. Thomas speaks for every doubter when he admits his inability to believe Christ's claim to deity. Yet John ends with Thomas's incredible confession at the feet of the resurrected Christ: "My Lord and my God!" (20:28). John wants us to know that Jesus of Nazareth is the incarnate God.

SUMMARY

Let's consider what we have discovered so far. In Ezekiel's and John's visions of God, they both saw a man on a throne represented by four living creatures: a lion, an ox, a man, and an eagle (Ezekiel 1; Revelation 4). These creatures represent the biblical concepts of a king, a servant, a human being, and God.

Then as God stepped onto planet Earth in the person of Jesus Christ, the Scriptures reflect on his fourfold nature, with four gospel portraits: Matthew, Mark, Luke, and John. In Matthew, Jesus is represented as the *Son of David*—the Lion King. Mark presents Him as the *Servant of Jehovah*—the Ox Servant. Luke paints a portrait of Him as the *Son of Man*—the Man who is totally human. Finally, John crowns the fourfold record with an amazing portrait of Jesus as the *Son of God*—the Eagle as the transcendent Being who has come from heaven.

FACES	NATURE	GOSPELS
Lion	King	Matthew
Ox	Servant	Mark
Man	Humanity	Luke
Eagle	Deity	John

4 Living Creatures • 4 Faces
4 Gospels • 4 Portraits

LOOKING IN THE MIRROR

The head, with its distinctive facial features, is the single most important identifying factor in determining who we are. Perched in the preeminent position above our frame, it assumes the prominent role of communicating with the rest of humanity. Drivers' licenses and passports display pictures of the face—not the body. When talking with another person, we focus on the face to read the expressions that enhance the meaning of words. Four of our five senses are exclusively in the head: seeing, hearing, smelling, and tasting. Inside the cranium the brain governs every aspect of the body and sits supreme over the entire functioning system. We groom the hair and face like no other part of the body, giving it our most careful attention. There's no question about it. The head is really "who we are."

In like fashion, Jesus Christ is enthroned as the Head over His body (Eph. 1:22–23; Col. 1:18) and is the undisputed focus of Holy Scripture (Luke 24:27, 44). As we watched the mosaic of the biblical books unfold earlier in our study, we noted the Gospels emerging into the supreme position of the head. This is fitting because, more than any other portion of Scripture, the Gospels reveal the full scope of who Jesus is.

Let's ask and answer a few more questions: Is there anything about the design of the human head that reflects the four dimensions of the gospel portraits? Where would we begin in our analysis of the structure and function of the head to discover a "quadraplex" of meaning? Again we find our clue in Ezekiel.

First of all, when describing the fourfold face of the man who is God, Ezekiel stresses features of the face (or head). The distinction between the four living creatures therefore is a *head*-thing. So we're on track in that regard.

Second, however, he mentions a division of the head into two spheres, which sets our course for viewing this analogy. He says: "As for the likeness of their faces, each had a human face. The four had the face of a lion *on the right side*, the four had the face of an ox *on the left side*, and the four had the face of an eagle" (1:10, emphasis mine).

Notice that all four of the living creatures had each of the four likenesses even though there is a clear distinction between the symbolic representations. This is unquestionably true of all four of the Gospels as well. Though Matthew clearly emphasizes Jesus' kingship, he in no way minimizes His servanthood or humanity and deity. He simply stresses the lion aspect of Jesus' character. The same is true of the other Gospels. All four likenesses are in each gospel, but one symbol is being highlighted above the others in each portrait.

Curiously, Ezekiel also mentions the side-placement of the lion and the ox. The right side of the face is said to look like a lion and the left side like an ox. These two creatures represent the first paradox—that the man is both a king and a servant. Somehow the two ideas seem to go together as two sides of the same face.

Matthew and Mark

Look at yourself in a mirror. Apart from abnormal imperfections like moles, birthmarks, and zits, do you see that the two sides of your face are symmetrical? What you have on the right side, you also have on the left: an eye, an ear, half a nose, and half a mouth. It's the same, yet different. Different in the sense that there are actually two distinct sides of your one face.

That's exactly what Jesus taught concerning the difference between a king and a servant. In essence He said that anyone wishing to become a leader must first of all learn how to serve. The disciples were arguing about who was going to become the leader of the group. Jesus interrupted their argument by saying, "If anyone would be first, he must be last of all and servant of all" (Mark 9:35). In other words, a good king rules by serving his people. Ruling and serving definitely go together as symmetrical concepts.

Jesus is presented in Matthew as the King on David's throne (the right side of the face). Mark describes Him as the Servant of Jehovah who gives His life for the people (the left side of the face). In Jesus Christ, both concepts blend together in perfect harmony—like two sides making one face.

Furthermore, this dual nature of Christ is reflected in His two advents. The first time He came in humility, as a Galilean peasant serving the people. He came as a servant. But when He returns again, the display of His kingly power will be awesome and majestic. The servant will come back as a king. Matthew and Mark are two sides of the same face.

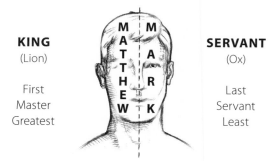

KING
(Lion)

First
Master
Greatest

SERVANT
(Ox)

Last
Servant
Least

Luke and John

Going back to Ezekiel's description of the faces (1:10), did you notice that the man and the eagle are not described in relation to sides of the face? Is there another way to divide the head? Sure. We can divide it horizontally, rather than vertically. Doing so, we get something very dissimilar and not at all symmetrical. The top portion (the cranium) houses the brain and is covered with hair. The bottom half is the face with all its distinctive features. The two halves are nothing alike.

Here's the question: will we find a reflection of the unique portraitures of Luke and John in this top and bottom view of the head? Surprisingly, yes!

Consider how the top and bottom portions of the head function together. The control of all actions and reactions centers in the brain, which is totally encased in a boney structure called the cranium or skull. Yet this epicenter of life is never seen—unless serious problems develop. Also, as if to isolate the brain in further obscurity, God covered the scalp with hair (at least for most of us). The brain is the most significant power source of life, yet it is never obvious and rarely seen.

Consider also the facial features that grace the lower part of the head—the mechanisms by which we reveal what is going on in the brain. The expressions of joy and sadness, pleasure and pain, compassion and anger, pity and disdain—all wrap themselves around the eyes, nose, and mouth like electrical impulses energizing each multicolored bulb on the Christmas tree. The many hues of emotion are reflected in the face. It is no accident that the words for anger and nose in the Hebrew language are the same, because anger is seen in the flaring of the nostrils. The mind communicates its thoughts by words articulated by the vocal chords, tongue, teeth, and lips—all in the lower part of the face. It's an ingenious design whereby the brain (in the upper part of the head) expresses itself through the features of the face (in the lower part of the head).

Let's look at Luke and John in light of this horizontal division of the head. We have seen that John's gospel is a portrait of Christ as the incarnate God. Every turn of the page reaffirms the declaration of Christ's deity. Yet when the religious leaders of Israel looked at Jesus, they couldn't see it. Jesus' deity was veiled in the covering of His human flesh. Deity was the most powerful aspect of His nature, but it was not obvious.

In fact, nowhere in John's gospel is Jesus' deity exposed to human view. John contains no transfiguration account except for John's single reflective comment on the experience he had with Peter and James—"we have seen his glory" (1:14). Nevertheless, the power of Jesus' deity determined everything in John's account. The problem for most people who saw Jesus was that His deity was encased in humanity and veiled by human flesh—similar to the brain encased in bone and veiled by hair.

So how were people supposed to understand that Jesus was God? According to Jesus, it was through His words and works.

Do you not believe that I am in the Father and the Father is in me? The words that I say to you I do not speak on my own authority, but the Father who dwells in me does his works. Believe me that I am in the Father and the Father is in me, or else believe on account of the works themselves. (John 14:10 – 11)

This is exactly how Luke interfaces with John. Luke emphasizes what can be seen through the humanity of Christ — His words and works. Functioning like the facial features as they reveal the unseen reality of the brain, Luke fleshes out the humanity of Christ through which we comprehend His deity. It is the full exposure of our Lord's humanity in Luke that is parallel to the analogy of the bottom portion of the human head.

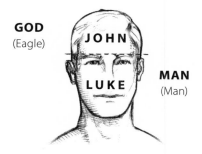

IT'S ALL IN THE HEAD

On the surface, the life of Christ is simple and easily grasped. Born in Bethlehem, Jesus lived a life of serving others and was ultimately crucified for claiming to be God. The details are a little more complicated of course, but like any other biography subject, Jesus was born … lived … and died. The nondiscerning eye has often seen it that way — in which case one blended narrative is all that is needed to tell the story. For most people the Gospels are merely redundant, complementary accounts enabling us to fill in details omitted by one or the other writers.

In God's plan, however, there could be no simple telling of the story — no single, yet complete, authoritative biography. To adequately understand Jesus' uncommon life, the world would need to comprehend *who He is*. And it would take a quatrain of portraits to do that. Thus four gospel portraits were written — each essential to portraying the full scope of the King-Servant who is the God-Man. Any study of the Gospels must begin with that observation.

The Gospels therefore are the apex of revelation. As the person of Christ is the *anticipation* of all Old Testament hope, so He is also the *reflection* of all New Testament proclamation. Christ is the Head of the body and sits enthroned in the Gospels over the whole corpus of Scripture.

And that is where God has positioned the human head—on top of the body, where it is both prominent and preeminent. Designed in symmetrical halves, the two sides of the head are a perfect analogy of the complementary concepts of leadership (Matthew-King) and service (Mark-Servant). Seen in horizontal halves, however, the upper cranium with its brain is a perfect picture of unseen deity (John-God)—while the lower facial features are an adequate display of our Lord's interactive humanity (Luke-Man). When it comes to the Gospels, it does seem that it is all in the head.

CHAPTER FOUR

BIFURCATED TRUTH

The Book of Acts

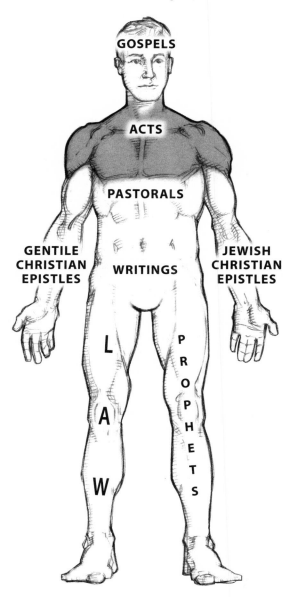

THE BOOK OF ACTS

When the Jewish leaders, in league with the government of Rome, put Jesus to death, they were confident that their problems with the troublesome prophet were over. He was dead and His followers had been scattered. Another glitch in their nefarious grasp of Israel's destiny had been successfully terminated. Jesus was history and Caiaphas the high priest was a hero. But only for a weekend.

Christ's resurrection on Sunday morning effectively dampened their enthusiasm and the postcrucifixion party came to a screeching halt.

"Is He really alive? Where did He go? What's the deal? . . . I thought we were done with this mess. His disciples must have stolen the body—that's the only thing that makes sense." Little did they know it was only just beginning.

Appearing to individuals and groups of people over a span of forty days, Jesus convinced His followers that He had truly risen from the dead. He persuaded them that His death marked the end of the beginning. God's plan was right on schedule, and there was more to come—much more! The Holy Spirit would soon come in a powerful demonstration of courage and renewed strength to equip the faithful for effective witness that would penetrate into every sphere of society.

Then Jesus ascended into heaven, and for ten days they waited. When the promise of the Spirit came, it was spectacular. Like fireworks on the Fourth of July, the little gathering of 120 followers of Jesus were set ablaze with passion from heaven, spilling out onto the swollen streets of holiday traffic. The ancient Feast of Pentecost had found its fulfillment, and the shockwaves of Christian witness would be felt all over the world. That's how the book of Acts begins.

RIGHT WHERE IT BELONGS

Beginning where the Gospels leave off at the resurrection appearances of Jesus, the book of Acts chronicles the historical foundation of the church as the continuation of Christ's work in the world. Dr. Luke, who wrote the Gospel of Luke, is the author of this book as well. So the Gospel of Luke and the book of Acts go together to form the first and second parts of the life of Jesus and the development of His spiritual body, the church.

It is important to observe from this that Acts is not a stand-alone book as some of the early church Fathers were prone to think (see Appendix 2). On the contrary, Acts has a vital connection to the Gospels and belongs right after the Gospels as the fifth book of the New Testament. This dual record of Luke and Acts establishes the chronological continuity between Christ's physical life on earth and his spiritual body in the church.

I	—	**CHRIST**	—	II
LUKE				**ACTS**
(His Physical Person)				(His Spiritual Body)

Building our study of the Gospels in the previous chapter, this Lucan connection of Acts with the Gospels establishes another significant aspect of the body analogy. In the mosaic of biblical books, Acts emerges in the position of the neck and shoulders. To what part of the head does the connection with the neck take place? Not at the top of the head (John) nor out of the right or left sides (Matthew and Mark). The union is clearly with the bottom half (Luke). If the body analogy is indeed the way God formatted the Scriptures, that is no accident. But for now let's just call it an interesting observation.

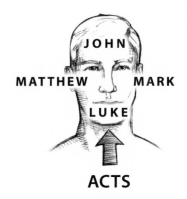

WHO'S GOT THE KEYS?

Even a quick analysis of the human body will reveal that it is symmetrical. Like the two sides of a face, what is on the right side of the body is also on the left. Each side has an arm, a hand, a leg, and a foot, and the backbone and sternum divide the torso into a right side and a left side. There are definitely two sides to who we are, and the two halves combine to form a single body. It's a perfect picture of Christ's body—the church.

The church is both Jew and Gentile—not either-or, but both-and. From a Jewish point of view, society is divided into two parts: a Jewish part and a Gentile part (that's the rest of us). In the days of Jesus and the beginning of the church, the Jews excluded the Gentiles from everything. Jew and Gentile just didn't mix—and that created huge problems for the neophyte church.

The reason for the problem of course was that Jesus made it crystal clear that His message was for everybody without distinction. The apostle Paul understood this and argued that the breaking down of the racial barrier was definitely a part of Jesus' agenda. "For he himself is our peace, who has made us both one and has broken down in his flesh the dividing wall of hostility ... that he might create in himself one new man in place of two, so making peace" (Eph. 2:14–15).

Getting the Jews and Gentiles to function together as a unit became a priority issue for the early church. According to Acts, this was accomplished in a number of ways. First, only one man was appointed by Jesus to open the door of the church for every group. To Peter, He said, "I will give you the keys of the kingdom of heaven, and whatever you bind on earth shall be bound in heaven, and whatever you loose on earth shall be loosed in heaven" (Matt. 16:19).

The use of a single figurehead to open the door of the body of Christ to both Jews and Gentiles signaled a common purpose for everyone and produced a unifying effect. The book of Acts actually begins by describing this use of the keys by Peter.

Chapter 2 of Acts opens with the celebration of the Jewish Feast of Pentecost and the descent of the Holy Spirit upon 120 Jewish believers in Jesus. This small group spilled out into the street proclaiming the gospel of Christ to thousands of Jewish pilgrims who heard the message in their native languages. People were amazed as they viewed this unusual and dramatic spectacle. In the midst of the ensuing confusion, Peter stood up and began speaking to the whole crowd. When he was done, three thousand people responded to his invitation to believe in Jesus as their eternal Savior. The church had begun, and the Jews were the first to enter. Peter had used his key and opened the door.

Sometime later a half step from Jew to Gentile was taken in the development of the burgeoning church. Philip the evangelist, one of the first deacons of the church, preached the message of Jesus in the cities of Samaria (Acts 8). Samaritans were an ethnic blend of Jew and Gentile and were considered a mongrel race by the Jews who ostracized them from Jewish society and worship at the Temple. In short, the Samaritans had developed their own independent religious system.

When Philip shared the good news of Jesus' death, burial, and resurrection with the Samaritans, many believed. Something was missing, though, because they did not receive the manifestation of the Holy Spirit as had their counterparts in Jerusalem. So they sent for Peter to come to Samaria to give his approval to what was happening. When Peter came and blessed them in the name of Jesus, the Holy Spirit came upon them just as He had at Pentecost. This is the only recorded delay between believing in Jesus and receiving the Holy Spirit—and it was all because Peter had to first come and use his key. From then on, there would not be two churches (one Jewish and one Samaritan), because Peter had demonstrated that they were both part of the same body of Christ.

The last group to gain entrance was the Gentiles. Later Paul would become the apostle to the Gentiles, but not before Peter had used his key to open the door for them. It happened in the house of Cornelius, a Roman centurion living in the city of Caesarea (Acts 10). Filled with religious tension, the situation unfolded like an intense drama.

Peter first needed to be convinced that his racial bias against the Gentiles was no longer fitting. Initially he balked at the idea. But a spectacular vision from God persuaded him that this was exactly what Jesus wanted him to do. Upon entering the house of Cornelius, Peter again shared the gospel of Jesus, and when everyone in the house believed, the Holy Spirit came upon them too—just like at Pentecost. It was obvious. God was receiving Gentiles into the body of Christ, and Peter was once again the common unifying factor. He had used the last key. All the doors were now open.

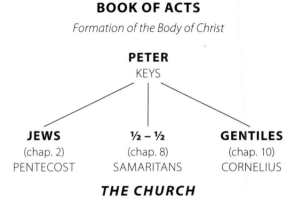

BOOK OF ACTS

Formation of the Body of Christ

PETER
KEYS

JEWS	½ – ½	**GENTILES**
(chap. 2)	(chap. 8)	(chap. 10)
PENTECOST	SAMARITANS	CORNELIUS

THE CHURCH

This is how the book of Acts begins. It chronicles the formation of the body of Christ, the church, and Peter's use of the keys to bring both Jews and Gentiles into one unified, harmonious body fellowship.

TWO HALVES OF THE BOOK

Like an apple cut in half, the book of Acts divides into two distinct parts. As you lay the book open, it becomes apparent that there is a "Peter half" and a "Paul half." Peter is the prominent figure in chapters 1–12, with the story having a definite Jewish flavor. Chapters 13–28, on the other hand, feature Paul in his missionary journeys into the Gentile world.

ACTS

JEWS	GENTILES
(chaps. 1 – 12)	(chaps. 13 – 28)
PETER	PAUL

Along with his use of the keys, Peter became a significant leader of the church in Jerusalem, which was primarily made up of Jews. The book of Galatians, for instance, refers to Peter (Cephas) as a pillar of the Jerusalem church (2:9) an apostle "to the circumcised" (2:8)—a term used to refer to the Jews. It is important to understand that even though Peter was the unifying factor for both Jews (chap. 2) and Gentiles (chap. 10), as well as the Samaritans (chap. 8), his primary ministry and focus was with the Jewish congregation in Jerusalem. The *first half of the book of Acts* (chaps. 1–12) is clearly about how the Jewish side of the body of Christ developed in Jerusalem.

The apostle Paul's conversion is described in chapter 9, but not until chapter 13 is he formally commissioned as an apostle to the Gentiles. In the plan of God, a prominent Jewish Rabbi would be used to introduce the gospel of Christ to the Gentile world. At this point Peter fades into the background, and Paul emerges as the powerful crusader for Gentiles in the church. *The second half of Acts* therefore is consumed with Paul's missionary exploits into Gentile areas.

Acts is indeed a bifurcated book. The two halves demonstrate how two distinct and formerly alienated groups were amalgamated into one harmonious body. The church of Jesus Christ is seen to be a miracle of unification —two sides but only one body.

TWO SPECIFIC NEEDS

Two different cultures ... two racial backgrounds ... two basic needs. That was the challenge for the Holy Land Experience (HLE), a themed Christian attraction in Orlando, Florida, when I was a part of the leadership team. Actually, the HLE offered just one experience for everyone, and people from all over the world were blessed by this ministry. But in the demographics of Orlando (as well as most of the state of Florida), Hispanics have become the second largest cultural group, with almost everything in Orlando bilingual —both English and Spanish. So the HLE adjusted to meet this challenge.

Many of the HLE employees were Hispanics who spoke fluent Spanish. The major venues and dramatic presentations could be heard in both English and Spanish. The HLE celebrated not only the customary American Christmas with an emphasis on Bethlehem and the birth of Christ; it also celebrated Three Kings' Day on January 6—the traditional Spanish observance —recognizing and fulfilling the needs of two distinct cultures.

That's the way it was in the early church. Jews were different from Gentiles. Each had specific needs. While insisting on only one fellowship within the unified body of Christ, attempts were made nonetheless to meet the unique needs of each group.

For Jews, the concern involved matters of "transition." Making the significant move from Moses to Jesus challenged the Jews culturally as well as theologically. For centuries, they had known God. Now the fulfillment of their Old Covenant anticipations had come and they were being asked to make the transition from God's old economy under the Law to the new relationship in Christ. This required major adjustment in their traditional thinking, and new revelation was needed to help them in this transition. Thus nine Jewish Christian Epistles (Hebrews–Revelation) were written, primarily by the apostles to the circumcision (James, Peter, and John; see Gal. 2:9), to facilitate the Jewish understanding of the new way, thereby assisting their transition from Moses to Jesus.

Gentiles presented an altogether different situation. Their cultures emphasized worship of pagan gods—not the Jehovah God of heaven. The Gentiles had no relationship to the covenants of promise and were truly without God in the world (Eph. 2:12). Having nothing to transition from, Gentiles were desperate to be transformed into a whole new concept of life. For them it was a matter of basic "transformation." Here nine Gentile Christian Epistles

(Romans – 2 Thessalonians) came from the pen of Paul the apostle to the "uncircumcision" (see Gal. 2:9), instructing the Gentiles as to how they could be spiritually transformed by believing in Christ.

BOOK OF ACTS
Two Major Groups

JEWS	GENTILES
(chaps. 1 – 12)	(chaps. 13 – 28)
PETER	PAUL
Transition	*Transformation*

Galatians 2:7 – 9

Jewish Christian Epistles **9 Books**	Gentile Christian Epistles **9 Books**
Hebrews through Revelation	Romans through 2 Thessalonians

Transition for the Jews and *transformation* for the Gentiles were not mutually exclusive ideas, however. Rather, they were complementary emphases. Jews obviously needed to be transformed by the new birth, and Gentiles needed an understanding of the transition from the old to the new. Yet because these two groups came from radically different backgrounds, facilitating their entrance into the body of Christ required a special emphasis for each. An equal number of New Testament epistles were provided in each case with instruction for their specific need.

SHOULDERING THE BURDEN

Like the book of Acts, the neck and shoulders act as a splitter or divider. In our home my wife and I each have a computer, and both of us use the Internet in our work. When our family went from a dial-up connection to a high-speed cable provider, we still needed a way for dual access to the Net. So we installed a router that split the connection, allowing each of us to exercise independent use of the same cable hook-up. To my technically challenged mind, that's amazing.

The neck and shoulders of the human body perform the same function as a router. One head sits on top of our frame, but both sides of the body receive the signal emanating from the brain. The connecting cord (the spinal cord) begins in the neck, with the signals surging down through the shoulder blades of the back, to the rest of the body. The spinal column, as it is called, splits the signal so both sides can operate independently as a complement to the other. In addition, the shoulders provide sockets for the arms and thus the two-sided body becomes a coordinated unit with an arm and hand serving each side of the body. That's the way the body works in connection with our head.

As we have gone through the basic framework of the book of Acts, you have no doubt observed that it functions in a similar manner to what I have described concerning the neck and shoulders. Connected to the Head (who is Christ) through the Gospel of Luke, Acts carries the message of Christ into the rest of the body. Acting like a router, Acts then splits the message into two distinct directions—toward the Jews and toward the Gentiles (with the Samaritans being a half step between the two).

Finally, in keeping with the shoulder imagery, two arms of epistles emerge from the historical background of the early church in Acts reaching out to both Jews and Gentiles. What Acts does for the Scriptures is a replica of the function performed by the neck and shoulders in our human bodies.

BIFURCATION OF THE BODY

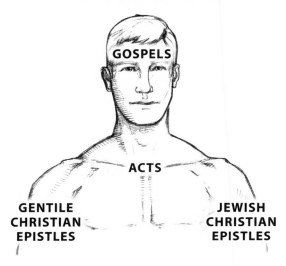

Perhaps you are beginning to see the interesting correlation between the form and function of the human body and the sequence and format of Holy Scripture. We obviously need to be careful not to spiritualize here by throwing caution to the wind in our excitement. Having said that, the analogy seems clear and unforced—at least to this point.

So let's proceed with the torso, the central core of our being. Before considering the Pastoral Epistles and the Poetical Writings, the torso as a whole seems to have an important spiritual lesson to teach us.

CHAPTER FIVE

THE BODY OF TRUTH
The Torso

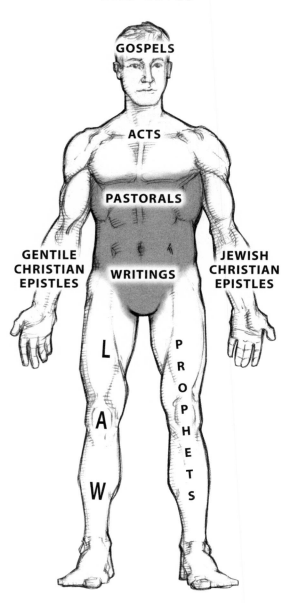

GOSPELS

ACTS

PASTORALS

GENTILE
CHRISTIAN
EPISTLES

WRITINGS

JEWISH
CHRISTIAN
EPISTLES

LAW

PROPHETS

THE TORSO

A curve ball arched toward the plate as the batter quickly surveyed his options. Arms and legs poised for maximum strength, shoulders level, hips loose, eyes focused—a split second of judgment convinced him that the spin would carry the ball across the strike zone. His grip intensified as the bat swung into motion. The wood circled around and connected with a crack that sent the ball into orbit.

Immediately legs and arms began to pump as the batter's feet propelled him toward first base … and then around second. Sprinting on, his eyes caught the third-base coach gesturing wildly with his hands in a downward motion. It was going to be close. He would have to slide. Sprawling headlong, his chest plowed dirt as billows of dust rose into the air. Extending his hand, his outstretched fingers touched the bag just ahead of the third baseman's mitt. Safe! He had slammed a triple.

Hands … arms … feet … legs … that's what it takes to play the game of baseball. One-armed batters and single-legged pitchers are conspicuously absent in America's favorite pastime. Paraplegics don't make the standard team.

But does that mean that someone in a wheelchair or who struggles to walk with iron crutches is not also a real person with potential for a meaningful life? Of course not! Why? Because legs, feet, arms, and hands don't make a person. Those things are wonderful provisions of life, for sure, but the essence of life is not in our limbs. Our head and torso define who we are and provide the fundamental source for life and living. Humans can compensate for the loss of a hand or foot, but they cannot survive without a torso.

In like manner, the Bible has a torso, and the message it communicates is essential to life with Christ and abundant living in His kingdom. It is in the Pastoral Epistles and in the Poetical Writings that we discover what it truly means to be a spiritual person.

LIFE AND LIVING

It is one thing to receive life and quite another to live the life you have received. In like fashion, becoming a Christian is only the beginning of being the Christian you have become. Life and living ... becoming and being ... belonging and participating—so many ways to express the idea of having something and enjoying what you have.

On one occasion Jesus told His followers that He had a specific purpose in mind by coming to them. He said, "I came that they may have life and have it abundantly" (John 10:10). *Life* is the Greek word, *zoē*, which refers to the principle of life—life as the essence of being. Jesus first of all came to bring us life—spiritual life with God.

But there was more. Jesus continued with an "and." A second reason for coming was on His mind, prompting Him to say "and have it abundantly." The Greek word translated *abundantly* actually means extraordinarily, remarkably, profusely. This extraordinary or remarkable life, according to *Strong's Concordance*, connotes a superabundant quantity and a superior quality. In other words, Jesus came not only to give us life, but to teach us how to live that life to the fullest. His purpose included both life and living.

These two concepts tumble through the Word of God as the basic framework for complete spirituality. Theologically speaking, justification comes first (whereby the sinner is declared righteous before God and is given eternal life in God's redeemed family). Sanctification follows as a label for the growing process (as the child of God progressively learns how to enjoy that new life with Christ). In justification, life is bestowed. In sanctification, living is encouraged. Reduced to its simplistic minimum, this is the biblical message of salvation for fallen humanity. Life and living are the essence of a spiritual relationship with God. Here is the lesson of the torso.

THE REAL YOU

So let's talk about *you* for a moment. Who are you?—intrinsically, that is. Your soul and spirit are the real you, of course. But the real you inhabits a body, and your body is the tangible expression of who you are. Your head, with its facial features and unique color and styling of hair, distinguishes you from other bodies to be sure. Yet when you get right down to expressing who you really are, how do you do that? One way is to point to your chest and say, "This is who I am. It's what is in my heart that counts. This is the real me in here."

The point is this: the physical heart isn't just a big muscle that pumps blood. It also represents the true identity of life. "I love you with all my heart" expresses a genuine commitment coming from the core of your being. The "heart of the matter" is getting down to the real issue. What's in your heart is the real you.

On the other hand, the ancients often reflected their basic feelings by referring to the viscera in the lower regions of the body. They would mention the kidneys or the liver, rather than the heart, as the true source of emotion. Today we may not say, "I love you with all my liver," but we do use expressions like "a gut reaction" or a "visceral response" or "I had a loathing in the pit of my stomach." The meaning is the same. What's real is what is deep down inside.

All of this identifying of the real you, whether contemporary or ancient, is localized in the torso. So let's probe this concept of life as represented by the organs of the body.

BLOOD AND FOOD

The torso is made up of two large cavities, each with its own distinct organs, that are separated from each other by a membranous wall called the diaphragm. Each chamber has its own specialized function, and there is no sharing or mixing of organs. The two systems benefit each other and are therefore complementary.

Thoracic Cavity — Blood

The upper part of the torso, the thoracic cavity, is where the heart and lungs perform their function. The primary organ is the heart, which shares the space with the right and left lungs. These crucial organs operate in a pressure-controlled chamber and are protected by the rib cage and sternum (breastbone).

Both the heart and the lungs perform a specific function — the circulation and purification of the blood. As a simple explanation, the heart pumps the blood, which the lungs purify. That's it. Just the blood ... that's their exclusive purpose.

CHEST
Heart — *pump*   **BLOOD**
Lungs — *purify*

Blood is the essence of life. That's what God said in His instruction to

Israel—"For the life of every creature is its blood: its blood is its life" (Lev. 17:14). Since life is in the blood, the chest cavity is devoted to one thing—life. As long as the blood flows and is regularly purified, there is life.

Is it a mere coincidence that blood is the crux of spiritual life as well? Apart from the blood of Christ there is no life with God. "For as much as you know that you were not redeemed with corruptible things ... but with the precious blood of Christ" (1 Pet. 1:18–19). In addition to being the source of life, the blood of Christ is the cleansing agent that purifies the sinner from all sin. "Without the shedding of blood there is not forgiveness of sins" (Heb. 9:22 KJV).

Just as the blood flows through the thoracic cavity in support of physical life, so the blood of Christ is the central focus of life with God. It does appear that the thorax is the symbol of life—both physical and spiritual. Blood is at the core of our being.

The Abdominal Cavity — Food

What about the lower chamber of the torso? The abdominal cavity houses the stomach, the intestines, and a host of other related organs that assist in the digestive process. Each of these organs is nourished by blood to give it life, but the function is totally different from the organs of the thoracic cavity. The key word here is not *blood*—it is *food*. And the purpose of the abdominal cavity's function is not so much life as the quality of living.

ABDOMEN
Stomach — *digest*   **FOOD**
Intestines — *absorb*

To a large extent, what we eat determines our physical welfare. Fast-food restaurants may be convenient, but too many fried foods (heavy in fats and carbohydrates) will put the cholesterol level off the charts. Weight will gradually increase, making the person a prime candidate for a heart attack. Too many sweets do a similar thing by maximizing triglycerides and creating the danger of diabetes or a stroke. Eating wrong things can inflict burdensome living.

On the other hand, fruits and vegetables, combined with a healthy portion of protein and fiber, will usually enhance life. Nutritionists understand that good living to a large degree depends on how a person eats.

Quantity of food is also an issue. Not enough food will result in malnutrition or anorexia. An overabundance of food will cause a person to be obese and less mobile. Yet the right amount of food in a balanced diet enables proper growth. What we eat certainly affects how we live.

When you think about it, spiritual living essentially works according to the same principle. A good spiritual diet for the Christian is fundamental to a healthy walk with Christ. Regular indulgence in the world and its system, with a once-a-week Sunday menu of Christ and His Word, leads to an up-and-down rollercoaster experience. Victories over the flesh, the world, and the devil are elusive, and defeat and failure occur regularly. It's like eating all your meals Monday through Saturday at a fast-food restaurant. Not healthy, to be sure.

But when there is a continual feasting on the Lord and the principles of His Word, Christian living takes on a healthy hue. The fruit of the Spirit increasingly pervades the realities of life, and the life of Christ begins to shine through the Christian experience. It all depends on what we eat, spiritually.

This is exactly how Jesus described the fullness of life with Him. He talked about it in terms of eating:

> I am the living bread that came down from heaven. If anyone eats of this bread, he will live forever. And the bread that I will give for the life of the world is my flesh.
> ... For my flesh is true food, and my blood is true drink. Whoever feeds on my flesh and drinks my blood abides in me, and I in him. (John 6:51, 55–56)

Jesus was obviously not talking about cannibalism. Using the physical analogy of eating, He used a word picture to describe communing with Him. I once heard a mother describe her son by saying, "He loves math. He eats it up." We all understand this manner of speaking. Jesus was saying that living with Him would be energized by eating Him up. You see, we take in spiritual nourishment when we are consumed with who Jesus is and what He does. That in turn causes us to grow spiritually as we experience the abundant living He promised.

The lower region of the torso in the abdominal cavity does seem to symbolize a quality of life. Abundant living with Christ is associated with proper spiritual food.

Dependent on the Head

Another interesting observation concerning the torso is that both the thoracic and abdominal cavities are serviced by the head. In fact, neither can function independent of the head. As we apply the body analogy here, we are reminded that both life and living are totally dependent upon Jesus Christ, who is our Head. Jesus actually told us this: "Apart from me you can do nothing" (John 15:5).

Bodies need oxygen to survive, and the carbon dioxide waste product produced by the body must be eliminated. The lungs perform this transfer, but breathing—the intake of oxygen and the output of carbon dioxide—takes place in the head. Inhaling and exhaling through the nose accomplishes the twofold process.

Years ago I came across a novel idea called "spiritual breathing." The concept was patterned after the exhaling and inhaling of normal breathing. First, a believer needs to exhale confession of sins to God, getting rid of the waste product of the soul. Then the person follows up by inhaling God's forgiveness to receive the revitalizing ministry of Christ. The purpose of spiritual breathing is to keep short accounts with the Lord in order to remain in close fellowship with Him. Not a bad idea.

So here's the point: physically and spiritually, life itself is sustained through the ministry of the head.

The same is true for the abdominal cavity and the quality of living. Food is the energy source for what we do. The only space in the human body for receiving food is the mouth. The stomach cannot feed itself, and the intestines (as well as the other digestive organs) have nothing to do unless the stomach has food to digest. The source of provision for the abdominal cavity is in the head.

The analogy here is crucial as well. Spiritually speaking, our source of nourishment is Christ, our Head. No other source is available. He alone can feed us what we need for spiritually healthy living. In both the physical and spiritual spheres, therefore, the abdominal cavity is desperate for what only the head can provide.

Putting It All Together

This, then, is the message of the torso. The essential structure of the human body illustrates perfectly the foundational truths of life and living with God.

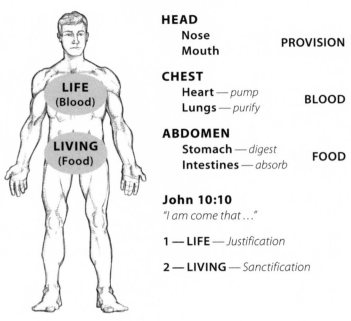

BODY OF TRUTH

HEAD
Nose
Mouth   **PROVISION**

CHEST
Heart — *pump*
Lungs — *purify*   **BLOOD**

ABDOMEN
Stomach — *digest*
Intestines — *absorb*   **FOOD**

John 10:10
"I am come that ..."

1 — **LIFE** — *Justification*

2 — **LIVING** — *Sanctification*

THE PASTORALS AND THE WRITINGS

What does all this have to do with the books of the Bible? A review of the mosaic design in chapter 1 will reveal the books that occupy central portions of the Old and New Testaments.

Coming between the nine Gentile Christian Epistles and the nine Jewish Christian Epistles in the New Testament are four personal books labeled the Pastorals. The combined teachings of these four books expose the concept of "life" for the body of Christ. As a unit they function in the same manner as the heart and lungs of the thoracic cavity.

The Old Testament has a central portion as well. The five poetical books are positioned between the seventeen books of the Law and the seventeen books of the Prophets. An analysis of their structure and function reveals that collectively the Poetical Writings develop the concept of "living" for the body of Christ. They function in the Scriptures as the organs of the abdominal cavity function for us physically.

In the next two chapters we'll take a closer look at these two groups of books. I think you'll be amazed at how the Pastorals and the Writings are beautifully illustrated by the complementary functions of the thoracic cavity and the abdominal cavity of the torso.

CHAPTER SIX

A CHEST-FULL OF TREASURE

The Pastorals

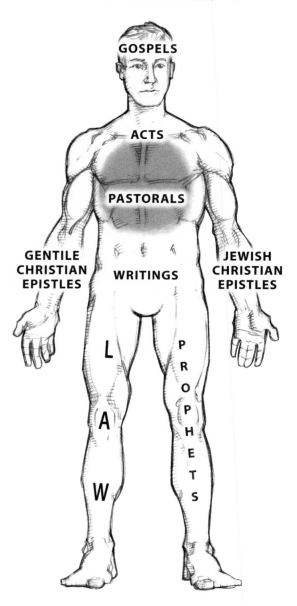

A CHEST FULL OF TREASURE

Most often we take our bodies for granted, but when something breaks down — an illness, an accident, a malfunction of some sort — suddenly our interest peaks and we want to know all we can about what went wrong and how it can be remedied. Then, when a health-care professional explains to us how the system functions, we are left captivated with wonder. The human body is without question a phenomenal work of scientific art by the sovereign Designer.

This is particularly true with regard to the mysteries of the heart. Think about the fascinating fact that our cardiovascular system works independently of conscious thought and deliberate attention. Beat after beat, minute after minute, 24/7/365 for a lifetime — the heart and lungs serve us with no request for appreciation. Until, of course, something goes wrong with the system, and suddenly we become all too aware of the treasure that functions within. The chest cavity is one of the wonders of the world!

A COMMON STRUCTURE

As the heart and lungs occupy the central portion of the upper frame of the torso, so the four Pastorals find themselves nestled into the upper part of the biblical torso. Four books (1 & 2 Timothy, Titus, and Philemon) functioning like a literary heart and lungs emerge between the arms of Jewish and Gentile epistles, all connected to the historical setting of the book of Acts. In a moment we'll probe the flow of thought in each of these four books, looking for an analogous correspondence with the workings of the heart and lungs. Before we do that, however, let's note a simple comparison of structure between the physical and literary systems.

The Pastorals are very personal books, written to individuals rather than churches. In that way they go together as a group. Timothy, ministering in Ephesus, received two of the books; Titus and Philemon, living in Crete and Colossae respectively, received one each. First Timothy (6 chapters) and 2 Timothy (4 chapters) are also larger books than Titus (3 chapters) and Philemon (1 chapter). So structurally speaking, the Pastorals exhibit one large unit divided into two unequal parts (1 & 2 Timothy) and two smaller unequal units that are not connected (Titus and Philemon).

Consider the anatomical structure of the chest cavity. The central organ is the heart—a single muscular unit divided into two unequal halves. The left side of the heart is bigger because it pumps blood throughout the entire body. The smaller right side pumps blood only to the lungs. In addition the cavity has two independent lungs. The left lung is smaller, with only two lobes, and the right lung is bigger with three lobes. And that's it. No other organs occupy the chest cavity. Just the heart, which pumps the blood, and two purifying lungs.

We haven't started looking at function yet, but structurally there is a startling similarity between the Pastorals and the organs of the chest cavity. One large unit operating with two halves (the Timothy epistles and the heart), and two separate units operating independently of each other (two lungs and two separate books—Titus and Philemon). The comparison of the Pastorals with the chest cavity is beginning to get interesting.

THE PASTORALS

Central Truth
New Testament

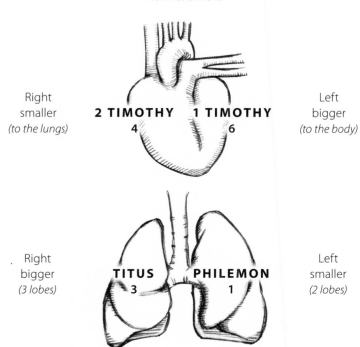

Right smaller
(to the lungs)

2 TIMOTHY
4

1 TIMOTHY
6

Left bigger
(to the body)

Right bigger
(3 lobes)

TITUS
3

PHILEMON
1

Left smaller
(2 lobes)

IS PHILEMON A PASTORAL?

Look at any Introduction to the New Testament, where the Bible books are grouped and analyzed, and Philemon will not be included with the Pastorals. Most often Philemon is categorized with the Prison Epistles (Ephesians, Philippians, and Colossians) because Philemon was also written by Paul during his Roman imprisonment.

Yet there are good reasons to include Philemon with the epistles to Timothy and Titus as a legitimate member of the Pastoral Epistles.

First, the book of Philemon was written to an individual who had personal concern for the church. Addressed to Philemon, the greeting also includes "and the church in your house" (v. 2). Paul, the author, obviously felt that the contents of the letter had a pastoral application for the church. As Timothy and Titus had concern for the churches in Ephesus and Crete, so Philemon shared an integral connection with the church in Colossae. None of these men was a pastor in the strict sense of the term. Therefore Philemon should not be excluded from this pastoral grouping because he was not a pastor.

Second, the letter to Philemon has a definite spiritual bearing upon the church. In other words, it has pastoral value. The forgiveness and acceptance of Onesimus as a brother (v. 16) had a great bearing upon the church that met in Philemon's house. Reconciliation is an important theme for the church and is a common pastoral issue. That is the essence of the book of Philemon.

Third, Philemon was included with the Pastorals by the early church, apparently for the above two reasons. Even in our Bibles today (which follow the traditional ordering of books), Philemon appears after the books of Timothy and Titus and is not grouped with the other Prison Epistles. Philemon was closely associated with the book of Colossians; they were both written at the same time to the same church and carried by the same messengers. Yet Philemon has never been grouped with Colossians in any of the ancient manuscripts. The early church deliberately segregated Philemon from the other Prison Epistles and placed it with the Pastorals. That's clearly where it belongs.

Fourth, Philemon was not excluded from the Pastorals until the eighteenth century. In 1703, D. N. Berdot was the first to use the term *Pastorals*. Twenty-three years later (1726), Paul Anton popularized the term as a reference to the books of Timothy and Titus. These men excluded Philemon from the Pastorals, apparently because they did not see it as having pastoral value. Berdot and Anton were, I believe, shortsighted. What is truly amazing, though, is that modern scholarship has followed their inept advice, and this has even been true in the evangelical community.

FOLLOW THE FLOW

What did the author intend to say by what he wrote? This question is crucial in deciphering any writing, but how much more important when seeking to understand the Word of God. Flow of thought establishes context, and context is the essence of meaning. The apostle Paul was a master of literature and a superb logician. His thoughts flow in meaningful progression so that the entire piece is a work of literary art. Following each biblical author's thought structure is the business of Bible study.

Paul wrote the Pastorals—all of them. So it is conceivable that the quartet of books written to Timothy, Titus, and Philemon have a meaningful connection. This is not to say that Paul patterned these books after the heart-lung analogy; that was more likely the superintending work of the Holy Spirit. Yet the theological concurrence and specific emphases in the combination of books are most probably by design, not happenstance. With little redundancy, each of the four books exhibits its own theme while adding significant overarching purpose.

So let's look at each book and probe the idea that the books work together as a comprehensive unit.

1 Timothy

Timothy served the church in Ephesus as a representative of the apostle Paul. Having been a regular companion of Paul, Timothy traveled extensively both with the apostle and on his behalf. Eventually when Paul left him in charge of the Ephesian church, Timothy needed specific instruction as to how the church should properly function. First Timothy is that manual of instruction.

This epistle could be labeled "Nourishment for the Body." As the body of Christ, the church needed to grasp its purpose in terms of spiritual nourishment and the application of that nourishment to specific congregational groups and situations. These in fact are the two ideas that form the essential sequence of the book. The end of chapter 3 obviously concludes a unit of thought; the six chapters of the book seem to divide evenly into two sections of three chapters each.

In keeping with the idea of nourishment for a healthy body, the first section reveals the *elements* of nourishment (chaps. 1–3); the second section deals with the *segments* of the body (chaps. 4–6) to which those elements are to be applied.

A careful reading of chapters 1–3 indicates that the elements of nourishment for the body of Christ are the Word (chap. 1), prayer (chap. 2), and a godliness as modeled by its leadership (chap. 3).

Chapter 1 is all about the Word of God and teaching the pure gospel of grace. Paul exhorts Timothy "not to teach any different doctrine" (1:3), to understand the limits of the law (1:8–11), and to remember that salvation is solely by the mercy and grace of God (1:12–17).

Prayer is the subject of chapter 2, as Paul begins, "First of all, then, I urge that supplications, prayers, intercessions, and thanksgivings be made for all people" (2:1). He goes on to say that "in every place the men should pray" (2:8) and that women should adopt the posture of prayer "with all submissiveness" (2:11).

Godliness is the result of the Word and prayer in the believer's life, and in chapter 3 Paul states that godliness should be supremely manifest in those who hold leadership roles in the church. Paul ends the chapter by saying, "Great indeed, we confess, is the mystery of godliness" (3:16).

When the church was first organizing itself in Jerusalem as recorded in Acts 6, the apostles requested that other men be found who could administrate the daily operations. In that way the apostles could give themselves to the foundational tasks of prayer and the ministry of the Word (6:4). According to the apostles, these are the core indispensable qualities for a healthy church ministry. We should not be surprised that the Word, prayer, and godliness are the elements emphasized in the opening chapters of 1 Timothy. They are indeed the critical elements of nourishment for the body.

In the second section of 1 Timothy, we notice an emphasis on various groups within the church to which the ministry of the Word, prayer, and godliness are directed. Skipping chapter 4 for a moment, we see that chapter 5 focuses on widows (women) and elders (men) with application toward gender differences in the fellowship. Chapter 6, on the other hand, calls attention to the economic contrast between masters (the rich) and slaves (the poor), telling both to keep their eyes on the Lord rather than on the issue of money.

Chapter 4 is a bit more oblique, but having noticed the gender (chap. 5) and economic (chap. 6) applications, it seemed natural to look for another category or specific grouping within the church. The chapter is devoted primarily to Timothy with regard to his personal acceptance by the congregation. In Acts 16:1 we see that Timothy's father was Greek, while his mother was Jewish, making Timothy a mixture of both races (or in a sense neither).

This raises the possibility of race as an underlying factor in the discussion. After all, the church of Jesus Christ is racially diverse, being neither Jew nor Gentile—and Timothy is a perfect example of that diversity. Also, the fact that the first paragraph of this chapter (4:1–5) addresses the problem of religious perversions (deceitful spirits and teachings of demons; 4:1), which came from both Jewish and Gentile backgrounds, seems to further suggest an ethnic application for the chapter. The point is clear. Timothy should expect the congregation to accept him on the basis of his godliness and recognition by the elders, not because he has come from any particular ethnic background.

So three applications appear in the second section of 1 Timothy: ethnic (chap. 4), gender (chap. 5), and economic (chap. 6). According to Paul's comments in Galatians 3:28, these three distinctions comprise the three major *segments* of the body—"There is neither Jew nor Greek, there is neither slave nor free, there is neither male nor female, for you are all one in Christ Jesus."

This simple scheme then, seems to describe the book of 1 Timothy. The initial three chapters present the basic *elements* for a healthy body fellowship. The final half applies those elements to each *segment* of the body.

1 TIMOTHY

Nourishment for the Body

A. The ELEMENTS of Nourishment
Chap. 1 — *The Word*
Chap. 2 — *Prayer* > **Acts 6:4**
Chap. 3 — *Godliness*

B. The SEGMENTS of the Body
Chap. 4 — *Ethnic*
Chap. 5 — *Gender* > **Gal. 3:28**
Chap. 6 — *Economic*

2 Timothy

Things don't always work out so well. Life is not ideal, and solving problems is a daily routine. That's what Timothy discovered when he tried to implement the instructions of Paul in his first letter. Not that everything had gone wrong, but people will be people, and the going was certainly not smooth. As a result Timothy became discouraged—even to the point of tears. So Paul wrote a second letter to encourage him. Second Timothy was written to help him with his difficult circumstances.

A quick reading of 2 Timothy immediately reveals that the overall theme is encouragement—not only for Timothy, but for the church as well. This book could be labeled "Encouragement for the Body." Like 1 Timothy, this second letter is in two equal parts. The problems are discussed in chapters

1 and 2, while solutions are offered in chapters 3 and 4. I have labeled the two sections the *refuse* of the body (chaps. 1–2) and the *refuge* of the body (chaps. 3–4).

Consider the *refuse* issue in the first two chapters. Timothy had certainly been hassled. In chapter 1 Paul acknowledges the difficulty of Timothy's situation by saying, "As I remember your tears" (1:4) and, "God [has] not given us the spirit of fear" (1:7 KJV). In fact Paul empathizes with the suffering Timothy has had to endure—for "which cause I also suffer these things" (1:12 KJV).

Added to hassles was the endurance of hardships. Paul addresses this issue in chapter 2 by challenging Timothy to "endure hardness, as a good soldier of Jesus Christ" (2:3 KJV). Paul is writing this letter from prison in Rome, where he has been confined for the sake of the gospel (2:9), and he wants to encourage Timothy to hang in there as Paul himself has done (2:12). The important thing, Paul goes on to say, is to cleanse oneself "from what is dishonorable" (2:21), "flee youthful passions" (2:22), and "have nothing to do with foolish, ignorant controversies" (2:23).

In chapters 1 and 2, then, Paul discusses the refuse Timothy has encountered within the church body and reminds him of the importance of cleansing himself lest he also become defiled.

The remainder of the book is about *refuge*—where to go to find answers to the refuse problem. Paul uses an interesting formation in this section. When a literary piece exhibits a mirror image in its structure so that the beginning and ending are the same and the central parts match in reverse order (A–B–C–C–B–A), it is a parallel comparison with an inverted sequence —an inverted parallel. Such a format moves from the issue toward the solution and from the solution back out to the issue. In other words, the emphasis is on the central portion and the application is at the beginning and the end.

Notice this pattern in chapters 3 and 4 of 2 Timothy. Chapter 3 begins with a description of the perverted culture (3:1–9) that has "the appearance of godliness, but denying its power" (3:5); chapter 4 ends with a parallel section on the conflicts produced by that culture (4:9–10). Then the power of true godliness as modeled by Paul's life is stressed (3:10–13) with another parallel emphasis on the results of his godliness (4:5–8). At the core of this issue is the Word of God (3:14–17) and a faithful proclamation of sound doctrine (4:1–4). In all of this, Paul is explaining that the answer to Timothy's problems is twofold: First, continue to live a godly life in the midst of the surrounding evil. Second, remain focused on the Word of God and the gospel of Christ as the core of his ministry.

2 TIMOTHY

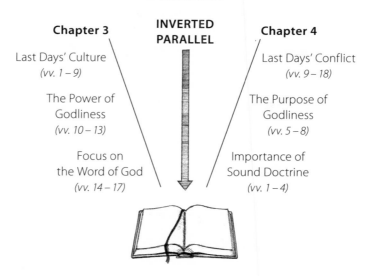

Chapter 3	INVERTED PARALLEL	Chapter 4
Last Days' Culture (vv. 1 – 9)		Last Days' Conflict (vv. 9 – 18)
The Power of Godliness (vv. 10 – 13)		The Purpose of Godliness (vv. 5 – 8)
Focus on the Word of God (vv. 14 – 17)		Importance of Sound Doctrine (vv. 1 – 4)

This appears to be the flow of thought in Paul's second letter to Timothy. So let's put it all together and lay it out clearly.

2 TIMOTHY

Encouragement for the Body

A. The REFUSE of the Body
Chap. 1 — *Hassles*
Chap. 2 — *Hardships*

B. The REFUGE of the Body
Chap. 3 — *Godliness &*
Chap. 4 — *Gospel*

Titus

Ministry on the island of Crete was a challenge. Immersed in the paganism inherited from the Minoan culture, the Cretans had a hard time grasping the concept of godly living. As a representative of Paul on the Island, Titus needed help in counteracting such self-indulgent ways. The entire Epistle to Titus is devoted to that concern. The book focuses on godliness, and Paul begins by clearly stating that point and "acknowledging of the truth which is after godliness" (1:1 KJV).

Paul opens the epistle with a comparison between the godly qualification for leadership in the church (1:5 – 9) and the ungodly behavior of the Cretans — many of whom professed to be believers in Christ (1:10 – 16). The theme of the chapter is that the true *measure* of godliness can be seen in the exemplary lifestyle of an elder who "must be above reproach" (1:7). In contrast, the Cretans "profess to know God, but they deny him by their works" (1:16). Paul is insisting that genuine faith in Christ will most definitely result in a new desire for godly living.

So how can the Cretan church become more godly? Chapter 2 explains the *means* of godliness by outlining a practical pattern for ministry. First, Titus needs to teach "sound doctrine" that will lead to godly behavior (2:1). Then spiritually mature men and women should instruct the younger men and women how to live according to God's Word (2:2–6). Titus himself is to be "a model of good works" (2:7) and encourage even the servants to "adorn the doctrine of God our Savior" (2:10). The motivation for all of this is the blessed hope of Christ's return (2:11–14) and realizing that the intended purpose of redemption is for believers to be "zealous for good works" (2:14).

Finally, like a child learning to adopt better behavior, Christians in Crete need to be consistent in practicing the new godly lifestyle. Hence, chapter 3 focuses on the *maintenance* of godliness. After being saved by the grace of God through Christ, they are expected to pursue godly living in every area of life (3:1–7). Paul concludes by reminding them that "they which have believed in God might be careful to *maintain* good works" (3:8 KJV, emphasis mine) and "let ours also learn to *maintain* good works for necessary uses, that they be not unfruitful" (3:14 KJV, emphasis mine).

Here then, is the flow of thought in Paul's letter to Titus. First he explains "the *measure* of godliness" (chap. 1). Then he gives instruction on "the *means* of godliness" (chap. 2). And finally, he exhorts with regard to "the *maintenance* of godliness" (chap. 3). The thrust of the book of Titus is clearly godliness.

TITUS

Godliness

Chap. 1 — **The Measure**
Chap. 2 — **The Means**
Chap. 3 — **The Maintenance**

Philemon

How did an ancient letter of appeal regarding the reconciliation of a runaway slave find its way into the collection of biblical writings? Sure, it was written by Paul, but as some have suggested, there doesn't seem to be a lot of spiritual value in the story. A lesson in Christian morals that rise above the norm, maybe—but beyond that, not much attention has been given to this short treatise dealing with a Christian response to slavery in the Roman Empire.

Unless there is more here than meets the eye.

It appears to me that the key to unlock the mysteries of the book of Philemon is found in its theme — reconciliation. In this book three principal characters emerge: Philemon, the master of the house; Onesimus, the runaway slave; and Paul, the mediating friend. When Paul wrote the letter, all three of these men were believers in Christ who knew what it was for a sinner to be reconciled with God. In fact, it becomes quite obvious in the way Paul frames his appeal that the divine reconciliation of a sinner with God has become the pattern for each step in the temporal process.

If that is true, and close study reveals that it is, the theme of this book may have a double application: a real-life story in the first century AD and a spiritual picture of eternal reconciliation between the sinner and God. The principles of divine reconciliation virtually leap off the page as Paul describes the foundation and process for reuniting alienated parties. Understanding God's fondness for analogy and Jesus' prolific use of parables to clarify spiritual truth, it should not surprise us to discover that the letter to Philemon may indeed be the grandest illustration of the gospel of reconciliation ever conceived.

Consider the scenario: Philemon is a wealthy landowner with sovereign control over the servants of his household in the same manner as God is the owner of all things with sovereign authority over every person in the world. As a loving master (vv. 4–7) Philemon mirrors the character of God, who is loving and just.

Onesimus, on the other hand, has a selfish heart and a rebellious attitude toward his master. Expressing his independence, this servant has run away from his responsibilities in Colossae and, by this act, incurred the death penalty of the Roman Empire. To rebel as a slave was a capital crime. How like us. In fact, Onesimus is a perfect picture of you and me, who have sinned against God, incurring the death penalty for our crimes — "For the wages of sin is death . . ." (Rom. 6:23).

Paul, the third party, is a personal friend of Philemon with a heart of compassion for Onesimus. Upon leading Onesimus to faith in Christ, Paul proceeds to make an appeal to Philemon to receive Onesimus back as a beloved friend rather than a servant (v. 16). Paul offers to pay Onesimus' debt (vv. 18–19) as a basis for Philemon's pardon. In all of this, Paul is the mediator of reconciliation between Philemon and Onesimus. And he performs this act of mediation while he himself is a prisoner of Rome (v. 1).

Is this not a perfect picture of Jesus Christ, our Mediator? As a prisoner of Rome, Jesus paid our debt. Intimate with the Father, He makes an appeal for our reconciliation, asking the Father to receive us as the Father would receive Jesus Himself (cf. v. 17). In fact, it is solely on the basis of Jesus' mediating work on our behalf, writing a letter of reconciliation with His blood, that we are accepted as a beloved one into the Father's house. The picture is complete and exquisitely beautiful.

Grasping the significance of this little book as a picture of the gospel helps us clarify the nature of our salvation. As Onesimus was reconciled to Philemon, not on the basis of any good works which he had done, but solely as a result of Paul's mediating provision on his behalf—so we too are reconciled to God because of Jesus' mediating work on our behalf without any merit on our part.

So if anyone asks, "How is it that I can be saved?" an appeal can be made to the book of Philemon: "In the same way that Onesimus was saved—by the mediating work of a Savior."

The book of Philemon is a picture story of the gospel, revealing how we can move from alienation to reconciliation.

PHILEMON

A Picture Story of the Gospel

Theme 1 — *Alienation*
Theme 2 — *Reconciliation*

THE HEART OF THE MATTER

Having analyzed each of the Pastoral Epistles, our next challenge is to discover if they work together as a unit. In keeping with the body analogy, let's probe the heart-lung system to see if this will help us in that discovery.

The workings of the chest cavity are relatively simple yet profound. Beginning with the heart, we find a two-directional pump with a receiving chamber and a pumping chamber on each side. These two sides of the heart receive blood and pump it in two different directions. The upper portion of each side has a receiving chamber (atrium), and each of the bottom sides is a pumping chamber (ventricle). Thus the one heart has two sides with a two-step function on each side.

The left side is bigger (more muscular), because it pumps blood throughout the entire body. Good oxygenated blood is received from the lungs into the left atrium (receiving chamber). Then that blood is transferred through a valve into the left ventricle (pumping chamber) where it is pumped out into the body. Arteries carry the good blood to the body, providing oxygen (O_2) to the cells. Veins, on the other hand, carry the dark, unaerated blood laden with carbon dioxide (CO_2) back from the body to the heart.

That's when the smaller right side of the heart begins to perform its function. The right atrium (receiving chamber) receives this tainted blood back from the body and transfers it via another valve into the right ventricle (pumping chamber). Then this blood is pumped a very short distance to both lungs. There the blood goes through a filtering process in which the old carbon dioxide (CO_2) is expelled and the new oxygen (O_2) is acquired. Once the blood is oxygenated again, it goes back to the left atrium and the process is repeated over ... and over ... and over.

HEART FUNCTION

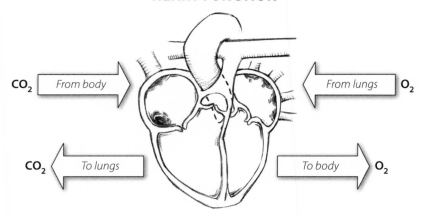

CO_2 | From body → | ← From lungs | O_2

CO_2 ← | To lungs | To body → | O_2

The Epistles to Timothy

As the heart is the central organ of the chest cavity, so 1 & 2 Timothy are the major structure of the Pastorals. Composed of two halves (1 & 2 Timothy), each book exhibits a two-part function—just as each half of the heart has a twofold process.

First Timothy is like the left side of the heart, where the good elements are first received and then distributed to every segment of the body. The first portion of the book, the "*elements* of nourishment" (chaps. 1–3), is analogous to the left atrium, where the good blood is collected and made ready for distribution. The Word, prayer, and godliness are exactly what the body needs for healthy living. The second section of 1 Timothy, the "*segments* of the body" (chaps. 4–6), delivers the good elements to each segment of the body of Christ: ethnic, gender, and economic. As you can see, 1 Timothy functions precisely as the left side of the heart.

Second Timothy, then, is a mirror image of the smaller right side of the heart. Timothy had to deal with a lot of bad stuff that came back from the body as he tried to implement the instructions of Paul in 1 Timothy. These bad reactions are collected and analyzed in the first half of the book: hassles (chap. 1) and hardships (chap. 2). This is exactly what happens with the "bad" blood in the right atrium. It is collected and prepared for expulsion to the lungs. Then all this bad material is sent to two purifying agents in the second half of the book: to "godliness" and to "the Word of the gospel" (chaps. 3–4; remember the inverted parallel). The right ventricle performs a similar function by pumping the "bad" blood to both lungs for the purpose of purification. The two halves of 2 Timothy, therefore, function exactly like the two chambers in the right side of the heart.

THE HEART

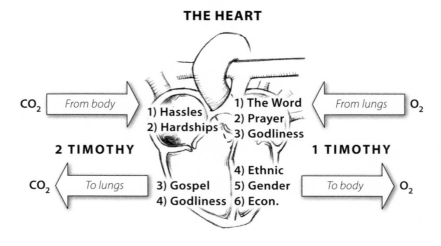

Titus and Philemon

Two elements of purification are emphasized in 2 Timothy 3–4. First, there was godliness—the need to counteract the godless behavior of the culture with the exemplary behavior of godly living. In our discussion of Titus, we saw that as the purpose and function of the book. Furthermore, as the right lung has three lobes with which to purify the blood, so Titus has three themes to clarify the subject of godliness. The *measure* of godliness comes first (chap. 1), then the *means* by which godliness is accomplished (chap. 2), and finally the importance of maintaining a godly life is addressed (chap. 3).

Also, as the pure blood returns from the right lung to the left atrium in the heart, so we discover the purified concept of godliness in Titus repeated in the first section of 1 Timothy. It is no accident that the qualifications for an elder (godly living) found in Titus 1 are also present in 1 Timothy 3.

The other purifying element mentioned in 2 Timothy 3–4 was the Word of God as supremely manifested in the gospel of Christ. As there is a second lung to purify the blood, so Philemon represents a second purifying book in the Pastorals. Remember, the left lung has two lobes. Even so, Philemon has two themes—alienation and reconciliation. Philemon, as we have noticed, is an exquisite picture of the gospel that acts as a purifier of the biblical concept of reconciliation. Understanding the details of the Philemon story helps to clarify the precise essence of the gospel. Again, as the purified blood returns to the left atrium in the heart, so the purified gospel in Philemon shows up as the primary element for nourishment in 1 Timothy 1.

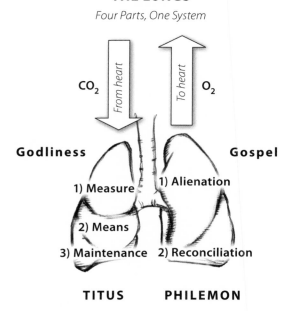

THE LUNGS

Four Parts, One System

CO_2 From heart To heart O_2

Godliness **Gospel**

1) Measure 1) Alienation

2) Means

3) Maintenance 2) Reconciliation

TITUS **PHILEMON**

FOUR PARTS, ONE SYSTEM

So, there it is! The Pastorals are indeed a finely tuned unit expressing the nature of life for the Body of Christ. As blood nourishes the human body to give us life, even so the Word ... prayer ... and godliness nourish the believer to give life. Through the processes of circulation and purification, the body remains healthy in order to perform its God-ordained function. The four Pastorals are truly a single system working in precise fashion, as are the organs of the chest cavity.

CHAPTER SEVEN

THE GOOD LIFE

The Writings

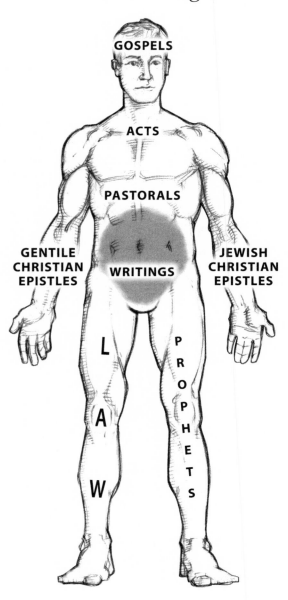

GOSPELS

ACTS

PASTORALS

GENTILE
CHRISTIAN
EPISTLES

WRITINGS

JEWISH
CHRISTIAN
EPISTLES

L
A
W

P
R
O
P
H
E
T
S

THE WRITINGS

The five books of the Poetical Writings (Job, Psalms, Proverbs, Ecclesiastes and Song of Solomon) are books for the soul. "But wait a minute," you say, "the whole Bible is for the soul, right? What's so unique about these five books that sets them apart as 'soulish'?"

For one thing, they are all written in a philosophical and poetic format that is different from the narrative style of the Historical Books and the prophetic style of the Prophets. It's not that the other books don't include elements of Semitic poetry and portions of proverbial wisdom. Rather, the Writings are totally devoted to and bound together as an artistic genre. For this reason they stand out as unique in the collection of biblical books.

Another peculiarity of the Writings is that they focus on an individual response to God rather than being a corporate national response. Although written by Jewish authors at the height of Israel's glory, the Writings are not about Israel as a nation. Israel isn't even mentioned. As others have observed, the Writings are at the heart of the Old Testament to show the heart of God for the individual.

Here we encounter the writings of kings—particularly King David and King Solomon. David wrote the largest portion of the Psalms; the books of Proverbs, Ecclesiastes, and Song of Solomon were the singular work of Solomon. Even Job, though living in an age prior to Israel's kings, was a man of great stature in the land of Uz. In special ways, then, the Writings are an introspective look into the souls of prominent men of God who were leaders in their generation.

African Americans speak of soul food and soul music as an expression of the inner feelings of their culture. In like manner, the Writings introduce us to "soul truth"—the inner reflections of spiritual leaders as they respond to God in the midst of life's circumstances.

Job, for instance, ponders the ultimate implications of suffering as he defends himself against lesser human philosophies of cause and effect. God finally interrupts the conversation of Job with his friends to clarify the divine perspective. The climax is an unexpected twist with a surprise ending.

The Psalms reflect a different approach to the dilemmas of life. They are not philosophical meanderings of the mind but conversations with God couched in poetic expressions of the soul. Whether times of joy, sorrow, fear, or praise, the psalmists reach out to God as the awesome provider and ever-present help. Inspired by the Spirit of God, these poets touch every circumstance of life and provide the words and thoughts for our own communication with God.

Solomon concludes the Writings with reflections upon three stages of life. Many speculate that he wrote the three books in response to the three stages of his own life. The last book, Song of Solomon, may have been his first inspired writing as he penned a youthful song commemorating the courtship and marriage of his first love. He called it "the Song of Songs" (1:1) in tribute to the wonder and grandeur of romantic love as the highest expression of selfless devotion.

Later, as a parent preparing his son for the complexities of life, he began the book of Proverbs by saying, "Hear, my son, your father's instruction, and forsake not your mother's teaching, for they are a graceful garland for your head and pendants for your neck" (1:8–9). Added to his fatherly advice are the other proverbial reflections on every conceivable subject as a compendium of wisdom for the pursuit of maturity. The book of Proverbs demonstrates that true spirituality is intended to filter into the practical dimensions of life.

Then, following this line of thought, Solomon supposedly looked back in a sort-of midlife crisis and concluded that most of his passions and pursuits were nothing more than folly. As a well-crafted artistic sermon by "the Preacher" (1:1), Ecclesiastes elucidates the vanity of all things independent of the Creator. Solomon's wealth, his many wives, and his indulgence in pleasures and possessions enabled him above all others to evaluate the total human experience in the light of ultimate worth. In conclusion, he decided that nothing matters beyond fearing God and keeping His commandments (12:13).

These are the Writings, sandwiched between the Historical Books of the Law and the record of the Prophets in the Old Testament sequence of books. Job, Psalms, Proverbs, Ecclesiastes, and Song of Solomon are a unique section of the Holy Scripture and carry a special message.

BOOKS FOR THE SOUL

Let's analyze each of these five books. Remember that our procedure is to understand what God has written before applying the body analogy. As we come to the Writings, we want to grasp the main theme of each book so we can see how it fits into the scheme of thought when compared to the other four books. First, we'll discover the *theme* and then consider the *scheme*.

Job

Suffering is clearly the theme of the book of Job. Having said that, we have only scratched the surface of the book's purpose. That Job suffered is a given. Understanding the reason God allowed him to experience such emotional and physical trauma is the greater issue. It is clear that Satan caused all of Job's problems, but what is also obvious from the very beginning is that God gave the go-ahead to Satan, permitting him to do what he did. Therefore God must take the ultimate responsibility for Job's suffering. Asking, "why would God do such a thing?" is the mystery that all of Job's friends tried to solve.

The first to respond to Job's misfortunes was his wife who also suffered the loss of her family and livelihood. My heart goes out to Mrs. Job, and I can understand her anger at what has happened. Her solution, however, is not helpful and misses the mark. In a depressed state, she advises her husband to "curse God and die" (2:9). Yet to get angry at God over the problems of life is to totally misunderstand the issue of human suffering.

Job's three friends (Eliphaz, Bildad, and Zophar) are the next to arrive, and the largest segment of the book (chaps. 3–31) is devoted to the discussion they have with Job.

Eliphaz sets the tone. "Remember: who that was innocent ever perished? Or where were the upright cut off?" (4:7). He voices the age-old philosophy that suffering is a consequence of wrongdoing and then assumes that the answer to the problem of suffering is to accept the punishment. Over and over again Job's friends try to convince him that he is being punished for his sins, but Job is not convinced. "What sin?" he asks. In retrospect he could not identify anything worthy of his suffering. Such a philosophy may explain some suffering, but not his.

Elihu, a younger man, waits his turn, and when the others have exhausted their arguments he voices another alternative: "Behold, God is exalted in his power; who is a teacher like him?" (36:22). In other words, "Job, God is trying to teach you something." To Elihu suffering is not for the purpose of punishment, but for the purpose of education. The solution to suffering, then, is to learn the lesson. Yet Job is still not convinced because he can't figure out what God is trying to teach him. Some suffering may have a didactic purpose, but that didn't seem to be true in his case.

Finally God broke His silence and confirmed Job's suspicions that his friends didn't know what they were talking about. God began by asking, "Who is this that darkens counsel by words without knowledge?" (38:2). As we read the four chapters of God's response (chaps. 38–41), we are surprised that God never tells Job the reason for which he suffers, nor does He tell Job about the deal that had been struck with Satan. God's explanation is merely a lesson on creation, as He demonstrates that everything He has ever done is characterized by intricate design and a carefully crafted purpose. Job gets the point: *he can trust God even when he doesn't understand what is happening.*

In the end Job repents of his arrogance in questioning the purpose of God in his suffering. He concludes by responding to God, "I had heard of you by the hearing of the ear, but now my eye sees you; therefore I despise myself, and repent in dust and ashes" (42:5–6). He is clearly brought to the end of trusting in himself. He no longer needs an answer. It is enough to simply trust in the Lord.

I have taken the time to work through the book of Job to substantiate what I believe to be the theme of the book. Beyond the surface reasons for suffering (which Job's friends suggested were punishment and learning), there appears to be a more basic purpose: suffering brings us to the end of ourselves. It reminds us of our frailty, our littleness, our mortality. It declares war on our ego. We are not so big now; we are not so important. Job's final response of utter humility and self-abnegation brings into focus the purpose of this book and clarifies its theme.

You see, there is an aspect of suffering that quickly puts life into perspective. Suffering helps us understand that life really isn't about us. It's about trusting the God of creation. To deny ourselves in the pursuit of Christ (Matt. 16:24) is an act of spiritual wisdom. Suffering convinces us that this is true.

> **JOB**
> *Dead to self*

Psalms

Who of us has not opened our Bibles to the Psalms in search of comfort amid the trials of life or for words of praise in worship? Poetry has always been the voice of the soul, but the poetry of the Psalms also enhances the spirit. Here we find expressions of human language worthy of the most intimate conversations with God. Whether listening to the divine voice or responding with vibrations of the heart, the Psalms carry us on angels' wings into the very throne room of heaven.

Speaking with mixed metaphors, J. Sidlow Baxter writes:

> The Book of Psalms is a limpid lake which reflects every mood of man's changeful sky ... It is a stringed instrument which registers every note of praise and prayer, of triumph and trouble, of gladness and sadness, of hope and fear, and unites them all in the full multi-chord of human experience."[1]

As an anthology of 150 separate poetic compositions, the Psalms cover a variety of themes and moods. Commentators have struggled to find a cohesive structure that would reflect a divine pattern of progressive thought. Authorship of the various psalms doesn't appear to help in this regard (75 are attributed to David, 2 to Solomon, 12 to Asaph [a musician in David's choir], 11 to the sons of Korah [a family of Levites], and the oldest psalm to Moses). That's a total of 101 psalms, leaving 49 as anonymous. Nor do the types of psalms (hymns of joy, psalms of thanksgiving, lament, praise, penitence, intercession, and imprecatory requests for divine retribution) seem to be arranged into an observable pattern. Apart from a few minor sequential psalms (i.e., the Songs of Degrees, Psalms 120–134), the compilation of psalms all appear to reflect a totally arbitrary collection of individual thought.

Yet, from ancient times, the Psalms have been handed down to us in a fivefold division, each part with a doxology similar to the others. Discussing the arrangement of the Psalter into five smaller books, Roland Harrison concludes, "While nothing is known for certain, of course, about the processes of compilation, the completed Psalter gives evidence of having been constructed carefully ... as follows:"[2]

Book I	Psalms 1–41
Book II	Psalms 42–72
Book III	Psalms 73–89
Book IV	Psalms 90–106
Book V	Psalms 107–150

Many have thought that these five books of psalms are a reflection of the Torah, the five books of Moses. Some have even suggested that individual themes can be found running through each book, mirroring the themes of the books of the Pentateuch. Whether this is food for thought or wild speculation, one thing becomes obvious by the concluding doxologies of this fivefold designation. The Psalms in their entirety are a unified collection of praises to the Lord God of Israel.

As mentioned, each of the five sections of the Psalms concludes with a doxology similar to the others (41:13; 72:18–19; 89:52; 106:48). Finally, the whole of Psalm 150 (the concluding psalm of Book V) captures the theme of the entire Psalter with 13 repetitions of "praise" to the Lord. This suggests that no matter who wrote each psalm or what its individual theme may be, every book of the Psalms and the Psalter as a whole are a wondrous reflection on the glory of God as the sustainer and provider of every human need. They are alive with the presence of the Lord.

Looking at the bigger picture, what is the sequence of overall themes from Job and Psalms? Like the book of Job, the book of Psalms deals with the troubles and pain of life. The Psalms do not wallow in philosophical speculation, however, but always lift the human spirit into the divine presence as the source of strength and courage. If the theme of Job is "death to self," the overriding theme of the Psalms is "alive to God." This dual truth is the "head" and "tail" of the spiritual coin, and the two books reflect in voluminous tones the single truth of Romans 6:11, "Consider yourselves dead to sin and alive to God."

THE WRITINGS OF SOLOMON

King Solomon, the son of David, is credited with writing the final three books of the Poetical Writings: Proverbs, Ecclesiastes, and Song of Solomon. Scholars continue to debate the extent to which he actually wrote each of these books, but most agree that his wisdom was unparalleled in the ancient world and that the basic thought structure of this wisdom literature is consistent with his authorship.

A Jewish midrash source actually claims (as mentioned earlier) that "Solomon wrote Canticles [Song of Songs], with its stress on love, in his youth; Proverbs, with its emphasis on practical problems, in mid-life, and Ecclesiastes, with its characteristic pessimism, in old age."[3] That can't be proven, of course, but it is an interesting thought in harmony with the tone and purpose of each book.

These ancient writings of wisdom literature exhibit a perennial relevance that is contemporary in every age. Proverbs, Ecclesiastes, and Song of Songs are never out of vogue. They express truths basic to life and foundational to godly living. Together they complement Job and Psalms in giving to us the full-orbed pattern of successful living from the divine perspective.

Proverbs

A proverb is a wise saying wrapped in a few specially chosen words. *Pro* (for) *verba* (words) suggests something pithy and condensed. The wisdom of a proverb is not only in *what* it literally says, but also in *how* it is said. The historical record of the kings reveals that King Solomon wrote three thousand proverbs (1 Kings 4:32) as a demonstration of the wisdom given to him by God. Many of those proverbs are included in the central portion of the book of Proverbs (chaps. 10–24).

Yet terse sayings of wisdom comprise only a portion of the book—albeit the major portion. The opening section of Proverbs (chaps. 1–9) is composed of a series of sonnets (short poems devoted to a particular theme) and the concluding chapters (25–31) exhibit a mixture of epigrams and proverbs, including wise sayings of Agur and Lemuel. The climax of the book is an exquisitely designed acrostic poem extolling the virtuous woman—each line beginning with the next letter in the Hebrew alphabet. In all, the book of Proverbs is a marvelous collection of rich and practical wisdom on every conceivable subject of human life.

Proverbs tells us how to live in a world of contrasting options and ethical choices. It is wisdom from God to help us discern "between good and evil, between virtue and vice, between duty and self-indulgence . . . between sham and reality, between truth and error, between the specious attraction of the moment and the long-range values that govern a truly successful life."[4] In the divine philosophy of life expressed in the book of Proverbs we are given instruction on how to live the life that is *"dead to self"* (Job) and *"alive to God"* (Psalms). It is the positive side (things to accept) of a life well lived.

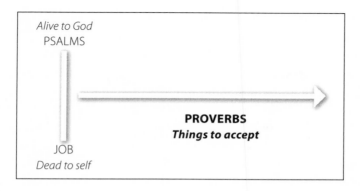

Ecclesiastes

> Ecclesiastes is an inspired confession of failure and pessimism, when God is excluded, when man lives under the sun, and forgets the larger part, which is always over the sun, the eternal and abiding things. If you want to know what a man of great privilege and of great learning and great wisdom can come to, read this record of a man who has put God out of count in his actual life.[5]

As J. Sidlow Baxter introduces his analysis of Ecclesiastes, he appeals to the above quote from G. Campbell Morgan because it sets a correct tone for pursuing the purpose of the book. The Preacher (referred to as Koheleth in the book) is not just decrying the vanities of life as though advocating a monastic existence void of all worldly involvement. Rather, he is putting the entire human experience into perspective by demonstrating the futility of trying to make sense out of anything independent of its relationship to God. In his quest for the ultimate good, Koheleth concludes that everything is empty and meaningless unless it is understood and experienced in the light of God's ultimate purpose and design.

It is not my purpose to analyze the book of Ecclesiastes, but I am interested in catching its overall emphasis. Ecclesiastes is a sermon. And, as with every good sermon, there is a main theme. As I've already indicated, the point of this sermon is to convince the reader that all human experience is meaningless apart from its orientation to fellowship with God.

In the words of Dillard and Longman, "While Qohelot [Koheleth] sounds unorthodox in the light of the rest of the canon, he represents a true assessment of the world apart from the light of God's redeeming love."[6] It is this connection with divine purpose that gives ultimate meaning to everything.

This is the Preacher's conclusion as the sermon winds to its climactic ending. It is as though his voice reaches a crescendo pitch, his finger gesturing the final point as he concludes, "The end of the matter; all has been heard. Fear God and keep his commandments, for this is the whole duty of man" (12:13).

Then, as though adding the exclamation point, he warns his audience to give serious thought to the matter: "For God will bring every deed into judgment, with every secret thing, whether good or evil" (12:14). The sermon is over. And, one hopes, a spiritual lesson has been learned.

So even though Ecclesiastes teaches us about things-to-reject in the pursuit of a meaningful life, its overall purpose is to instill positive wisdom by the means of negative learning. Knowing what *not to do* is as important as knowing *what to do* in any circumstance of life. As Proverbs teaches us what to do, Ecclesiastes teaches us what not to do. In this way, these two books are the head and tail of the same coin—the wisdom of God for life. Together they help us understand how to live a godly life that is "dead to self' (Job) and "alive to God" (Psalms).

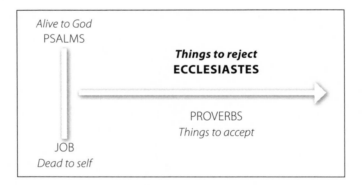

Song of Songs

Listen to popular music and you'll soon notice that most songs are devoted to the subject of love—enjoying love, losing love, and trying to find love. The Bible trumps pop culture by extolling a virtuous love rooted in the love of God that surpasses any contemporary secular song. That is why the love poem attributed to Solomon is called the Song of Songs (1:1). Actually that superlative expression suggests not only that this is an excellent song, but that it is the best song of all songs.

It is the best song because it lifts the level of romance from the human experience into the divine chambers of perfect love. Yet many contemporary commentators seek to diminish the analogous dimension of human love with divine love in the poem. Dillard and Longman, for instance, say, "The book's primary aim is not to portray the relationship between God and his people, but rather to extol sexual love between a man and a woman."[7]

This seems shortsighted for several reasons: first, because the book is included in the sacred canon of Scripture; second, because the poem is called Song of Songs (many songs exalt the wondrous rapture of romantic and sexual love — so, what makes this one different?); third, because God likens His relationship to Israel, as well as Christ's relationship to the church, to the marriage bond. Since this is a biblical analogy and since this song is a biblical book, why would we not immediately assume a connection between the physical and the spiritual?

When considering the idea that this is a poem of human love and nothing more, J. Sidlow Baxter observes:

> This theory leaves the inclusion of the book in the sacred canon an inexplicable anomaly. When we remember how the Hebrews venerated their sacred Scriptures, and how careful they were that only inspired writing should be included in the canon, we cannot believe that the Song of Songs should have been given its decided place in the Scripture simply on the ground of literary merit. Not one of the books is there simply as a piece of literature. Each has its place because of its religious character ... the very canonicity of the poem, therefore, argues its spiritual significance.[8]

Recognizing that the Song of Songs has a definite historical basis, it is also consistent with the rest of Scripture in having a religious purpose and a spiritual intent. It is also significant to note that the Jewish people read the Song of Songs as they commemorate the Passover. Passover is the first feast in the annual Jewish cycle and celebrates the superlative love of God for His people in delivering them from bondage and death into a special relationship with Himself. The Jews clearly see the love of Solomon for his bride as typifying the sacrificial love of God as reflected in the Passover.

Thoughts like these led the eminent scholar Gleason Archer to conclude: "This love affair is understood to typify the warm, personal relationship which God desires with His spiritual bride, composed of all redeemed believers who have given their hearts to Him."[9]

The Song of Songs is an idyllic poem rather than a drama of consecutive events (although overall, it does tell a romantic story). "An idyl ... is ... a short descriptive or narrative poem ... which gives to familiar or everyday scenes a tinge of romance."[10] From the royal wedding in chapter 1 to the renewal of love at Lebanon in chapter 8, the Song of Songs is a poem of courtship, betrothal, and meditations on the wonder of love. Each idyllic section contributes to the final expression of the lovers:

> Many waters cannot quench love,
>   neither can floods drown it.
> If a man offered for love
>   all the wealth of his house,
>   he would be utterly despised. (8:7)

Because the Song of Solomon shifts from an early romantic encounter of the Shulamite maiden with her shepherd lover to the royal entourage of King Solomon coming for his bride, some have suggested a competition between the shepherd and the king for the love of this girl. Yet Solomon had numerous flocks overseen by undershepherds—and it is not inconceivable that Solomon might disguise himself as a shepherd to woo the love of this beautiful country woman. Furthermore, this was probably the first love of Solomon's life, since no mention is made of his harem of concubines and wives. The fact that he later became a polygamist does not therefore detract from the purity of first love expressed in this poem as an analogy of the perfect love of Christ for His bride.

Consider for a moment the divine scheme in the romantic pursuit of Christ for His beloved. The Gospels portray two comings of the heavenly Lover—the first as a humble shepherd (the Good Shepherd; John 10) to woo the trust and love of His bride; the second, as the glorious King of Kings to whisk away the object of His love to His palace in the sky. The story of Christ's love does indeed parallel the account of Solomon's love as both a shepherd and a king in the Song of Songs.

Also, as a shepherd Christ came for Israel as well as for the church. And as a king He will also come for both. In fact, the New Jerusalem (His palace in the sky), adorned as a bride for her husband, has twelve foundations likened unto the apostles and twelve gates representing the twelve tribes of Israel (Rev. 21:9–14). It seems that the bride of Christ is not only the church, but all of the redeemed for whom He shed His precious blood as an exquisite demonstration of His unending love. Referring to the entire celestial city composed of Israel and the church, the apostle John writes, "Come, I will show you the Bride, the wife of the Lamb" (Rev. 21:9).

So the Song of Songs uses the dramatic story of Solomon and the Shulamite maiden to portray the glorious union of Christ and His beloved. It is the climactic crescendo of the human drama for all who have put their trust and hope in Christ, the divine Savior and Lover of their souls. In this way the Song of Songs reflects the intimate spiritual union of walking with Christ.

There could be no more fitting conclusion to the five books of the Poetical Writings than Song of Songs. As a song of intimate union, it caps the sequence of God's design for a life well lived—dead to self (Job) and alive to God (Psalms), realizing that along the way there are things to accept (Proverbs) and things to reject (Ecclesiastes), all for the purpose of leading us into the fulfilling experience of fellowship with God through intimate union with Christ (Song of Songs).

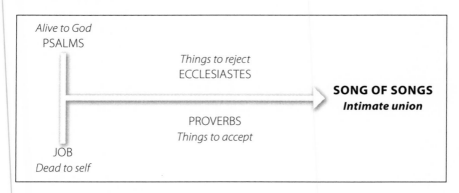

A UNIVERSAL TRUTH

A pattern of spirituality is repeated in the Old Testament and the New Testament as a guide for those who are looking for direction in life. Whenever favorite verses are shared as a testimony to the faithfulness of God, these invariably surface as being among the most meaningful in the Bible. I'm referring to Proverbs 3:5–6 and Romans 12:1–2.

It is interesting to notice the similarity of sequence within the structure of each set of verses. Beginning with a strong positive challenge, they each insert a memorable negative warning before sharing another positive assertion, all of which is intended to produce the desired result of fellowship with, and guidance from, God.

	Proverbs 3:5–6	**Romans 12:1–2**
Beginning challenge	Trust in the Lord with all your heart	Present your body a living sacrifice to God
Negative warning	Lean NOT on your own understanding	Be NOT conformed to this world
Positive assertion	In all your ways acknowledge Him	Be transformed by the renewing of your mind
Desired result	He shall direct your path	That you may discover the will of God

Note that the similar pattern of these verses follows the exact sequence of thought we saw in the five books of the Poetical Writings. A formula for

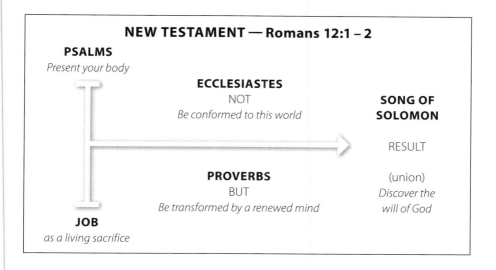

success in the spiritual life appears to emerge from a comparison of these verses with the five profound concepts of Job, Psalms, Proverbs, Ecclesiastes, and Song of Songs.

Having observed the similar pattern in these verses and seeing the correlation of concepts with the five books of the Writings, perhaps you will agree that this appears to be more than coincidence. A sequence has emerged that gives evidence of divine design and purpose. Job, Psalms, Proverbs, Ecclesiastes, and Song of Songs display a unit of thought far beyond their individual themes that guides us through the process of living life with God. It seems we have discovered another exquisite system in the body of Truth.

FOOD FOR THOUGHT

"You are what you eat"—have you ever heard that? Actually, it's the unofficial slogan of nutritionists everywhere. If you eat foods saturated with fat, they warn, you can expect to become an overweight person with a multitude of health problems; a diet heavy in simple carbohydrates and sugars could contribute to diabetes or a stroke. Good eating, on the other hand, helps ensure good health. In many ways, you are indeed what you eat.

So why do so many people ignore the warnings? The answer is obvious —because the bad stuff tastes so good. Donuts and pastries, hamburgers and fries, pizza, Slurpees, and cakes—these not only have a wonderful taste; they are inextricably tied to our convenient way of life.

Why take time to cook a healthy meal when you can grab a hamburger, fries, and Coke on the run at a McDonald's drive-thru? We all know that the fast-food industry has thrived on "tastes good" (which means "loaded with fats and sugars") and "available quickly" (which caters to our busy lifestyles). That's why a great percentage of Americans are overweight and sickly. It's a sad picture and a trend that's hard to break.

What is true physically is also true spiritually. Christians who engage in a heavy diet of TV, movies, pop-novels, and cultural indulgence tend to be spiritually anemic and susceptible to a whole list of spiritual ills. They never seem to be able to get it together because life is always falling apart. God seems to be distant, and life with Christ is perceived as a puzzle. They prefer a quick God that they can grab on the run.

On the other hand, believers who feed regularly on God's Word, with a healthy diet of prayer and continued fellowship with Christ, are the strong and mature among us. They tend to see the bigger divine picture and understand the enabling power of the Spirit of God. What blows others away seems to strengthen them. They enjoy a spiritual health that the indulgent can only wish they had.

You see, it all goes back to diet. Eating well spiritually really *does* appear to be the key to a spiritually successful life. Physical health and spiritual health are truly parallel concepts. In fact, it is fascinating to observe how the five books of the Poetical Writings function in a similar fashion to the abdominal organs that process our food.

The Stomach

The largest structure in the midriff area is the stomach. We've all noticed the overweight male who looks like he swallowed a basketball (a graphic image of how big the stomach is, or can be). In the assimilation of food, the stomach is the first organ to become engaged in the process (other than the tongue, teeth, and saliva in the mouth). It is the gathering bin for all that is ingested. In fact, the stomach performs a death-to-life function that is very much like the tandem spiritual process accomplished by the books of Job and Psalms.

Remember that the overall theme of Job relates human suffering to the objective of bringing us to the end of trusting in ourselves. In like fashion, food enters the stomach having been completely demolished as it is ground up, pulverized, and masticated by the teeth and saliva in the mouth. When it arrives in the stomach its individual identity has been completely altered. Then the acidic environment of the stomach further breaks down the food so that its former state is no longer recognizable. Just throw up once, and you'll get my point.

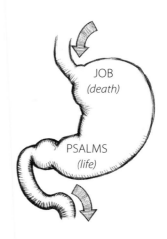

The purpose of crushing and otherwise mutilating our food is not to destroy its effectiveness, but to render it more useful for sustaining the life of the body. It becomes beneficial only after it has (so to speak) suffered. Then in an amazing twist of purpose, the principle of death ushers in the incredible hope of life—just like the Psalms, which turn our thoughts from self-despair (in Job) to the glorious life-giving God. Suffering is part of the picture; but really it's all about life.

On one occasion Jesus put it this way, "Truly, truly, I say to you, unless a grain of wheat falls into the earth and dies, it remains alone; but if it dies, it bears much fruit. Whoever loves his life loses it, and whoever hates his life in this world will keep it for eternal life" (John 12:24–25). This is just the way the procedure works. It's not rocket science—but it *is* smart living.

Another consideration is that the stomach can process only what we put into it. The digestive death-to-life principle operates with anything we eat, but the value to the body is greatly enhanced or seriously diminished, depending on what we eat. Upon feeding five thousand people with a little boy's lunch of bread and fish, Jesus said,

> I am the living bread that came down from heaven. If anyone eats of this bread, he will live forever. And the bread that I will give for the life of the world is my flesh ... truly, I say to you, unless you eat the flesh of the Son of Man and drink his blood, you have no life in you ... For my flesh is true food, and my blood is true drink. (John 6:51, 53, 55)

Jesus was certainly not talking literally about eating and drinking Him. What He was saying was that personal fellowship with Him on a daily basis is the spiritual equivalent of eating well every day. When we ingest Him, the death-to-life principle of Job and Psalms produces a healthy, vibrant Christian.

As in the combined themes of Job and Psalms, the stomach tells the story of death for the purpose of life. This is the most basic and fundamental concept of the spiritual life. To experience a life well lived in fellowship with Christ, we must die to self so that we can become alive to God.

The Intestines

Numerous organs (e.g., the liver, spleen, pancreas, gall bladder, kidneys, and bladder, etc.) are contained within the abdominal cavity. In one way or another, these organs are involved in the digestion and elimination processes. Yet only two major structures are directly involved in the assimilating of food —the stomach and the intestines. The stomach breaks down the food, and the intestines pick and choose what is good and what is not. The beneficial elements are absorbed into the blood as they flow along the intestinal tract, and waste material is rejected and eventually eliminated.

Twenty-five feet long and one inch in diameter, the small intestine is "something of a miracle of biological packaging in the way it is coiled up and fitted into the abdominal cavity."[11] The first twelve-inch section, called the duodenum, is the place where pancreatic and duodenal enzymes transform the acidic mix coming from the stomach into an alkaline environment that enhances the absorption process.

On the internal surface of this lengthy journey of food through the small intestine, numerous finger-like projections called villi house the absorption cells that assimilate the nutrients into the bloodstream for the nourishment of the body. What is rejected is eventually deposited into the colon, the much shorter large intestine; finally, the unwanted material arrives at the rectum, where it is eliminated. The entire process is a miracle of creative genius.

Perhaps you have noticed the similarity of this procedure with the function of Proverbs and Ecclesiastes. After receiving the death-unto-life product from Job and Psalms (correlating with the stomach in our analogy), the wisdom books of Solomon tell us what to receive and what to reject as we travel through life. The book of Proverbs absorbs one bit of wisdom after another as nutrients necessary for a healthy spiritual life. On the other hand, Ecclesiastes is constantly telling us to reject the unwanted philosophies of life that are not beneficial for fellowship with God. In this, the intestinal action of the human body mirrors the function of these tandem books—Proverbs and Ecclesiastes.

Organs of Sexuality

It has always been of great interest to me that God crafted the organs of sexuality (both male and female) by which we express intimacy to be positioned at the very place where the digestive process comes to a conclusion.

Think about it! God's creative reasoning is limitless when it comes to designing how things will work. Procreation of the human race could have been accomplished by an exchange of fluids in a kiss — or any other of a hundred ways. For example, the tiny amoeba reproduces by simply dividing in half. One moment there's one amoeba, and then suddenly there are two. Considering the modern fascination with cloning possibilities, dividing in two is an interesting scenario.

But God's intellect is governed by His wisdom. He does all things by deliberate purpose and design. So when God created the man and the woman, desiring that they procreate the human species, He made a conscious choice as to where He would place the sexual organs. The fact that these organs are located where they are raises an intriguing question: did God have this analogy between the Living Word (the human body) and the Written Word (the inspired books of Scripture) in mind when He did that? As we observe the amazing similarities between the two entities, we may think perhaps He did.

Which brings me to the application of the positioning of the Song of Songs. As we compared the sequence of thought for successful spiritual living in Proverbs 3:5–6 and Romans 12:1–2, we saw that intimate fellowship with God was the concluding reward in each passage. This gives me confidence in suggesting that the Song of Songs is located right where it belongs in the sequence of the Poetical Writings.

When we understand and accept the death-to-life message of Job and Psalms, leading to the acceptance and rejection pattern of Proverbs and Ecclesiastes, we discover a wonderful intimacy with God in Christ. As a result of this relationship we can enjoy Him with a new depth of appreciation and wonder. His direction for our lives resonates with a renewed sense of clarity, reminding us that His purpose for us is good, acceptable, and perfect (Rom. 12:2). It is the means by which we "grow in the grace and knowledge of our Lord and Savior Jesus Christ" (2 Pet. 3:18). And it really is no longer about us. It's about Him.

GRASPING THE BIG PICTURE

Here again we have an excellent example of how important it is to grasp the big picture in each grouping of biblical books. We saw how the Gospels work together as a unit to reveal the magnificent nature of the fourfold Christ. The Pastoral Epistles do not stand alone as separate entities but share an intricate function in which all four of the books bear an integral part in demonstrating the life of God for the body. So in both the Gospels and the Pastorals, each set of books is a system of truth in which every part is necessary to the functioning of the whole.

Now we have discovered this same principle in the Writings. Remove any one of the five books, and the design is incomplete. All are necessary in telling the story of how to live the spiritual life in perfect fellowship with God. The order of the books is crucial in developing the sequence of thought. Job, Psalms, Proverbs, Ecclesiastes, and the Song of Songs are indeed a collection of writings with a combined message for spiritual living that is relevant in any age.

PICTORIAL SUMMARY

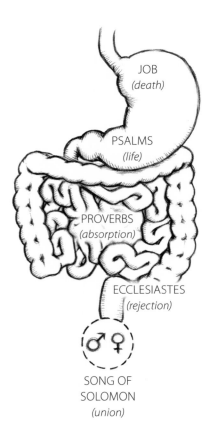

PART 2

REACHING
THE WORLD

CHAPTER EIGHT

A TRILOGY OF MOTION

The Epistles

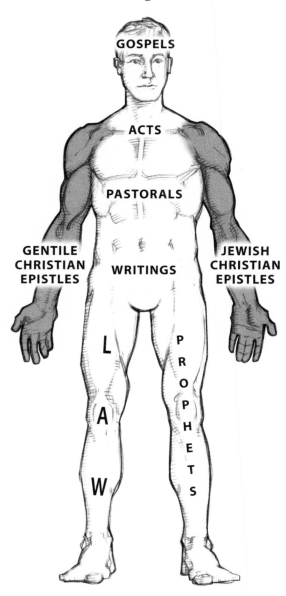

THE EPISTLES

Can you imagine life without arms? That's not a pleasant thought. But just pretend for a moment that hands and arms were not part of the human anatomy. You'd be in a fix to do anything. Your legs could move you around, but once you got to where you were going, you'd be hard pressed to carry out what you went there to do.

Life would be seriously diminished without arms and hands—no push and pull to accomplish work, no helping hand to reach out to others, no arms to hug and caress, no fingers to play the piano or write a message—so much of life as we know it would be impossible. Reduced to a penguin existence, we would find ourselves waddling about, catching food with our mouths while huddling together to keep warm. Thinking about that makes me appreciate hands and arms more than ever. Face it—arms and hands are amazing creations of God that grace our lives in phenomenal ways.

That would be the dilemma of the Bible with no epistles. Twenty-two brief writings in the form of letters, these special books of the New Testament are a fine tuning of the gospel message. It is through the Epistles that the Holy Spirit reaches out with a refining touch of faith, hope, and love to the peoples of the world. The books of Romans through Revelation are not just wonderful literature; they radiate with significant and essential importance. The body of divine truth would be severely handicapped without them.

WHAT IS AN EPISTLE?

The joke is that biblically illiterate folks may think that an epistle is the wife of an apostle. Not exactly! An epistle is a formal letter meant to be read by more than one person. As such, all epistles are letters—but not all letters are epistles.

Everett Harrison, a professor of New Testament, quotes A. Deissman as the authority on the distinction between a letter and an epistle:

His contention is that even though the letter and the epistle may be similar in form, they represent two distinct types of writing. Whereas the epistle is a conscious literary effort designed for publication, the letter is private in character, written for a specific occasion and certainly not designed for posterity.[1]

The point here is that epistles were written in the form of a letter addressed to a particular person or group of people. What was said was often very personal, and the content of the letter usually dealt with practical issues in the lives of the recipients. In these respects, an epistle is like a letter.

Of the twenty-two epistles in the New Testament, the four Pastoral Epistles are most like traditional letters. Addressed to individuals (Timothy, Titus, and Philemon), these letters are very personal in contrast to the inclusive nature of the other church epistles. The only exceptions are 2 & 3 John, which were addressed to "the elect lady" and "Gaius" respectively. Even these letters were widely circulated, however, and because of that are legitimately called epistles.

In the case of an epistle, the person or group receiving the letter was encouraged to share the letter with others—as when the Colossian church was told to pass its letter on to the church in Laodicea which, in turn, was exhorted to read the letter that had been sent to Laodicea (Col. 4:16). James wrote his letter to "the twelve tribes which are scattered abroad" (James 1:1 KJV), obviously intending for the letter to circulate among the Jews dispersed throughout the area. Furthermore, those letters written to churches certainly had a collective audience in mind with a message that was appropriate to other churches. In this way the letters were epistles meant for a broader group. In the providence of God, these epistles would eventually be read by all the churches and would be passed on through the centuries to believers in every age—including our own.

> "Paul's letters are not creations of the moment, dashed off in a hurry, but have behind them much careful thought. Time was required to compose them. They differ, therefore, from the improvisations that constitute an ordinary letter." In a true sense they are the works of an artist.[2]

Epistles, then, are a distinct genre of literature; as far as the Bible is concerned, they are unique to the New Testament. Observing that no book of the Old Testament is cast into the epistolary form, Dr. Edmond Hiebert suggests a reason for the epistles being a New Testament phenomenon.

Under the law, prophets delivered *oracles* to the *people*, solemnly setting

forth their authoritative pronouncements with a "thus saith the Lord."
With the inauguration of the age of grace, the apostles wrote *letters* to the
brethren in a spirit of loving intimacy, setting forth the significance and
implications of their new position in Christ.[3]

ARRANGING THE EPISTLES

Even a cursory examination of the Epistles reveals that they are given to us
in two specific divisions. Paul's epistles are grouped together, and come first.
Then the books not written by Paul are in a collection together at the end of
the New Testament. In the case of Paul's letters, they in turn are presented
in two parts: first, his writings to the churches (Romans – 2 Thessalonians)
followed by his personal letters to Timothy, Titus, and Philemon (the Pastoral
Epistles). The Pauline Epistles being grouped this way is both natural and
deliberate.

Someone might ask, "Why do Paul's letters come first? After all, Peter and
John were apostles long before Paul, and they were involved in founding the
church in Jerusalem before Paul even got saved."

The answer may at first seem a little disappointing. St. Jerome (d. 420)
appears to have established the general order of the New Testament books
when he translated them from the Greek language into Latin for the Roman
Church (see Appendix 2: "Everything Is in Order: New Testament"). When
it came to the Epistles, Jerome was evidently encouraged by the ecclesiastical authorities in Rome to put the Pauline book of Romans first to reflect
the supremacy of the Roman Empire and the Roman Church. All of Paul's
letters were kept together as a unit and emerged as the first grouping of New
Testament epistles.

That may appear to be contrived and manipulative, but we must remember that the sovereign providence of God in the arranging of His Word
allowed this to happen. In fact, it would never have happened if He had not
wanted it to. God takes even carnal human choices and turns them to His
purpose.

Think about what this arrangement did for the logical progression of the
gospel in the Bible. After Jesus accomplished our redemption as recorded in
the Gospels, and after that message was communicated throughout the Mediterranean world in the book of Acts, the next important function would be
to present a clear explanation of what the gospel message entails. No epistle
does that better than the book of Romans.

The books of Peter and John (and the other non-Pauline epistles) deal with matters of Christian living in the midst of persecution, hardship, and apostasy. These provide a fitting conclusion to the New Testament with the book of Revelation (written by John) capping the Scriptures with an exciting climax to the gospel story. To put this group first would have violated the sense of natural sequence and logical progression.

All of Paul's epistles to congregations, on the other hand, are a fine tuning of the gospel and its implications for the church. Thus, it appears that Paul's letters are right where they belong, fulfilling the natural pattern of logical thought in the progressive revelation of the gospel. Maybe Jerome understood this as a grander motive in the orderly arrangement of the Epistles than the ecclesiastical desire to put Rome first.

NOT IN ORDER OF WRITING

Having already dealt with the Pastoral Epistles in chapter 6, it remains for us to consider Paul's church epistles and the other non-Pauline epistles. In terms of balance and symmetry, as highlighted in the opening section of this book, we notice that both divisions of the Epistles comprise nine letters.

Paul's Church Epistles	The Non-Pauline Epistles
Romans	Hebrews
1 Corinthians	James
2 Corinthians	1 Peter
Galatians	2 Peter
Ephesians	1 John
Philippians	2 John
Colossians	3 John
1 Thessalonians	Jude
2 Thessalonians	Revelation

Neither list of epistles has come down to us in the chronological order in which the letters were written. For instance, Paul wrote 1 & 2 Thessalonians first, but they come last in the biblical order. The letter to the Romans, now positioned first, wasn't written until after Paul had penned his letters to the Thessalonians and to the Corinthians and probably his letter to the Galatians. Likewise, James is thought by many to be the very first epistle written, but it is positioned after the book of Hebrews (to say nothing of the fact that the Jewish Epistles were placed after *all* of the Pauline letters). Something other than the time of writing drove the placement decisions.

One explanation suggests that the books were grouped according to size.

> It is obvious that the present order of these epistles was determined by the length of the epistles. The longest, Romans, stands first; and the shortest, Philemon, stands last. The letters addressed to the churches appear in the order of their length, and the epistles to individuals follow in the same order. This fact has caused some critics to declare that the present order is haphazard and destitute of any real significance.[4]

While this is generally true with the Pauline Epistles, the pattern does not follow with the non-Pauline epistles where 2 Peter (3 chapters) is followed by 1 John (5 chapters) and ends with the longest book of all, Revelation (22 chapters). In fact, following the above quote, D. Edmond Hiebert adds, "the present order is not haphazard, but has real meaning and value."[5]

So what shall we make of the way the Epistles are arranged? A careful examination of the content of each letter reveals a spiritual order of doctrinal progression. Each grouping begins with a masterful book introducing the complex unfolding of the *work* of Christ in Romans (Pauline grouping) and the *person* of Christ in Hebrews (non-Pauline grouping). And both groupings end with the hope of Christ's return in the Thessalonian epistles (Pauline grouping) and Revelation (non-Pauline grouping). J. Sidlow Baxter, who observed this meaningful sequence, adds a further reflective thought:

> This order of these "Church" epistles never varies in any of the manuscripts. It is the same everywhere, without exception. It would seem as though the Holy Spirit was just as careful about the arrangement of these precious letters as about their original inclusion in the sacred canon.[6]

A MATTER OF ETHNIC NEED

Before looking more closely at the content of the Epistles to determine their specific subject matters, let's consider why there are two major groups of nine epistles each. The most obvious fact is that nine were written by Paul and nine were not: the Pauline group and the non-Pauline group. Since the second group is composed of multiple authors, and none of the letters was written to a specific church, the non-Pauline group has traditionally been called the General Epistles. This merely convenient designation adds nothing to the true identity of this non-Pauline group.

To grasp the significance of these two sets of epistles, we must go back to our study of the book of Acts (chap. 4). There we saw that the huge challenge of the early church was knowing how to blend Jews and Gentiles into one body fellowship. The first part of the book of Acts (chaps. 1–12) explained how the church of Jesus Christ began among the Jews and flourished in Jerusalem. The remainder of the book (chaps. 13–28) concentrated on the ministry of Paul as he established churches among the Gentiles throughout the Mediterranean area.

This amalgamation process took time, but it was ultimately effective. Later, writing to the Ephesians, Paul described this incredible achievement: "For he himself is our peace, who has made us both one and has broken down in his flesh the dividing wall of hostility" (2:14).

As both Jews and Gentiles responded to the message of God's grace in Christ, each group had specific needs for clarification of the gospel as a result of its unique circumstances. The Gentiles, for instance, had no hope of eternal life and were without God in the world (Eph. 2:12). They knew nothing of the covenants of God and His providential care. What they needed was a basic description of how to be saved from their sins through faith in the sacrificial death of Christ. Gentiles were prime candidates for Paul's instruction in the book of Romans.

The other Pauline church epistles were appropriate for them as well— teaching them how to walk by faith, how to love one another as members in the body of Christ, and how to live with hope in the expectation of Christ's return. As the apostle to the Gentiles, Paul was supremely fitted for communicating these truths to the Gentiles.

Of course, the Jewish community was desperate for all of this too, but its situation was different. It had been nurtured in the law of God and the sacrificial system of substitutionary atonement. Having the knowledge of the true God, they reveled in the covenantal relationship He had established with them. The concepts of sin and redemption were not foreign to them.

What was not clear to the Jews, though, was that Jesus was the fulfillment of their ultimate hope. This theme dominates the book of Hebrews, which became important instruction for the Jews. They needed to know that salvation in Christ was infinitely better than compliance with the law, that their veneration of Moses was not nearly as worthy as the exaltation of Christ, and that the priesthood of Aaron was merely temporary when compared to the everlasting priesthood of Christ. They needed to know that Christ had become the fulfillment of their entire system and salvation with

God depended on believing in His Son. James, Peter, and John refined the application of that message for the Jewish Christian community so it could be prepared for all that commitment to Christ entailed.

You see, apart from Hebrews (which is anonymous) and the little book of Jude (the brother of James and half brother of our Lord), the so-called General Epistles were all written by apostles of the Jerusalem church; these were the apostles to the Jewish circumcision (Gal. 2:9). In fact, the order of these non-Pauline epistles follows the order given in Galatians 2:9—first James, then Peter (Cephas), and finally John.

It is evident that the nine General Epistles were meant for Jewish believers and their unique needs. The recipients of the book of Hebrews were obviously Hebrews. James wrote to the "twelve tribes in the Dispersion" (1:1), and John contrasted his audience to the Gentiles (3 John 7). J. Sidlow Baxter comes to this very conclusion in his book *The Strategic Grasp of the Bible*: "In all these nine epistles, either the address is directly Jewish, or the standpoint is noticeably so."[7]

What do we have, then, in these two groups of epistles? It appears that God has addressed the needs of the two major elements of the burgeoning church—Gentiles and Jews. For the Gentiles the message was clearly that of *transformation*—how to be *transformed* from a lost sinner to a saved child of God. Instruction for the Jews, on the other hand, took the form of *transfer-mation*—how to *transfer* their entire understanding of Old Testament truth to its glorious fulfillment in Jesus Christ.

These emphases were not mutually exclusive but were complementary. Jews certainly needed to be transformed and Gentiles had to grasp how the Old Testament was fulfilled in Christ. Yet, this balance of truth was given in two unique groupings of epistles reaching out simultaneously to both Gentiles and Jews.

This arrangement of epistles therefore can be legitimately labeled the "Gentile Christian Epistles" (9 books—Romans–2 Thessalonians) and the "Jewish Christian Epistles" (9 books—Hebrews–Revelation). These two groups of epistles truly fulfill the dual ethnic need of Gentiles and Jews for the refining of the gospel message. As with two arms reaching out to the world, these symmetrically uniform sets of epistles provide a complementary balance of "transformation" truth and "transfer-mation" truth for all people.

WHAT ABOUT MAJOR THEMES?

As the director of Biblical Research and Education for Sola Scriptura, I had the privilege of working with the Van Kampen Bible Collection, one of the largest private collections of biblical manuscripts, artifacts, and ancient Bibles in the world. Since the first acquisition in 1986, it took approximately fifteen years to complete the task of amassing the desired material and cataloging the resources of this priceless treasure. Collecting, however, was just the beginning of the process.

In 2001 the decision was made to make the collection available to the public through an organized display at the Scriptorium: Center for Biblical Antiquities in Orlando, Florida. At that point careful attention was given to theming the collection. After all, not too many people are interested in walking through a museum of musty old books and hard-to-read manuscripts from faraway places unless the items are displayed in an attractive and meaningful way.

So themed rooms were designed to reflect the historical background of various pieces. Rare artifacts were placed in the context of ancient Babylon with its Ishtar Gates; old papyri and vellum scrolls were enlivened in the ambience of ancient Egypt with the pyramids visible in the distance; and the significance of vernacular codices (the first bound volumes of biblical texts) could be readily grasped in the setting of a medieval bindery room. It's all very impressive, with fourteen beautifully themed environments highlighting God's providential oversight and preservation of the biblical text throughout the ages.

This is essentially what happened with the Epistles when they were written by the apostles. The task of authenticating and collecting Paul's letters happened rather quickly, but the Hebrew Christian Epistles took longer. Eventually all of the manuscripts were arranged in a specific sequence to reveal the progressive unfolding of the New Testament message. Upon closer examination, we discover that theming was apparently an important consideration.

The first book in each grouping set the tone for all that follows it. Romans heads the list of Gentile Christian Epistles and introduces us to the wonder of Christ's *work* in saving and sanctifying the sinner. Hebrews, on the other hand, is more about the *person* of Christ as a fitting introduction to the Jewish Christian Epistles. The *person* and *work* of Christ are at the core of the New Testament gospel as the two groups of epistles reach out to touch a lost world with the message of saving grace.

In any analysis of the Epistles, Romans and Hebrews are the masterworks.

THE REMAINING EPISTLES

Following the lead of Romans and Hebrews, the remaining eight epistles in each group all gather around three specific themes. Central to the epistolary literature are the subjects of faith, love, and hope. It is no coincidence that Paul sees these three qualities as the essential foundation of Christian living. "So now faith, hope, and love abide, these three; but the greatest of these is love" (1 Cor. 13:13).

Many have observed this thematic grouping while looking at Paul's church epistles. For instance, W. Graham Scroggie sees this progression:

> 1 & 2 Corinthians, Galatians—"Polemical, dealing with Christian Faith"
>
> Ephesians, Philippians, Colossians—"Philosophical, dealing with Christian Love"
>
> 1 & 2 Thessalonians—"Prophetical, dealing with Christian Hope"[8]

D. Edmond Hiebert expresses the same analysis in slightly different terminology:

> 1 & 2 Corinthians, Galatians—Soteriological [faith in the gospel]
>
> Ephesians, Philippians, Colossians—Christological [love for the Savior]
>
> 1 & 2 Thessalonians—Eschatological [hope in Christ's coming][9]

Referring to the same group of books, J. Sidlow Baxter concurs with Scroggie and Hiebert:

> These three groups of the "Church" epistles are a trinity in unity. Having regard to their respective emphases, we may say that in the first group *faith* looks back at the cross and is strengthened. Then in the second group *love* looks up to the Bridegroom and is deepened. Finally, in the two Thessalonian epistles *hope* looks on to the coming and is brightened. (emphasis mine)[10]

Once this pattern is grasped, the internal significance of these Gentile Christian Epistles is readily apparent. But what about the Jewish Christian Epistles? Can this same sequence of themes be seen in the non-Pauline books? The answer is a definite yes!

The book of James, for instance, has been contrasted to Galatians as provoking the other side of faith. Whereas Galatians emphasizes salvation by faith without works, James argues for a salvation that manifests itself with works. It took a while for Martin Luther to accept the book of James because he misunderstood this obvious contrast between the two books. In like fashion 1 & 2 Peter are an application of living faith to the challenges of suffering and apostasy, respectively. It is not hard to see the theme of *faith* in the first trio of James and 1 & 2 Peter.

A common designation for the epistles of John is that they are the Epistles of *Love*. As Hiebert observed, "It is obvious that the Johannine epistles form a distinct group."[11] Most evangelical Bible teachers would agree that their overriding theme is love.

Finally, Jude and Revelation cap this set of epistles with their message of *hope* in the return of Christ. Revelation is obvious in this regard, but including Jude as a book of hope may take a little convincing. The book of Jude is a warning to apostate teachers that their judgment is coming when Christ returns.

> And Enoch also, the seventh from Adam, prophesied of these, saying, Behold, the Lord cometh with ten thousands of his saints, to execute judgment upon all, and to convince all that are ungodly among them

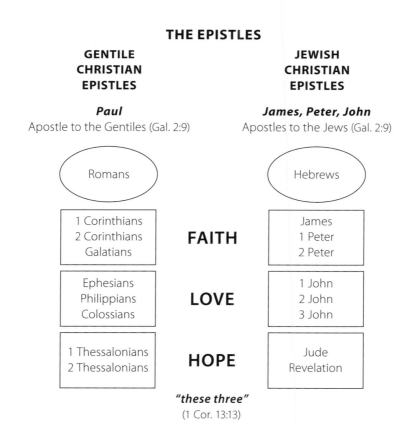

THE EPISTLES

GENTILE CHRISTIAN EPISTLES	JEWISH CHRISTIAN EPISTLES
Paul	*James, Peter, John*
Apostle to the Gentiles (Gal. 2:9)	Apostles to the Jews (Gal. 2:9)

Romans		Hebrews
1 Corinthians 2 Corinthians Galatians	**FAITH**	James 1 Peter 2 Peter
Ephesians Philippians Colossians	**LOVE**	1 John 2 John 3 John
1 Thessalonians 2 Thessalonians	**HOPE**	Jude Revelation

"these three"
(1 Cor. 13:13)

of all their ungodly deeds which they have ungodly committed, and of all their hard *speeches* which ungodly sinners have spoken against him. (Jude 14–15 KJV)

In this respect the book of Jude is certainly like the book of Revelation as it reveals the judgment that will fall upon an ungodly world at the coming of Christ. Both Jude and Revelation are apocalyptic books. Thus the Jewish Christian Epistles conclude in the same manner as the Gentile Christian Epistles, with two books highlighting a message of hope for the people of God.

Whether or not this theming of the Epistles was deliberately intended in the human process of their arrangement is beside the point. It is evident that a divine control determined the outcome. That a trilogy of Christian graces can be seen in both of the epistle groupings, in the same sequential order, suggests strongly that this was the work of God.

MOSAIC ANALOGY

Hands and Arms

Following the introduction of the mosaic analogy in chapter 1, we probed the application of that analogy with respect to the head (Gospels) and torso (Pastorals and Writings) to determine the legitimacy of the concept. We took great care to understand the text of Scripture before venturing a comparison to the corresponding area of the human anatomy.

The time has come to turn our investigative gaze on the application of the analogy to the Epistles. They appear in the mosaic design as the upper torso appendages—the arms and the hands. Without forcing the analogy, can we observe a natural affinity between the Epistles and these appendages?

An initial obvious correlation presents itself: we have two arms, and the Epistles are divided between two groups—the Gentile Christian Epistles and the Jewish Christian Epistles. From the point of view of the New Testament church, only two groups comprise the body of Christ—Jews and Gentiles. The Epistles reach out to each of these specific groups fulfilling the dual purpose of uniquely ministering to both. And as our two arms function together as complements to each other, so the two groups of epistles work as a duality in unity.

The hands, of course, are the most striking aspect of our arms. In fact, the whole purpose of the arms is to extend and rotate the hands so they can accomplish the myriad tasks required of them. Exquisitely crafted by God, hands are amazingly agile structures with an importance exceeding their size. When looking for a similarity to the hands within the Epistles, Romans and Hebrews seem to loom with that kind of significance. As we anticipate the study of these books in the next chapter, you may be surprised at how intricate and precise the structure of Romans and Hebrews are as a reflection of God's design in the human hands.

Thinking of the rest of the Epistles as mirroring the function of the arms, I initially considered the possibility of eight segments in the anatomy of each arm to match the eight remaining books in each of the Gentile and Jewish groups. That only produced frustration and confusion. Then I remembered that the Epistles are grouped around three themes (faith, love, and hope) that correspond to three basic functions of the arms: working, embracing, and reaching out. Living faith is active, like the arms in constant motion (working faith); caring love embraces the object of its affection, like arms encircling the one who is loved (embracing love); uplifting hope reaches out, like arms stretched forth to encourage (reaching hope). Things were beginning to fall into place.

Noticing how the epistles of faith and love were arranged in groups of three, I narrowed my investigation to look for three significant aspects of arm design and function. What stood out immediately is that the upper arm is the symbol of strength, with its biceps-triceps muscles and singular bone structure.

STRENGTH

(upper arm)

"You have a mighty arm."
(Ps. 89:13)

The lower portion of the arm, on the other hand, has a dual function, with two bones (the radius and ulna), creating the ingenious function of rotation. When rotated downward, the arms are in a "push" mode, and when rotated upward, a "pull" mode. Speaking simplistically, every motion of the arms is a combination of pushing and pulling.

ROTATION
(forearm)

"Underneath are the everlasting arms.

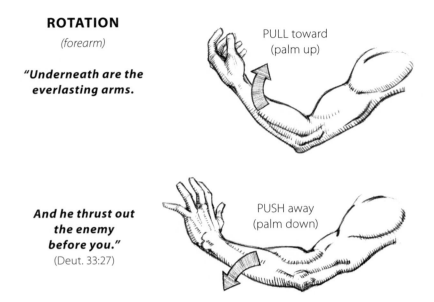

PULL toward
(palm up)

And he thrust out the enemy before you."
(Deut. 33:27)

PUSH away
(palm down)

With this in mind, we are in a position to observe whether the arms are a reflection of the way the Epistles work. If we see the epistolary themes of *faith, love,* and *hope* as three separate arm functions (working, embracing, and reaching out), the segments of strength, push, and pull are readily apparent in each thematic group.

In the *first category of faith*, for instance, Galatians is the strength book of the Gentile Christian Epistles; James is the corresponding strength book of the Jewish Christian Epistles. Remember harmonizing Galatians and James was the single greatest struggle for Martin Luther in his pursuit of the means of justification.

On the Gentile side, 1 & 2 Corinthians provide a combination of push and pull, with 1 Corinthians pushing away things related to faith that are wrong in the church and 2 Corinthians pulling toward the body of Christ the essence of legitimate apostolic authority in matters of faith and practice. Peter's epistles perform the same function on the Jewish side, with 1 Peter reflecting a positive (pull toward) response of faith to the trials of life and 2 Peter reflecting a rejection (push away) of false authority in the church. We will examine in more detail this interplay of push-away and pull-toward functions in the faith epistles in chapter 10.

This threefold pattern is repeated in the *Epistles of Love.* Since we will scrutinize the interrelationship between these six books in chapter 11, I'll simply state here that Ephesians and 1 John are the strength books. Philippians and Colossians rotate the pull and push within the Gentile area, and 2 & 3 John do the same in the Jewish area.

Last, we encounter *the books of hope* and immediately notice only two in each section. I propose that when the arms are reaching out to express the encouragement of help and hope, the muscles of the upper arm are totally relaxed. Could this be why there are no strength books in the Epistles of Hope? The combination of push and pull are very noticeable, however. First Thessalonians (pull) and 2 Thessalonians (push) as well as Jude (push) and Revelation (pull) will be our subject in chapter 12.

PURSUING THE EPISTLES

With all of this as a general background for the Epistles, we now have the opportunity to probe these books in more detail.

In the next chapters we will embark on an incredible excursion through one of the most intriguing portions of God's Word. Understanding how the Epistles work together to present a full-orbed analysis of the *person* and *work* of Christ in the realms of faith, love, and hope will allow us to delve more deeply into these marvelous books. Without question, they radiate a divine aura that speaks loudly of the fact that these books are truly "crafted by God."

So let's begin with the hands, as we consider the books of Romans and Hebrews.

HELPING HANDS

Romans & Hebrews

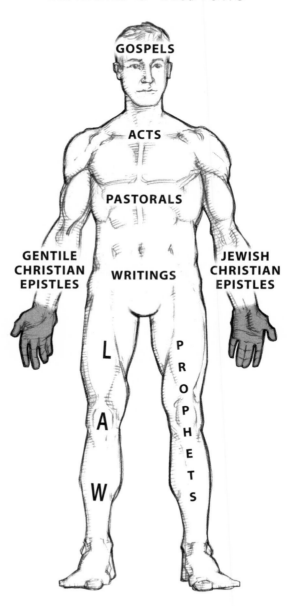

HELPING HANDS

"Hey, would you mind giving me a hand with this?" You've probably heard that expression. Lending a helping hand (rather than a foot) is the appropriate expression for giving assistance. This phrase recognizes the uniqueness of the hand to accomplish tasks, even though the rest of the body also participates in the process.

Years ago before I pursued the ministry, I held a job as a surgical technician at Children's Hospital in Chicago. I assisted pediatric surgeons in their efforts to save and improve young lives. Observing the skilled hands of an accomplished surgeon performing a delicate procedure often left me with a sense of awe.

The same can be said of watchmakers and sculptors and gourmet cooks and cabinetmakers and gifted pianists. All amaze us with the dexterity and precision of their hands and persuade us that of all the gifts of God to humanity, the hand is one of His greatest masterpieces.

THE HANDS OF GOD'S REVELATION

Try to imagine your arms without hands. For the Bible student, that would be like envisioning the Epistles without Romans and Hebrews. These books head their respective columns of epistles (see diagram on p. 115) precisely because, like the hands with their respective arms, they completely fulfill the purpose and function of their particular epistolary grouping. As the hands are the glory of the arms, so Romans is the glory of the Gentile Christian Epistles and Hebrews is the glory of the Jewish Christian Epistles.

Arms and hands fulfill the wishes of the body. The head determines the body's purpose, and the arms swing into action, extending the hands to perform the functions of that purpose. It's all one coordinated effort. Normally speaking, what the body intends to do, the hands accomplish.

That is essentially how the Bible functions. The overriding purpose of Scripture is to scratch the itch of mankind's alienation from God (which is actually a lethal wound, more than an itch). So the purpose of the Bible can be distilled into one concise statement: *Jesus Christ is the exalted Creator and Savior of the world, and His provision of salvation is the only hope for mankind.* Romans and Hebrews scratch that itch.

As we shall see, this is also the message of the Epistles, with each New Testament letter refining that theme as an extension of the biblical gospel. Yet the lead books of Romans and Hebrews are the most complete and articulate expressions of this message in their dual emphasis on the *person* and *work* of Christ. Think for a moment about the special emphasis in each of these two books.

Salvation Is the Only Hope for Mankind

Romans, like no other epistle, captures the complete scope of Christ's *work*. The great doctrines of salvation are arranged in logical progression from the lost condition of humanity in the early chapters (1–3) to the grand themes of salvation by grace through faith (chaps. 4–5), our unique position in Christ (chaps. 6–7), and the extent of our ultimate security (chap. 8). After illustrating the surety of our salvation by appealing to God's saving work among the Jewish people (chaps. 9–11), Romans concludes with an application of those truths to the significant areas of life (chaps. 12–16).

You will notice however that not much is said about the person of Christ. The emphasis is clearly on His great work of salvation. Romans is the monumental book on soteriology—the doctrine of salvation—a detailed explanation of the fact that *His provision of salvation is the only hope for mankind.*

Creator and Savior of the World

Hebrews, on the other hand, is devoted almost exclusively to the exaltation of Christ's *person* as the Son of God and only qualified Savior. The meaning of the atonement and the death of Christ as a replacement for the old covenantal system and sacrifices are clarified, but specifically in the context of our Lord's high-priestly role. The emphasis is clearly and emphatically on who *He is* as the person who is qualified to do what *He did.*

The book climaxes with an appeal for the reader's response to the person of Jesus as the giver of hope, the sustainer of life, and the object of worship. Hebrews is the masterful treatise on Christology—the doctrine of Christ. It is the full embodiment of the theme of Scripture *that Jesus Christ is the exalted Creator and Savior of the world.*

So here's my point: the theme of biblical revelation is that Jesus Christ is the exalted Creator and Savior of the world (Hebrews), and His provision of salvation is the only hope for mankind (Romans). This dual emphasis on the *person* and *work* of Christ resonates in harmonious balance between these two books. As the hands work together in coordinated fashion, so Romans and Hebrews function together as the dynamic duo portraying the two significant aspects of the one glorious gospel.

SIMILAR BUT DIFFERENT

As we continue to think about the hands, we notice that they complement each other—for they reflect opposite symmetrical patterns like a mirror image. Romans and Hebrews are like that. They are similar but different.

We have already considered the fact that these two books emphasize different aspects of the one gospel message—Romans, the *work* of Christ, and Hebrews, the *person* of Christ. Yet they facilitate each other in the same way that our two hands work together. It takes both books to get a grip on the core truth of Scripture.

But Romans and Hebrews are also similar in striking ways. Let's consider a few.

Literary Similarity

The arguments of the two books employ a common format. (I will develop this more fully in the next section.) Suffice it to say at this point, the scheme for each book is cut from the same pattern.

First, the full scope of the particular doctrine in each book is systematically developed: *Soteriology*—Christ's work—in Romans (chaps. 1–8); *Christology*—Christ's person—in Hebrews (chaps. 1–7).

Following these initial beginnings, each book inserts a parenthetical section to further clarify the doctrinal subject. Romans 8 concludes with a proclamation of the Christian's secure position in the love of Christ. This is then illustrated by God's dealing with the Jews and the nation of Israel (chaps. 9–11). In like fashion, Hebrews expands upon the high-priestly role of Christ in chapter 7, by extolling the better quality of the New Covenant over the Old, as well as the more effective nature of Christ's ultimate and final sacrifice (chaps. 8–10).

Finally, each book concludes with practical applications of its thematic argument to various areas of life. Romans challenges the reader to a consistent understanding of how salvation in Christ impacts every phase of life (chaps. 12–16). Hebrews in turn asks the reader to consider how a relationship with the person of Jesus Christ dramatically changes the believer's worldview (chaps. 11 – 13).

	SIMILAR FORMAT		
	Doctrinal Development	Parenthetical Clarification	Practical Application
Romans	1 – 8	9 – 11	12 – 16
Hebrews	1 – 7	8 – 10	11 – 13

Authorship Similarity

Have you ever seen a tandem truck moving down the highway — a single cab with two trailers hitched to the same truck? That is an apt visual picture of Romans and Hebrews. As both trailers are controlled by one driver, so both books appear to have been crafted by a single mind.

All agree that Paul wrote the book of Romans. "Romans claims to have been written by Paul (1:1), and there has been no serious challenge to this claim,"[1] write Carson, Moo, and Morris. The driver in our cab pulling the first trailer of Romans is definitely the apostle Paul.

The question is, then, who's driving the second trailer of Hebrews? Nowhere in the book itself does the author mention his name. The writing is anonymous. Using our analogy, you will notice on our tandem truck that the second trailer is not actually hooked to the cab that empowers it, but to another coupling behind the first trailer.

Hebrews has never been conclusively identified with any particular author, and in that sense it resembles a tandem trailer not hooked directly to a cab. No other book in the New Testament shares this characteristic. Yet everyone who studies the book understands that the recipients knew who wrote it. And the early church seemed to know as well. For the first several centuries the church acknowledged that Paul was the author of Hebrews.[2] According to the early church, the human author in the cab of divine revelation for both Romans and Hebrews was the apostle Paul.

Not everyone in later centuries has agreed with this early church tradition. Appealing to perceived differences in vocabulary, style of writing, and uncharacteristic exclusions and emphases, Bible scholars have offered their own ideas on who wrote Hebrews. One of the first to do so was Tertullian of Carthage (AD 150 – 222) who postulated it might have been Barnabas. Others since then have suggested a variety of possibilities: Luke, Apollos, Silas, and even Priscilla. The problem with all this speculation however is that no uniform agreement exists among the scholars, and each suggestion faces as many problems as the next.

Here is not the place to argue the pros and cons of the authorship of Hebrews. I am simply pointing out that "the Pauline *tradition* is much weightier than is generally allowed."[3] After this statement, J. Sidlow Baxter argues rather convincingly that Paul was indeed the author of Hebrews, calling attention to the fact that even those who think someone else wrote it are forced to admit that Paul's influence can be readily seen throughout the book.

In the third century, Origen suggested an alternate to Paul yet indicates that the thoughts were the apostle's. More recently, Dean Alford, although not in favor of Pauline authorship, wrote that the general cast of thought was Pauline. D. Edmond Hiebert (a contemporary scholar) argues strongly against Paul as the author but nevertheless admits that Hebrews "arose within the Pauline circle of influence."[4]

Either directly as its author, or indirectly as a major influence, Pauline thought drives the book of Hebrews. It does appear that Romans and Hebrews are analogous to a tandem two-trailer truck.

Recipient Similarity

Considerable evidence supports the theory that Romans and Hebrews were written to the same group of people living in Rome. A major Gentile city, Rome provided refuge for a large population of Jews. The church in Rome undoubtedly reflected this ethnic mix.

When it comes to the book of Romans, Carson, Moo, and Morris conclude, "Paul addresses in Romans a mixed community of Jewish and Gentile Christians."[5] Reflecting on the testimony of Ambrosiaster (fourth century), Everett Harrison observes, "At the beginning Jews formed the nucleus, but ... a considerable group of Gentiles ... very soon became an important element in the church."[6] The very fact that Paul addresses both Gentiles and Jews in the book of Romans, with a whole section devoted to the Jewish question (chaps. 9–11), indicates the reality of this racial mix in the Roman church.

Coming to the book of Hebrews, then, we should not be surprised to find that the book seems to be addressed to the same Jewish believers in Rome. Other destinations for the book have been suggested (e.g., Alexandria, Antioch, and Caesarea) based on possible authorship by Apollos, Barnabas, and Luke, respectively. But credence for these conjectures has never been substantiated. Leon Morris went so far as to conclude, "There do seem to be more reasons for connecting the letter with Rome than with any other place."[7]

Why then would a special letter be written to the Hebrews in Rome after the great letter of Romans had already been written to the whole church in that city? The answer revolves around the severe persecution of Christians in Rome by the demented emperor Nero. His hostilities were not directed toward the Jews and their synagogue but only against the Christians and the church. According to *Foxe's Book of Martyrs*, "Nero even refined upon cruelty, and contrived all manner of punishments for the Christians that the most infernal imagination could design."[8]

These persecutions at the hand of Nero began to weed out the noncommitted professing Christians from the Roman church, including those professing Hebrews who preferred to return to the sanctity of Judaism and the synagogue. Consequently the Christian Hebrews were troubled by the problem of desertion by some, on the one hand, and the challenge to personal commitment, on the other. They needed to understand that the person of Christ was greater than anything Judaism had to offer. This appears to have been the circumstance that spawned this special letter to the Hebrew Christians in Rome.

Here is another way, then, that Romans and Hebrews demonstrate an affinity for each other. They both seem to have been written to the same general group of people.

Dating Similarity

A similarity in the dates of writing is more interesting than it is crucial; it merely suggests that Romans and Hebrews were written for the same generation. The books seem to have been written within a decade of each other.

Romans was written first, having been penned around AD 57 when the political and social conditions in Rome were relatively stable. Ten years later Emperor Nero set the city on fire and blamed it on the Christians, using them as scapegoats for his mentally deranged activity. During this time Hebrews was written, between AD 65 and 67. These books therefore were historically sequential, involving the same generation of believers in the city of Rome.

Summary

Reviewing the similarities between Romans and Hebrews helps us appreciate the dual nature of these two incredible New Testament epistles as they elucidate the twofold aspect of the gospel—the *person* and *work* of Christ. Since both books seem to have been written to believers in Rome, by the same or a similar author, with an identical literary format, and within a few years of the other—the affinity between them is as natural as the two physical hands working together.

A CLOSER LOOK AT STRUCTURE

Although the hands are mirror images of each other (as opposites), their basic structure is the same. Both hands have a thumb, four fingers, and a palm. God designed the two hands to be identical. He did the same with Romans and Hebrews.

Structure, or format, adds meaning to the text. As with the human body, so with the biblical text—form serves function. God's design is always specific to accomplish a particular function, and that design reveals the mind and purpose of His intent. If we understand the format, we will have a more comprehensive grasp of God's purpose.

As I pointed out in the previous section, Romans and Hebrews manifest a common structural design. Each begins with a thorough analysis of its particular doctrine: Romans 1–8, the *work* of Christ (soteriology), and Hebrews 1–7, the *person* of Christ (Christology). To use Paul's words in 2 Timothy 3:16 (KJV), "All scripture . . . is profitable for doctrine" or teaching. God wants us to understand the truth about salvation and the Savior. Romans and Hebrews are His magnum opus on these two subjects.

But God never intended for doctrine to be simply a matter of knowledge. Paul elaborates in the same verse, "All scripture . . . is profitable for doctrine, for *reproof*, for *correction*, for *instruction in righteousness*" (emphasis mine). Righteousness is right behavior, and *that* is the ultimate goal of doctrine. The purpose of sound doctrine has always been to reprove our errant ways, to correct our course of action, and to establish a disciplined pattern of righteous living. Knowing the truth is not enough. God expects a direct correlation between knowing the truth and living the truth.

This is why both Romans (chaps. 12–16) and Hebrews (chaps. 11–13) end with a strong and comprehensive section on application. In the format of these books God is revealing that the divine purpose of each doctrine is to elicit a response that will influence the reader's behavior. Numerous scenarios of application are proposed to expose the practical intent of each doctrine.

Finally, a middle section serves as a bridge between the doctrinal portion and the practical application: Romans 9–11; Hebrews 8–10. In each case what appears to be a parenthetical break in the argument extends the flow of thought to establish a logical foundation upon which to build the life applications. I will elaborate more fully on this below; for now I note that by the use of this literary technique, God assures the reader that the connection between the doctrine and the application is both a logical sequence and a beneficial consequence.

From the divine perspective, faith is not a blind leap in the dark but "the assurance of things hoped for, the conviction of things not seen" (Heb. 11:1). So let's examine more deeply the arguments of these two monumental books, keeping in mind this doctrine-to-application structural pattern.

ROMANS

When reading the apostle Paul, we quickly discover that he is a master of logic and sequential thought. With Paul, it is always first things first as he builds his case point upon point.

Romans is a classic example of Paul's amazing ability to be clear, thorough, and concise when presenting a reasoned argument. In fact, he tells us at the outset what he will attempt to prove—that salvation from sin is a provision of God's grace to be received by faith (Intro: 1:1–17).

Doctrinal Development (Chaps. 1–8)

The Depravity of Humanity's Lost Condition (1:18–3:20)

Salvation is the theme in Romans, so Paul begins by analyzing the sinful condition from which all men and women need to be saved. Before we can appreciate the wonder of God's provision for salvation, we need to understand the reality of our desperate plight! Whether Jew or Gentile, Paul argues that all are condemned because of our sinful state before a righteous God. We are hopelessly lost and in need of someone to save us.

Justification through Faith in Christ (3:21–5:21)

The solution to our grievous problem surprises us. We discover that the burdens of religious ritual and humanitarian goodness are eliminated as the pathway to forgiveness: all is reduced to humble faith. The remission of our sins and a just standing before God (justification) are provided solely through faith in the provision of Christ's death on our behalf. As Abraham was justified through faith, so are we. Paul explains that to be saved is to enjoy a new position in Christ, whereby our old position of condemnation in Adam is nullified.

Sanctification by the Spirit of God (6:1–8:39)

Our spiritual growth as believers in Christ is based on the fact that our old nature has been crucified with Him. As a result, we are no longer servants to sinful inclinations; rather, we now enjoy a whole new freedom whereby we can choose to serve Christ. Yet a battle continues to rage within the believer with regard to choices between good and evil. Only by yielding to the power of God's Spirit within us can we experience victory in this spiritual struggle. In spite of the suffering we all endure as members of the human race, we know that ultimate goodness and eternal life will triumph in Jesus Christ. Furthermore, nothing can separate us from His love when we belong to Him by faith.

Parenthetical Clarification (Chaps. 9 – 11)

Before Paul applies the doctrine of salvation to the practical issues of life, he pauses to address a major concern. At the end of chapter 8 Paul declares that nothing can separate us from the love of God that is in Christ Jesus. How then can he explain what happened to Israel? Didn't Israel experience a separation from the love of God? So is it possible for a person who is saved to lose his or her relationship with God and be cast away in the same manner as Israel? This is the question Paul seeks to answer in chapters 9 – 11.

Paul begins his explanation in chapter 9 by reminding us that God chose Israel to be His people; they did not choose Him. Therefore the longevity of their relationship with God is based on God's sovereign choice, not on Israel's unreliable response. True, Paul is talking about the nation of Israel, but he is also clarifying the point he made at the end of chapter 8, that people of faith are secure in Christ's love. God's love is rooted in His unchanging character, so that the believer's relationship to Him is permanent.

Next (chap. 10) Paul wants his readers to know that when a believer sins (as Israel did), God continues to pursue the errant sinner to bring about repentance and restoration of fellowship. Finally (chap. 11), God does not cast away His people, but after a period of chastising will bring them back — as He will one day do with Israel.

In all of this, Paul continues his argument from chapter 8 that we, like Israel, are truly secure in God's love if we have been genuinely saved by His grace. Paul understood that before he could lead these Roman believers to engage as people of faith in the practical affairs of life, he had to first of all settle the question of security.

Practical Application (Chaps. 12 – 16)

Insecurity breeds restlessness and a lack of stability. Security, on the other hand, creates an atmosphere of confidence and freedom to take risks. This, I believe, is why Paul clarified the matter of security before challenging his audience to live out their salvation in the practical dimension of life. Only then was he ready to give an exhortation for sacrificial living: "I appeal to you therefore, brothers . . ." (12:1).

Verses 1–2 of chapter 12 set the tone for this "application section" by appealing to a level of sacrificial service that is not conformed to the world's way of thinking. Instead, salvation in Christ makes it possible for the believer to have a whole new mind-set for discovering and doing the will of God. This includes numerous scenarios:

Chapter 12 — to those within the body of Christ and people in the world

Chapter 13 — to human government and one's neighbor

Chapter 14 — to those who are less mature in the faith

Chapter 15 — to ministry and Christian service

Chapter 16 — to personal relationships with valued friends

Obviously this is a simplistic summarization of Paul's specific challenges for the application of salvation truth. For our purpose, it is sufficient to understand that the final section of Romans is a demonstration on how the doctrine of salvation works itself out in daily life.

HEBREWS

As mentioned previously, the book of Hebrews is anonymous — the name of the human author never mentioned. Curiously, all the book's references to the Old Testament are also anonymous. The book quotes extensively from the Greek version of the Hebrew Scriptures but never names the human author of the quotation. The consistent nature of this pattern suggests a deliberate intent on the part of the writer.

Even a surface reading of the book of Hebrews reveals the reason for this pattern of anonymity. The emphasis throughout the book is clearly on the person of Christ and the fact that He has spoken (1:2). As the light of the moon and stars retreats into obscurity in the presence of the sun, so all human involvement in the writing of Scripture diminishes before the magnificent glory of the Son of God.

The author of Hebrews will not tell us his name because who he is doesn't matter. His only concern is to magnify Christ so that we will become enthralled with the wonder and majesty of the Savior. The author gladly bows out of the picture so as not to obscure our view of this beatific vision.

Here is another clue to the theme of Hebrews. It is all about the *person* of Jesus Christ. The author wants us to fully grasp that Jesus is the divine Son of God who is the only qualified Savior.

Doctrinal Development (Chaps. 1 – 7)

For Jews in the church who were contemplating a return to Judaism to escape the persecution of Nero against the Christian community in Rome, it was imperative that they understood the seriousness of this decision. Since Jesus Christ, the Son of God, was infinitely superior to all the pillars of ancient Judaism, they would be jumping from the frying pan of temporal persecution into the fire of eternal damnation. To abandon Christ for the antiquated system of Mosaic Law and its ritualistic religion was to lose any hope of eternal salvation.

This is why the author of Hebrews begins with a strong doctrinal section that exalts the preeminence of Christ over angels, Moses, and Aaron. The first seven chapters explode upon the reader with the most dazzling, thorough, and precise display of Christology to be found in the Word of God. The author argues that leaving Jesus for something infinitely less makes absolutely no sense — even under the pressures of persecution.

Christ Is Better than the Angels (chaps. 1 – 2)

Our first clue to the opening comparison between Christ and the angels flows clearly out of the author's initial statement concerning God's ultimate revelation: "Long ago … God spoke to our fathers by the prophets, but in these last days he has spoken to us by his Son" (1:1 – 2). The comparison with angels is really about the superior status of the new revelation given by the Son over the old revelation that was mediated by angels (cf. Gal 3:19). So here's the point: if the Old Testament message of the Law had serious consequences, the New Testament message of salvation in Christ is far more serious in its ramifications — "how shall we escape if we neglect such a great salvation?" (2:3). Christ's exaltation over the angels demonstrates the superiority of the gospel of salvation in Christ over the Torah of Judaism.

Christ Is Better than Moses (chaps. 3 – 4)

The anchor of Judaism was Moses and the Old Covenant of law. The author continues therefore by describing how Christ is superior to Moses because Moses was merely a servant in God's house, whereas Christ is the builder and master of that house. Even Joshua, Moses' successor, brought the people of Israel only into a temporary rest. But Christ brings the people of faith into a permanent, eternal rest. With this strong argument, the author challenges the Hebrew Christians to look beyond Moses and Joshua to see the fulfillment of all they prefigured in Christ. Jesus Christ is worthy of devotion and commitment because He is far better than Moses.

Christ Is Better than Aaron **(chaps. 5 – 7)**

As the first high priest of Israel, Aaron established the earthly priesthood system foundational to Judaism. Christ, however, was called to a higher priesthood that left Aaron and his posterity in the shadows. After a brief interlude (5:11 – 6:20) designed to challenge the Jews to think more clearly (as those who are mature), the author presents an incredible argument for Christ's more exalted priesthood, patterned after the King-Priest Melchizedek, not after Levi and Aaron. Christ is indeed far more impressive than Aaron.

Parenthetical Clarification (Chaps. 8 – 10)

The author of Hebrews includes a clarification section after his doctrinal presentation to prepare his audience for the final practical application. In the first part of the book he concentrates on the magnificence of Christ who, in every way, is better than the grandest aspects of Judaism. To clarify that claim and further drive home the point, he describes how this glorious Person has produced a better covenant (chap. 8), ministers in a better sanctuary (chap. 9), and has provided a better sacrifice (chap. 10). This emphasis on what Christ has done qualifies Him to be the only adequate Savior. In other words, what He has done (chaps. 8 – 10) validates who He claims to be (chaps. 1 – 7).

Practical Application (Chaps. 10 – 13)

Commentators seem to agree that a major shift in the argument occurs at verse 19 of chapter 10. Just as in Romans 12:1, where the practical section begins with the word *therefore,* so in Hebrews 10:19 we read, "Therefore, brothers ..." From this point on, the author's concern is to apply the great truths of Christology to the current issues of life.

First (chap. 10), if Christ is the only worthy Savior, it doesn't make sense to not assemble with other believers (vv. 19 – 25), to willfully sin by turning from Christ (vv. 26 – 31), and to lose confidence in Christ's ability to meet their needs (vv. 32 – 39). Furthermore, the author encourages them (chap. 11) to consider the many faithful men and women of God from the past who received hope in hard times through faith, as an incentive for them to do likewise. The discipline of faith is something to rejoice over (chap. 12), because the chastising work of God demonstrates that they are indeed His children. Finally (chap. 13), he reviews a number of moral and spiritual implications of the life of faith to motivate his readers toward a positive response to the total sufficiency of Christ.

Here again, as with Romans, I have offered a simplistic generalization of these concluding chapters, intending only to highlight the fact that the book of Hebrews concludes with a practical section on application. The author helps these struggling Hebrews to understand that Christ is the answer to the most pressing issues of their lives.

A GRIPPING DESIGN

Throughout this chapter I have been comparing the books of Romans and Hebrews to the human hands. In the mosaic analogy, both the Gentile Christian Epistles and the Jewish Christian Epistles extend as arms of specialized revelation out of the historical perspective of the book of Acts. Within these groupings of epistles, two formidable books, Romans and Hebrews, emerge as foundational masterpieces to articulate the basic message of each group. Comparing these books to the hands as the ultimate refinement of the epistolary arms seems like a reasonable assumption.

The task before us now is to examine the structure and function of the hand to see if we find any likeness to the literary design of the books. As we have seen, the two books exhibit a similar format, even as the two hands are mirror images of each other. With this observation in mind, let's probe more specifically into the anatomy and physiology of the human hand to see if we are on track with this aspect of the mosaic concept.

The Human Hand

A web site that specializes in orthopedic information begins its discussion of "Hand Anatomy" with these words: "Few structures of the human anatomy are as unique as the hand."[9]

Unique indeed! What an amazing array of hinges, levers, and power sources graces the human hand. With twenty-seven bones in each hand (54 total = ¼ of the skeletal bones) and a grid of muscles extending from the forearm in conjunction with the intrinsic muscles of the palm (there are no muscles in the fingers, only tendons), the hand is truly a complicated living machine. A complex and rich vascular network of arteries and veins team up with the median, ulnar, and radial nerves to energize the various hand functions. Furthermore, two of the largest areas (about 25 percent) of the motor cortex of the brain (the part that controls all movement in the body) are devoted to the intricate workings of the hands. This obvious importance of the hands to the body, with all their remarkable complexity, makes the hands a worthy representation of the significance and finesse of Romans and Hebrews to the Scriptures.

Perhaps the most impressive function of the hand is its ability to grasp objects and hold them in its grip. The prehensile thumb, working in opposition to the independent fingers, is the genius of this unique ability. Whether exercising the gripping strength of swinging a five-pound sledgehammer or the delicate finesse of threading a needle, the hand routinely navigates a variety of maneuvers.

What makes this possible is the thumb-palm-fingers design. Observe how the thumb, with its large base muscle, provides strength to the grip. In turn, that strength can be applied to any one of the four fingers or to any combination of them as the tasks vary. Located between the powerful thumb and the finger applications, the palm provides a significant pocket connecting the thumb to the fingers so that things can be held or gripped. Each part of this multifaceted mechanism (a strong thumb, multiple fingers working with the thumb, and a middle connecting palm) is necessary for the hand to carry out its designed purpose.

AN AMAZING ANALOGY

The above description of the hand is strikingly similar to the form and function of both Romans and Hebrews. The two books do indeed operate in the same manner as the hands.

Take Romans, for instance. The opening treatise on the doctrine of salvation (chaps. 1–8) approximates the size and purpose of the thumb. This is the strength of Romans and provides the fundamental teaching on the work of Christ. Then, in the final section (chaps. 12–16), this powerful doctrine interacts with a number of specific practical concerns in the same fashion as the thumb, providing strength to the various fingers. Doctrine working with many applications is curiously like the thumb working with numerous fingers.

Finally, between the doctrine section and the application section, snuggles the connecting interlude on the believer's security (chaps. 9–11). Functioning like the palm, this parenthetical clarification allows the powerful truth of salvation to interact effectively with the various elements of practical service.

When Jesus wanted to express how secure His followers were in His care, He used this very analogy. In the context of His role as the Good Shepherd, Jesus said that His sheep "shall never perish, neither shall any man pluck them out of my *hand*" (John 10:28 KJV, emphasis mine). Being in the palm of

His hand is to be eternally secure. There's no question that the hand is an incredible picture of the book of Romans.

And Hebrews follows the same pattern. Beginning with a complete development of the person of Christ, the author methodically establishes Jesus' credentials as the divine Savior (chaps. 1–7). This also is beautifully illustrated by the strength of the thumb. Then, as the author applies this truth of who Christ is to the various occasions of concern for the Hebrews (chaps. 10–13), we are reminded once again of the analogy of the thumb touching the various digits.

The middle interlude in Hebrews (8:1–10:18) gives a glimpse of how great Jesus is as evidenced by the monumental things He accomplished—a New Covenant, a better sanctuary, and a final sacrifice forever. This ties the doctrine and practice of the book of Hebrews together, like the palm connecting the thumb and fingers.

This picture of the ultimate sacrifice of Christ in the palm of Hebrews is a poignant reminder that our Lord's hands were pierced in the crucifixion: "A company of evildoers encircles me; they have pierced my hands" (Ps. 22:16). His hands bear the scars of our salvation. As for Romans, the hand is a striking analogy of the book of Hebrews.

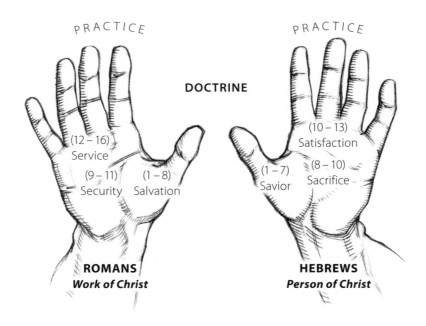

FINAL THOUGHTS

Romans and Hebrews are the monarch epistles of the New Testament, expressing the *work* and *person* of Jesus Christ respectively. In their presentation of tandem truths of the Christian faith, these books are, in my opinion, the most important in the Bible for touching our needy world with the message of the gospel.

"The hands are ... two intricate, prehensile, multi-faceted body parts ... [which] are the chief organs for physically manipulating the environment,"[10] declares the Wikipedia Internet free encyclopedia. Perhaps it would be appropriate to borrow the sense of this statement by restating it this way: Romans and Hebrews are the chief organs for spiritually manipulating the human environment.

Salvation and a Savior—what powerful and essential truths with which to reach out to the world!

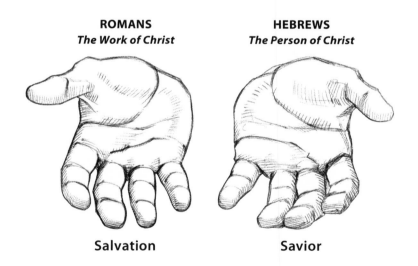

ROMANS	HEBREWS
The Work of Christ	*The Person of Christ*

Salvation   **Savior**

CHAPTER TEN

CONNECTING WITH REALITY

The Epistles of Faith

1 & 2 Corinthians, Galatians, James, 1 & 2 Peter

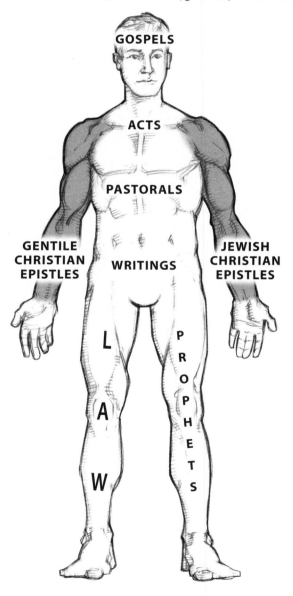

THINKING ABOUT BELIEVING

Disney parades are spectacular. Each afternoon in the Magic Kingdom of Disney World, wide-eyed children and their equally excited parents line the corridor from Frontier Land to Main Street to experience the wonder of a parade. Take, for example, the Dream Come True parade. Costumed dancers, fabulous floats, and fantasy characters flow along in magical process as everyone celebrates the bewitching music of "Just Believe."

The words, "just believe in all you imagine ... just believe and your dreams will come true," seem so welcome to commonplace ears. What a wonderfully entertaining experience it is, wrapped in the hopes of a bright tomorrow. The repetitious refrain is so simple, yet so mystically profound. *Just believe*—and all you can imagine will come true. After all, Mickey Mouse, Cinderella, and Peter Pan said it was so.

This is what happens in Disney World, which is why they call it the Magic Kingdom. As the ferry or monorail returns you back toward home and reality, however, you quickly realize it was all just make-believe. Parades are wonderful diversions of momentary escape from the challenges of life, but in the real world believing in believing is just as unreliable as falling in love with love. There's no substance in it. So, apart from what happens in Disney's Magic Kingdom, "just believe and your dreams will come true" isn't really a formula for success.

All this is pertinent to the subject of faith. Faith is simply another word for believing, and believing is only effective if the object of faith is anchored in reality. Even strong faith in something not reliably true will ultimately lead to despair. Believing in believing works only in the Magic Kingdom; in like fashion, faith in faith is religious fantasy that works only in never-never land.

In a broad sense, this is the message of the Epistles of Faith (1 & 2 Corinthians, Galatians, James, and 1 & 2 Peter). Collectively these epistles unfold the mechanism of faith by revealing the essential elements of a faith that truly connects with spiritual reality. Hollow faith (based on believing in believing) is exposed for what it is—a naïve confidence in that which cannot deliver.

REVIEWING THEMES

As I introduced the New Testament Epistles in chapter 8, I isolated the books of Romans and Hebrews as the capstone revelations for the *work* and *person* of Christ respectively. In chapter 9, I summarized the unique message and complementary balance of these two books. A picture emerged of the Bible reaching out with helping hands to the whole world (both Jews and Gentiles) with the crucial message of a majestic Savior and His marvelous work of redemption.

Now we come to the eight remaining epistles in the Gentile division and in the Jewish division, which correspond to two human arms in the mosaic design. In chapter 8 we saw that each set can be thoughtfully divided into the dominant themes of faith, love, and hope. The sequence for both the Gentile and Jewish books is the same: books of faith, followed by books of love, and finally books of hope.

GENTILE CHRISTIAN EPISTLES	THEME	JEWISH CHRISTIAN EPISTLES
1 Corinthians		James
2 Corinthians	**FAITH**	1 Peter
Galatians		2 Peter
Ephesians		1 John
Philippians	**LOVE**	2 John
Colossians		3 John
1 Thessalonians	**HOPE**	Jude
2 Thessalonians		Revelation

Our challenge now is to take each thematic group of books and explore its individual contribution to the overall theme. In this chapter, we'll consider the books of faith. Then we'll turn to the books of love and hope.

THE TWO SIDES OF FAITH

Quoting from the observations of several Bible expositors in chapter 8, I demonstrated that the books of 1 & 2 Corinthians and Galatians within the Gentile Christian Epistles and the books of James and 1 & 2 Peter within the Jewish Christian Epistles have *faith* as their characteristic theme. These two sets of three epistles each balance the concept of faith and help us to grasp the essential elements of a faith that is vibrant and effective.

So let's further examine these six books as epistles of faith. How does each book's particular variation on the theme balance our understanding of this great spiritual virtue?

The Epistles of Faith	
GENTILE CHRISTIAN EPISTLES	**JEWISH CHRISTIAN EPISTLES**
1 Corinthians	James
2 Corinthians	1 Peter
Galatians	2 Peter

First of all, notice that each grouping comprises a single book (Galatians and James) and a set of double books (1 & 2 Corinthians and 1 & 2 Peter).

The dual books of 1 & 2 Corinthians and 1 & 2 Peter emphasize that a standard for right and wrong is rooted in the character and revelation of God. Choices have consequences. In these books, good behavior is commended while bad behavior is exposed and corrected. A dynamic tension exists between *pushing away* the bad and *pulling in* the good. In fact, push and pull readily describes the central flow within both of these sets of books.

All of this casts a meaningful reflection on the subject of faith. The Corinthian books and Peter's epistles refine the concepts of faith introduced in Galatians and James.

First, let's compare the two single books. Historically, Galatians and James have been hard to reconcile because they appear to present contrastive views on the subject of faith.

Martin Luther loved Galatians, the book that gave him a proper understanding of justification[1] by faith alone. On the other hand, he wanted to exclude James from the canon of Scripture, because it seemed to advocate justification by works. Only later in life did he recognize the complementary nature and vital necessity of both books. Galatians and James are indeed the key books on the subject of faith, and they need to be studied together.

Galatians

How much clearer could it be? The apostle Paul's explanation of the grace nature of salvation in Romans was precise and powerful: because mankind is totally depraved in its sinful condition, no amount of good behavior or religious ritual can atone for its sin. Salvation is by faith alone in the finished work of Christ. Period!

Yet religionists and moralists (the Judaizers in Paul's day) have continued to insist that salvation is a complicit effort between what Christ did for us and what we must do for ourselves. He did His part; now we must do our part to obtain the coveted salvation blessing. That is the insidious error that seeped into the Galatian churches, and Paul responded with stern condemnation:

> I am astonished that you are so quickly deserting him who called you in the grace of Christ and are turning to a different gospel—not that there is another one, but there are some who trouble you and want to distort the gospel of Christ. But even if we or an angel from heaven should preach to you a gospel contrary to the one we preached to you, let him be accursed. As we have said before, so now I say again: If anyone is preaching to you a gospel contrary to the one you received, let him be accursed. (Gal. 1:6–9)

In Galatians Paul presents a well-reasoned argument intent on thoroughly dismantling the Judaizers' legalistic thinking. Judaizers were Jewish religionists who sought to incorporate the law observances of Judiasm into the new message of faith in Christ. Faith plus works to gain the favor of God was their mantra, and Paul saw it as deceptive error. As he said to the Romans, grace plus anything is no longer grace (11:6). Truth declares that salvation is solely by the grace of God through faith in Jesus Christ apart from any human effort (Eph. 2:8–9).

Paul actually calls the Galatians fools for believing that works of the flesh could contribute to their righteous standing before God (3:1). He goes on to say, "Now it is evident that no one is justified before God by the law, for 'The righteous shall live by faith'" (3:11). Paul's whole Epistle to the Galatians thunders this message—*salvation is through faith alone*, apart from works.

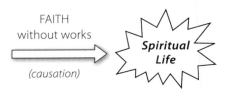

FAITH
without works

(causation)

Spiritual
Life

The thought structure of Galatians is uncomplicated and forthright.[2] Paul starts by establishing the *authenticity* of the gospel in the first two chapters. He received the gospel by direct revelation from God, and this was confirmed by the apostles in Jerusalem (chap. 1). Even Peter and Barnabas had to admit that the Judaizers were wrong and Paul was right (chap. 2).

Next Paul demonstrates the absolute *superiority* of the gospel of grace to any system of works. A "grace only" gospel provides a new position of sonship with God, which is better than the servant relationship of works (chap. 3). Furthermore, the privileges of this new position are incalculable: as adopted sons we become joint heirs with Christ (chap. 4).

Finally, Paul exhorts the Galatians, saying, "For freedom Christ has set us free; stand firm therefore, and do not submit again to a yoke of slavery" (5:1). The practical application of liberty in Christ is explained in terms of the motivation of love and the empowerment of the Spirit (chaps. 5–6).

Galatians is indeed a foundational book for defending the truth of the gospel that salvation is solely by the grace of God through faith alone, apart from works. In his *New Testament Survey*, Robert Gromachi begins his analysis of Galatians with these statements:

> Galatians has been called both the Magna Charta of Christian Liberty and the Christian Declaration of Independence. Out of its pages grew the Protestant Reformation for it was by study in Galatians that Luther's heart was opened to the truth of justification by faith alone.[3]

James

The early church was predominantly Jewish. Jerusalem was the epicenter of Christianity, yet there were other communities of Jewish believers. The twelve tribes of Israel were initially scattered at the time of the Assyrian and Babylonian captivities. On Pentecost (as recorded in Acts 2), many descendants of those dispersed Jews, making a pilgrimage back to Jerusalem, became believers in Jesus Christ through the preaching of Peter before they returned to their far-off cities. Known as the Jews of the Diaspora (or Dispersion), these believing Jews established Christian communities all over the ancient world.

Persecution and extreme poverty drove other believing Jews from Jerusalem during the early years of the church; these also sought refuge in the communities of the Diaspora. As the presiding bishop of the Jerusalem church, James felt a pastoral responsibility for all these Jewish saints—many of whom he knew personally through contact in Jerusalem. So when James addressed his epistle, "To the twelve tribes in the Dispersion" (1:1), he was writing to these Jewish believers scattered throughout the world.

Writing earlier than any other New Testament writer, James was concerned about a common problem among Jewish believers living in hostile environments. Persecuted because of their faith in Christ, it seems that they had fallen into a negative spirit of complaining about their problems and retaliating with verbal abuse against their persecutors. They had become lax in demonstrating Christian character. With no joy in their walk and no love in their talk, the reality of their profession of faith in Christ had become suspect.

Referring to the recipients of his letter as "my brothers" (1:2), James is convinced that they are genuine Christians. So when he writes to them about faith, he is not referring to faith in Christ for salvation, but to their walk of faith as followers of Christ. He encourages them to be "doers of the word, and not hearers only" (1:22), so that their testimony as Christians will be pure and vibrant. It is in this sense that faith without works is not a genuine faith (2:14–18). He is not telling them how to *become* Christians, but how to *be* the Christians they have become.

> The *argument* of the epistle is that true Christian faith must express itself in practical goodness. Hence, all the way through, the emphasis is on good works ... There is no contradiction between Paul, with his primary emphasis on faith, and James, with his insistence on good works. James is not arguing for good works as a *means* to salvation, but as the *product* of salvation.[4]

James wants his readers to know that genuine faith produces spiritual fruit. People of faith find joy in trials, overcome temptations, and live out the teachings of God's Word (chap. 1). They are not prone to showing partiality (chap. 2), and they know how important it is to control their tongues as a manifestation of heavenly wisdom (chap. 3). Being sensitive to the dangers of worldliness, they resist the advances of Satan in order to live according to God's will (chap. 4). Furthermore, those who live by faith understand the dangers of riches, the rewards of patience, and the power of prayer for spiritual healing (chap. 5). All of these things are strong evidences of true faith in Christ.

A Crucial Distinction

A comparison of Galatians and James reveals an important distinction between faith without works for salvation and faith with works for Christian living. Faith alone in the completed work of Christ with no addition of human effort is the means of God's provision for salvation. That is the message of Galatians. Genuine faith, on the other hand, will always manifest itself in good works as a testimony of redemption. James is the writer who highlights this aspect of faith.

In this way both Galatians and James are necessary to complete the message of faith. One without the other is only half the story. Paul argues strongly in the book of Galatians for the *exclusion* of works in faith, while James is equally adamant for the *inclusion* of works in faith. Both are right, depending on which side of salvation is under consideration. No wonder Martin Luther experienced a period of quandary when comparing these two books.

THE "FAITH SET" OF THE GENTILE CHRISTIAN EPISTLES

Galatians and 1 & 2 Corinthians are the "faith set" of the Gentile Christian Epistles. The lead book is Galatians; as we have seen, Paul here argues for faith as the sole means of salvation. The real contrast in Galatians, however, is between the spirit (the realm of faith) and the flesh (the source of works). These two are not only in contrast to each other; they are actually at war (5:17).

This then is the push-and-pull factor. Paul strongly exhorts the Galatian believers to *push away* the flesh and to *pull in* the spirit as the basis for exercising faith without works. In light of this, it is interesting to observe how the Corinthian epistles pick up these alternate themes and expand on how the push-and-pull concepts affect the body of Christ. First Corinthians is a corrective epistle with an emphasis on *pushing away the works of the flesh*. Second Corinthians is a positive defense of Paul's apostolic authority with an emphasis on *pulling in a discerning spirit*.

First Corinthians

Corinth had a reputation for being the "sin city" of the first-century Greek world, and almost every aspect of the Corinthian church bore the taint of fleshly thinking. When writing to the Corinthians Paul admitted, "But I, brothers, could not address you as spiritual people, but as people of the flesh" (3:1). The tension between the flesh and the Spirit so prominent in Galatians was also evident in the Corinthian church—and the flesh was winning.

From beginning to end, Paul's first letter to the Corinthians bears the stamp of severe but loving correction. Although the letter is graced with many positive thoughts, the overall tone is negative. In one scenario after another, Paul challenges their thinking and behavior by telling them to push away their fleshly ways.

The book naturally divides into two parts as Paul responds to both a verbal and written report:

Concerns in Response to a Personal Report (chaps. 1 – 6)

A report had come to Paul from the house of Chloe (1:11) that disruptive divisions existed within the church. Boastful claims made by various groups had divided the assembly into elitist factions that essentially destroyed the spirit of unity (1:10–4:21). These prideful exaltations were a hypocritical farce covering a multitude of flagrant evils—incest, lawsuits, and impurity (5:1–6:20). Catch the negative flavor of Paul's scathing rebukes:

3:3: For you are still of the flesh. For while there is jealousy and strife among you, are you not of the flesh and behaving only in a human way?

5:2: And you are arrogant! Ought you not rather to mourn?

5:6: Your boasting is not good.

6:5: I say this to your shame.

Corrections in Answer to a Formal Letter (chaps. 7 – 16)

A major indulgence in *sexuality* characterized the Corinthian society. It is therefore no surprise that the church in Corinth addressed this problem as the first question in their letter to Paul (see 7:1). Paul responded with a lengthy discussion on the sanctity of marriage and concerns about celibacy (7:1–40). Also, sacrificial animals offered to the pagan gods usually ended up in the meat market, raising serious questions about the spiritual ramifications of eating this meat. So Paul carefully laid out the principles governing such *doubtful issues* and concluded that the glory of God was the major concern (8:1–11:1).

The next question dealt with two specific issues related to worship—the *role of women in worship* and the problem of selfish behavior in the observance of the *Lord's Table*. Again Paul offered corrective instruction on the importance of proper decorum (11:2–34). Furthermore, *spiritual gifts* given by the Holy Spirit for the benefit of the body of Christ were being misused for self-exaltation. Paul urged them to give priority attention to *love* and to the primacy of *teaching* through the gift of prophecy (12:1–14:40).

Finally, doctrinal error concerning the *resurrection* had also crept into the assembly. Paul straightened them out in no uncertain terms (15:1–58). He ended with an appeal to the Corinthians' *generosity in the collection* for impoverished saints before he concluded with special remarks and greetings (16:1–24).

In reading and assessing these sixteen chapters, two things stand out: Paul truly cared about the spiritual welfare of the Corinthian believers, and he wanted to correct their errant ways. First Corinthians is indeed a corrective epistle with a negative push-away-the-flesh tone intended to produce a positive result.

Second Corinthians

Paul wrote the First Letter to the Corinthians from the city of Ephesus. Later he traveled north to Troas, anticipating a meeting with Titus, who had recently been in Corinth. Paul was hoping to get a report from Titus concerning the effect of his letter upon the Corinthian church. But Titus was unable to meet him, at which point Paul contracted an illness that almost took his life.

By the grace of God, Paul recovered and later met Titus in the Macedonian city of Philippi. There Paul learned that his letter to Corinth had been well received, and some of the problems had already been resolved. This would have brought the apostle great encouragement, except that Titus also informed him that false teachers had recently infiltrated the Corinthian church and were challenging Paul's authority. This news precipitated the Second Letter to the Corinthians, in which Paul defended his apostolic authority and laid down the principles for discovering true godly leadership.

Notice a few of the insidious accusations being leveled against Paul by these arrogant, self-serving intruders into the Corinthian church:

> He was bold only from a distance (x. 1, 2). His outward appearance was base, and his speech contemptible (x. 1, 10, 11). Compared with themselves he was inferior, despite his pretensions (x. 12–15); and what he preached was a poor edition of the Gospel (xi. 4); and the Corinthian church was a poor-grade church in so far as it was Pauline (xii. 13, xi. 7–9). He was not truly an apostle (xi. 5, xii. 11, 12). He did not have the qualifications or credentials which *they* (from Jerusalem) could boast (xi. 22–[28]). Even in his refusing financial support there was a hidden simulation and an admission of inferiority (xii. 16–19).[5]

Actually, Paul was reluctant to defend himself but knew it was necessary for the well-being of the church. Throughout the epistle, his sufferings for Christ emerge as his ultimate credentials. Robert Gromacki recognized this dominant theme: "These expedient disclosures reveal that Paul suffered far more for the cause of Christ than any man would imagine. His sufferings became his main defense against the unjust charges. What had his enemies suffered for Christ? That was his countercharge."[6]

The world and its system appeal to the flesh for fulfillment. In the realm of the spirit, however, worldly experiences become secondary to the all-consuming passion for God's purposes in the world and life. The spiritually minded person is therefore willing to suffer deprivation, inconvenience, and rejection for the cause of Christ. Paul may have been weak in the flesh, but he was certainly strong in the spirit—in contrast to his critics who boasted about their strength in the flesh, even though they were woefully weak in the spirit. This in essence is the difference between godly leaders and false teachers.

This message is at the core of 2 Corinthians. Although Paul answers his critics, he exhibits a greater concern for the believers in Corinth who need to be discerning in this matter. We see this in his exhortation to the Corinthians—that they pull toward them the life of the spirit as the means of unmasking the imposters and that they honor those who seek the glory of Christ.

> 3:6: [God] who has made us competent to be ministers of a new covenant, not of the letter but of the Spirit. For the letter kills, but the Spirit gives life.

> 3:17: Now the Lord is the Spirit, and where the Spirit of the Lord is, there is freedom.

Thus Paul's desire to vindicate his apostleship in 2 Corinthians seems secondary to his concern for the spiritual welfare of the Corinthian church. His major purposes are to develop within them discernment for all things spiritual and to encourage a willingness to live in the realm of the Spirit.

In chapters 1–5, Paul draws attention to his own life and ministry as a living demonstration of sacrificial service and genuine compassion for Christ's sake. He then exhorts them to follow his example of using material things for spiritual purposes (chaps. 6–9). Finally, he exposes the pretensions of the false teachers and reveals the true nature of his own spiritual credentials (chaps. 10–13).

None of Paul's other epistles matches the insight of 2 Corinthians into the apostle's heart and passion. As J. Sidlow Baxter so beautifully expresses it: "It was written with a quill dipped in tears, from the apostle's 'anguish of heart,' and contains more of human pathos than any other of his letters."[7] Second Corinthians is the quintessential book for discovering how to live life in the Spirit.

Summary — The Gentile Christian Epistles' "Faith Set"

GALATIANS

Faith without Works

by SPIRIT . . . not by FLESH

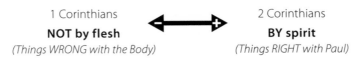

1 Corinthians		2 Corinthians
NOT by flesh		**BY spirit**
(Things WRONG with the Body)		*(Things RIGHT with Paul)*

THE "FAITH SET" OF
THE JEWISH CHRISTIAN EPISTLES

The "faith set" of the Jewish Christian Epistles includes the books of James and 1 & 2 Peter. We have seen how the lead book of James lays out a concept of faith that includes works as the outworking of genuine salvation. For James, faith is not a static concept, but a living, breathing extension of a dynamic relationship with God through Jesus Christ. It is a personal faith that manifests itself in righteous thoughts and actions.

James personalizes the object of faith. According to James, a person is either drawing near to God through the exercise of faith or is succumbing to the influences of the devil in a denial of faith. This stark contrast is at the heart of James's message: submit to God (+) and resist the devil (–). "Submit yourselves therefore to God. Resist the devil, and he will flee from you. Draw near to God, and he will draw near to you" (4:7 – 8).

Here, then, are the push-and-pull factors that are further developed by Peter. First Peter is a *positive book* stressing the importance of submitting to God in times of suffering. On the other hand, 2 Peter is a *negative book* with strong exhortations to resist the devil by pushing away the false teachers. James sets forth the full scope of a working faith, while Peter's epistles rotate the concept for a closer look at submitting to God (+) and resisting the devil (–).

First Peter

You will remember that James wrote his book to the Jewish Diaspora: "To the twelve tribes in the Dispersion" (1:1). These Jewish exiles living in "Pontus, Galatia, Cappadocia, Asia, and Bithynia" (1 Pet. 1:1) were experiencing great trials and persecution as a consequence of their faith in Christ.

James wrote to these Jewish believers challenging them to remain consistent in their walk with Christ by demonstrating the works of faith. Peter, on the other hand, saw their desperate need for encouragement and sought to draw their attention to the example of Christ, and the faithfulness of God, as motivation for a positive spirit. "Suffering" is the pervasive theme in 1 Peter, and encouraging a godly response to suffering is the purpose of the letter.

> The key word of the Epistle is "suffering." It occurs sixteen times . . . Peter challenged the believer to follow the example of Christ and to suffer patiently (2:20) for the sake of righteousness (3:14), for well doing (3:17), with rejoicing (4:13), as a Christian (4:16), and according to the will of God (4:19). The suffering motif permeates the Epistle and forms the background for Peter's exhortations.[8]

Suffering comes in a variety of forms and degrees of severity. It also has physical and emotional components with varying durations. Yet the most sinister aspect of suffering is not its raw experience, but in the havoc it wreaks upon the human spirit. Disorientation (loss of focus) and discouragement (loss of hope) are two of the by-products of suffering, which in turn lead to irrational thinking and to despair. Even committed Christians can question the faithfulness of God and the value of patience and personal integrity in times of suffering. This appears to be the underlying rationale to this compassionate letter from Peter to the suffering saints.

After a brief introduction, Peter draws his readers' attention to their ultimate destiny in Christ as the essence of their hope. He reminds them that they are "born again to a living hope" (1:3) that includes "an inheritance that is imperishable, undefiled, and unfading" (1:4). He notes that the trials they are experiencing are the means of testing the genuineness of their faith, which God considers to be more precious than gold (1:7). In all of this, Peter infuses a powerful message of hope as the antidote to a slumping spirit.

Having begun with an emphasis on eternal salvation as the foundation of hope, Peter (much like James) challenges his readers to focus on holy living (1:22–25) and spiritual growth through the study of God's Word (2:1–10). In any scenario of suffering caused by others, the natural impulse is to rebel and retaliate — or at least question the legitimacy of what is happening. Peter is careful to remind these believers that submission to rightful authority always trumps any desire for personal reaction (2:11 – 3:7). The principle of godly submission is always of paramount concern. Furthermore, a willingness to suffer for the sake of righteousness is considered good in the sight of God (3:8 – 17), for it emulates the suffering Christ endured for us (3:18 – 22).

One of the hardest sufferings to endure is the self-inflicted suffering when a believer says no to a besetting sin (4:1 – 6). Instead of indulgence in sinful ways, readers are encouraged to commit themselves to prayer, hospitality, and Christian service (4:7 – 11). The ultimate response to suffering, however, is for "those who suffer according to God's will [to] entrust their souls to a faithful Creator while doing good" (4:19).

Peter concludes with a challenge to the elders to help the people understand how their suffering will turn to glory as it did in the life of Christ (5:1). With sincere humility and a servant spirit, leaders are to care for the flock by resisting the devil who is the perpetrator of their suffering (5:2 – 11). In fact, from an eternal perspective, their suffering will last only for a short time, after which God will "restore, confirm, strengthen, and establish" them (5:10).

This brief Epistle of 1 Peter is a gem of spiritual encouragement for all those who suffer. With positive thoughts on submission to God in all circumstances, Peter uplifts their spirits to rejoice in Christ.

Second Peter

Peter wrote a second letter to the same people. He writes: "This is now the second letter that I am writing to you, beloved" (3:1). Like Paul in 2 Corinthians, Peter was concerned about false teachers having infiltrated the Jewish Christian assemblies. He knew that nothing is more damaging to the cause of Christ than heretical teaching foisted upon gullible people by deceptive and deviant pretenders. Unlike Paul who wrote to the Corinthians a positive apologetic on spirit-led leadership, Peter penned a flaming epistle excoriating the villains and exposing their damnable heresies. Baxter notes: "In this second letter, the deep concern is to rescue these early Jewish Christian assemblies and their members from the wily errors and corrupting influences of false teachers who were bringing in 'destructive heresies'" [2:1].[9]

This was double jeopardy for these Jewish believers of the Dispersion. Not only were they enduring immense physical and emotional suffering for their association with Christ (1 Peter), they were now also facing the spiritual peril of a severely damaged faith (2 Peter). Knowing that his beloved friends were in danger of being cast upon the rocks of seductive error, Peter's tone here is different from that of his first epistle. His readers were in desperate straits and in serious need of being warned.

In this second epistle Peter sounds a siren to raise a spirit of caution concerning the imminent peril of these believers. Borrowing from the perceptive analysis of Robert Gromacki, I note that Peter gives three blasts of warning:[10]

1. Safeguards against the Apostasy (chap. 1)
2. Description of the Apostates (chap. 2)
3. Refutation of the Apostasy (chap. 3)

Peter first exhorts his readers to take the offensive by pursuing spiritual growth as a guard against simplistic naïveté. A sincere commitment to Christ and the study of His Word is the surest way to avoid the shipwreck of their faith.

After this positive beginning, Peter launches into the main purpose for his writing: "But false prophets also arose among the people, just as there will be false teachers among you, who will secretly bring in destructive heresies" (2:1). These emissaries of Satan were attempting to influence the churches with their damnable counterfeit teaching. Peter gives a forceful and condemning description of these greedy, malicious perpetrators of evil. This second chapter ends with an illustration that characterizes the imposters as dogs and pigs (2:22).

The third blast of the siren exposes the lunacy of the critics' taunts as they deliberately ignore the plain teaching of God's Word. The fiery judgment of "the day of the Lord" (3:10) will consume their hollow voices when God terminates their influence and establishes His righteous kingdom on the earth.

Satisfied that the three warnings were sufficient to ensure their safety, Peter concludes his letter with a final exhortation: "You therefore, beloved, knowing this beforehand, take care that you are not carried away with the error of lawless people and lose your own stability. But grow in the grace and knowledge of our Lord and Savior Jesus Christ" (3:17–18).

In our positive-and-negative-pole analysis, 1 Peter was a positive epistle to encourage the people in the midst of suffering, while 2 Peter emphasized a negative warning against apostate teachers. The exhortation in 1 Peter was to draw near to God through submission to His faithful care (+). Second Peter, on the other hand, sounded a solemn warning to resist the devil by rejecting his ministers of error and deception (–). Peter's epistles therefore rotate the push-and-pull concepts introduced by James, expanding on what it means to draw near to God (1 Peter) and to resist the devil (2 Peter).

Summary — The Jewish Christian Epistles' "Faith Set"

JAMES

Faith with Works

Submit to God ... Resist the devil

1 Peter		2 Peter
Submit to God		**Resist the devil**

ARMS AT WORK

So how is all of this pictured by the structure and activity of human arms? At the end of chapter 8, I discussed the strength of the upper arm in conjunction with the rotational concept of the forearm as an apt illustration of the Epistles of Faith. Here I pursue that idea to see if we can turn speculation into a more confident observation. Having reviewed the books of faith, we are now in a better position to determine if the body analogy works here as well as in previous groupings.

As the biceps and triceps provide strength for the activity of the arms, the books of Galatians (Gentile Christian Epistles) and James (Jewish Christian Epistles) are the strength books for the Epistles of Faith. Together these two books articulate the full scope of faith: faith without works for salvation (Galatians) and faith with works for Christian living (James). These two books contain the muscles of truth for applying actions of faith to any spiritual endeavor.

The forearms turn the strength of the upper arm into the push-and-pull functions that allow for the variety of tasks performed by the arms. In our brief study of both the Corinthian and the Petrine Epistles, this push-away and pull-toward concept has been prominent. On the Gentile side, 1 Corinthians had a negative thrust (pushing away the works of the flesh), while 2 Corinthians expressed a positive pull-toward message of appreciating the primacy of the Spirit. Peter's epistles (on the Jewish side) followed the identical pattern, with 1 Peter stressing the positive encouragement of drawing near to God in times of suffering, and 2 Peter giving a negative, strong warning to push away and resist the influence of the devil.

It seems the pattern of the arm functions mirrors precisely the configuration of these sets of books. The concept of faith in presenting to the world the work and person of Christ (Romans and Hebrews — the hands) is fully realized by the combination of specialized functions performed by Galatians and 1 & 2 Corinthians as they draw out the message of faith in Romans — and by James, and 1 & 2 Peter as they refine the faith concept in Hebrews.

Another observation relating to the unique movement of the forearms is reflected in the way the Corinthian and Petrine books work together. To experience this movement, join me in a brief exercise of the arms. Hold your arms straight out in front of you, with your palms facing upward in a pull-toward position. Rotate your forearms so that the palms are facing downward in a push-away position. As you do this, watch the rotation process. Do you see that the rotation of each arm is opposite to the other? Your arms do not rotate in the same parallel direction; rather, when your left arm rotates right, your right arm rotates left. The pattern of rotation for each arm is reversed.

Look at the twin set of faith books again, and you will see opposite patterns. First Corinthians is a negative book (–), while 2 Corinthians is a positive book (+). Peter's epistles are in the reverse order. First Peter is a positive book (+), and 2 Peter is a negative book (–). This rotational phenomenon of the books is certainly interesting in light of the way our forearms function.

One other observation addresses another possible question with regard to the sequence of these books. In the Gentile set, Galatians (the strength book) comes after the Corinthian epistles; in the Jewish set, James (the strength book) is located first, before Peter's epistles. Can anything be found in the analogy that might explain this difference?

Here, I proffer a suggestion that may provide insight. We often talk about the "walk of faith" as a way of expressing the idea that faith is an active concept in the pursuit of life. If you go for a walk, notice the action of your arms. They do not swing in a parallel fashion; that is, they do not both go forward and then backward at the same time. The arms swing opposite one another for purposes of balance. As the left arm goes forward, the right arm swings backward, and then the process is reversed.

Now freeze the action at the height of the forward and backward swing and observe the positions of the forearms in relation to their corresponding upper arms. Do you see how, in the extended forward arm, the forearm is in front of the upper arm — while in the backward extension, the upper arm is first, followed by the forearm?

Believing that the body analogy is a valid concept, I was not surprised to discover that this motion of the arms in their working mode pictures the reverse pattern in the two sets of faith books. In the first set of books (Gentile), the forearm books of 1 & 2 Corinthians come first, with the strength book of Galatians following. In the second set of books (Jewish), the strength book of James is first followed by the rotational books of 1 & 2 Peter. Could it be that by this sequential arrangement God is saying that faith must be filled with energizing life in an active pursuit of the things of Christ? It's worth pondering.

WORKING FAITH

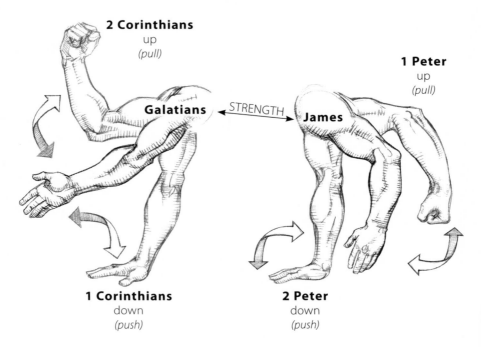

There you have it: the *faith books* operating in the same manner as the arms in working activity. The similarity of the books in their position and function to the arms in their anatomy and physiology is curious, if not captivating. It certainly provides a way to remember these books.

An obvious question comes to mind. Is all of this by divine intent, or is it by random chance? You probably know what I am thinking.

CHAPTER ELEVEN

EMBRACED BY LOVE

The Epistles of Love

Ephesians, Philippians, Colossians, 1, 2, & 3 John

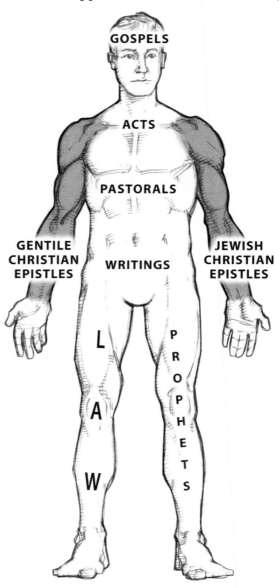

EXALTED LOVE

Flower children of the 1970s sang a favorite song as though it expressed the panacea for all ills — "What the world needs now is love, sweet love; it's the only thing that there's just too little of."

I was there and can testify to the sincerity of their intentions. That the remedy was simplistic and naïve seemed to be beside the point. They really believed that *if* we would just love one another, all the problems plaguing humanity would dissolve like sugar in tea. And they were right — *if* it weren't for the little word *if*.

"*If* we would just love one another" just isn't going to happen — not in a sinful world that continually runs amuck in the mud of human depravity. On the microscale of close personal relationships … maybe. But on the broader perspective of international affairs, it seems that we are worse off today than we were in the 70s.

Hippies were idealists who rejected materialism because it had robbed them of the loving attention of their parents. Yet, confusing lust for love, they simply traded the evil of materialism for sensual indulgence in drugs and unbridled sex. Pregnant with debauchery, they birthed a culture of irresponsibility and selfish pursuit that had its own problems with the concept of love. Now, forty years later, we're still struggling with the love thing.

You see, love is actually a complicated issue. The word is thrown about as though we all know what we're talking about. But defining what we mean by "love" is a crucial part of the discussion. The great English apologist C. S. Lewis wrote a book titled *The Four Loves*, in which he explained that the word *love* can mean numerous things. The Greeks had different words to refine the concept of love — *eros*, the erotic love of passion; *philos* the filial love of family and friends; and *agape*, the deeper love of ultimate commitment. So, in any situation, which love is it?

Hippies immersed themselves in erotic and filial love, but the only love that can save the world is the *agape* love emphasized in the Word of God. "For God so loved the world, that he gave his only Son, that whoever believes in him should not perish but have eternal life" (John 3:16). Here is the supreme example of sacrificial commitment that raises love to its highest level.

This is the love spoken of by Paul (Ephesians, Philippians, and Colossians) and John (1, 2, & 3 John) in the Epistles of Love. Romantic love and the love of friendship fall into the shadows as these books catch the rising sun of *agape* transcending all other love. Verse by verse, we bask in the warmth of this love of God for His people, drawing out a reciprocal love from the hearts of those who trust Him. This exalted love is the enthralling theme of the Epistles of Love.

LOVE IN TWO DIMENSIONS

Jerry and Mindy were in love. After dating for six months, Jerry popped the question, "Mindy, will you marry me?" Mindy's eyes sparkled as marital excitement gripped her heart. "Oh, Jerry . . . yes. Of course I will marry you!"

Soon a beautiful ceremony sealed their commitment to each other and an official license gave testimony to their relationship as husband and wife. It was wonderful to be married. Enjoying a mutual commitment of life gave a sense of security to their love.

Over the next several years, Sara and Patrick were born. Children are a special blessing from God. But the responsibility of raising them is time consuming and often emotionally draining.

Jerry was busy with work. Balancing kids, home projects, and community involvement left Mindy in a perpetual state of exhaustion. As a couple, they were spending less time together. Passionate love drifted into marital complacency. It wasn't fun anymore—just lots of work.

In all of this, the relationship was still intact. Both were committed to their marriage. But they lacked the personal touch that adds the mystery and magic to any relationship. They weren't close anymore. Life was too busy for that.

Having a relationship is one thing. Pursuing fellowship in that relationship is quite another. *Relationship* and *fellowship*—these are the two dimensions of commitment in love. The tension that can exist within these two dimensions as experienced by Jerry and Mindy is a struggle in many marriages. In fact, it is also a fundamental concern in our spiritual marriage with Christ. Having a relationship with Him is crucial for our salvation. But it is in the personal dimension of fellowship that the joy of our mutual commitment is experienced. Bottom line: no fellowship, no joy.

In this comparison between *relationship* and *fellowship* we encounter the unique emphases emerging out of the two sets of love epistles. In the Gentile

Christian Epistles' "love set" (Ephesians, Philippians, and Colossians), Paul exposes what a relationship with Christ looks like. The balancing concept is then developed by John in the Jewish Christian Epistles' "love set" (1, 2, & 3 John) as he unfolds the crucial dynamics of fellowship that brings joy to our relationship with Christ.

So with this background, let's look at these six books to discover God's perspective on the full scope of *agape*. We will follow our agreed-upon motif of allowing each book to speak for itself before observing how these Epistles of Love work together in the embracing function of human arms.

Epistles of Love	
GENTILE CHRISTIAN EPISTLES	**JEWISH CHRISTIAN EPISTLES**
RELATIONSHIP	FELLOWSHIP
Ephesians	1 John
Philippians	2 John
Colossians	3 John

In my initial observations on these two sets of books, I quickly saw that the lead books of Ephesians and 1 John are the epic epistles on the subject of divine love. In a special league with Romans and Galatians, the Epistle to the Ephesians is one of the great doctrinal treatises in the Word of God. Beginning in the heavenlies with a view of God's sovereign perspective on the salvation process, we seem to fly on angels' wings through towering spires of divine truth before swooping down into fertile valleys of specific application that are currently overrun with spiritual warfare. It's a breathtaking ride that leaves the reader in awe of God's majestic love.

Though not as dramatic as Ephesians, the First Epistle of John is spectacular in its own way. Known as the Epistle of Love, 1 John transports us into the warm embrace of God's love as anchored in the tangible presence of a divine Savior and invites us to share in His life. In the joy of this exalted experience, we learn to love with His love. John reminds us that to entertain the idea of fellowship with God is to embrace the incredible.

Here are two books, then, to help us understand superlative love. Let's examine them in more detail.

Ephesians

Relationships are an important part of life. The human experience was designed for social interaction. God said, "It is not good that the man should be alone" (Gen. 2:18). Surface connections are part of this experience, of course, but God intended something far deeper when He gave Eve to Adam. An intimate sharing of life with another person in the context of an enduring relationship seems to be a fundamental need of humanity.

The opportunity to give and share with another person describes the biblical concept of *agape*. Yet we are wide eyed with wonder to learn that God wants this kind of love to exist between us and Him as well. A transcendent relationship of *agape* between God and man is the ultimate design of God's eternal plan. The core message of the book of Ephesians wraps around this theme.

So what does an intimate relationship with Christ look like? Paul tells us in Ephesians that it is similar to a great marriage—only better! In fact, he says, human marriage is patterned after this exalted image of Christ's relationship to His people. "Husbands, love your wives, as Christ loved the church and gave himself up for her" (Eph. 5:25). But let's begin at the beginning to get a better perspective on this relationship.

Most commentators agree that Ephesians is divided into two major parts —often reflected as the *doctrinal* division (chaps. 1–3) and the *practical* division (chaps. 4–6). The indicator for this analysis is the prayer (3:14–19) and doxology (3:20–21) at the end of the doctrinal chapters. The second practical part is, in turn, divided into two areas—our *spiritual walk* with Christ (4:1–6:9) and our *spiritual warfare* with the forces of evil (6:10–24).

Years ago I ran across a little book that summed up these divisions with the simple words, "Sit, Walk, Stand."[1] Watchman Nee took these words from the text of Ephesians and showed how they reflect the trifold dynamics of our relationship with Christ.

OUR *POSITION* IN LOVE — *"SIT"*
(Ephesians 1–3)

Sitting is the posture of rest that describes our *position* in Christ as the fundamental aspect of this relationship. The *doctrinal* portion of the book (chaps. 1–3) is highlighted by the words of Paul in 2:4–6: "But God, who is rich in mercy, for his great love with which he loved us ... hath raised us up together, and made us *sit* together in heavenly places in Christ Jesus" (New Scofield, emphasis mine). Sitting together is the idea of companionship and mutual commitment as the foundation of a secure relationship.

God's Love FOR Us (chap. 1)

As the actions of parents determine the birth of their children, God chose us for this special relationship with Christ and in love planned our future (vv. 1–12). Consequently, when we believe in Jesus Christ as our Savior, the Spirit of God seals our union with Christ (vv. 13–14), so that we actually become a part of His spiritual body (vv. 15–23).

God's Love **IN** *us (chap. 2)*

Even though we were spiritually dead, God in His love has made us alive together with Christ (vv. 1–9). This prepares us to do the good works that please God (v. 10), who inhabits us through the Spirit (vv. 11–22).

God's Love **THROUGH** *us (chap. 3)*

After unveiling the mystery of Jews and Gentiles becoming one in the body of Christ (vv. 1–13), Paul prays that we will be strengthened by the Spirit to comprehend the full dimension of Christ's love (vv. 14–19) so that we will be filled with the fullness of God. This, in turn, enables Him to do through us what is above and beyond anything we could imagine (vv. 20–21).

Think about all of this. In the first section of Ephesians, all the elements of the divine-human love relationship are established. God the Father initiates our union with Christ; then, when we believe, the Holy Spirit seals the union so that we can rest assured ("sit") that we belong to Him. Then, because of His great love for us, God infuses life into our spiritually dead condition and prepares us for loving participation with Christ in all that He is and does. Because we are so intimately united in the body of Christ, the Holy Spirit fills our hearts with Christ's love so that God can accomplish His purposes through us. Here is an amazing relationship, literally made in heaven! It defines our *position* in Christ.

OUR *PERCEPTION* OF LOVE — "WALK"
(Ephesians 4:1 – 6:9)

As we consider our wonderful union with Christ, Paul encourages us next to "walk in a manner worthy" of this relationship (4:1). First (chap. 4), he wants us to understand that we are endowed with special gifts that enable us to fully participate in Christ's love. Second (chaps. 5–6), this provides an incentive for us to "walk in love" in the same way that Christ loves us (5:1–2) so that every human endeavor—personal, marriage, family, and work—is characterized by the expression of this love. Living consistently as "children of light" (5:8) is the ultimate *perception* of what it is to participate in Christ's love.

OUR *PROTECTION* OF LOVE — *"STAND"*

(Ephesians 6:10 – 24)

Because of satanic influence in our world, pure love is always under attack by evil forces. This is why Paul exhorts us to "be strong in the Lord and in the strength of his might" (6:10). Walking together is the positive side of any relationship, but standing against intruding, negative influences is a necessary protective action. Twice we are told to put on the "armor of God" (6:11, 13) to withstand the devil and his evil intentions. The Word of God and prayer (6:17 – 20) are the offensive weapons to counteract these forces of evil. This last section, then, is all about *protection* of this relationship.

Having set forth this simplistic analysis of the book of Ephesians, let's graph the component parts so that we can see them more clearly.

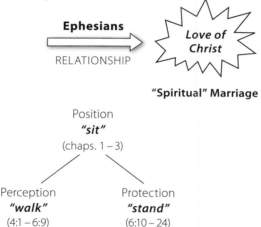

First John

John assumes that his readers already have a *relationship* with Christ because he calls them his "children" (2:1, 12 – 13, 18, 28; 3:7, 18; 4:4; 5:21) and his "beloved" (2:7; 3:2, 21; 4:1, 7, 11). As he concludes the letter, he specifically says, "I write these things to you who believe in the name of the Son of God" (5:13).

These believers well knew what it was to have a relationship with Christ. They didn't seem to understand, though, how to experience joy in the outworking of this relationship. That is why John begins the epistle by stating his purpose to develop the idea of fellowship so that they could know fullness of joy (1:3 – 4).

Entering into a relationship with Christ is the precursor to enjoying fellowship within that relationship. On the other hand, fellowship is the enjoyable consequence of union with Christ. First John analyzes the elements of *fellowship* in the same way that Ephesians unveiled the component parts of a *relationship*. In this way, Ephesians and 1 John are the flip sides of the two dimensions of love.

A quick reading of 1 John reveals a tumbling of reoccurring thoughts that seem to defy a clear-cut analysis with specific divisions. In this way, 1 John is not at all like Ephesians. Yet certain recurrent and repetitive themes are clearly evident. Quite frankly, fellowship is like that. Whereas a relationship can be defined in specific criteria, fellowship is more fluid and dynamic, with formidable issues continually balancing one another. If we approach 1 John with this mind-set, we will not be disappointed with its structure.

John begins his epistle by establishing that Jesus is a real flesh-and-blood person with whom we can enjoy personal fellowship (1:1–4). John himself had experienced this fellowship as an apostle of Christ; he had seen Him, heard Him, and touched Him. John wants his readers to understand that fellowship with Christ is more than a mystical vision. It is real.

The basic element of genuine fellowship, according to John, is truth. No relationship can survive in the context of lies. For this reason, John begins with a categorical statement on the nature of God. "God is light, and in him is no darkness at all" (1:5). Light reveals what is true and right, but evil and falsehood can survive only in the dark. This affirmation forms the foundation of John's message.

So how do we react to that? This is the underlying question in 1 John. A positive response to the truth is the essential indicator of true fellowship with God (1:6–10). As we walk in the light and agree with God about the need to confess our sinful condition, we enter into joyful fellowship. If we identify with the dark side and disagree with God, we are guilty of calling Him a liar —and that breaks any sense of togetherness.

The key element of obedience as a positive reaction to truth occurs consistently throughout 1 John. Chapter 2 opens with this emphasis (vv. 1–6).

Commitment to truth characterizes those who are genuinely related to Christ, and obedience to that truth forms the basis of joyful fellowship.

Acknowledging that Jesus Christ is the Son of God is for John the essence of truth, and any rejection of Christ's divine nature is the foundation of lies (2:18–29). Living a purified life that exalts righteousness honors the truth (3:1–10), and obedience to the Lord's commandments demonstrates a sincere desire to fellowship with Him (5:1–15).

No relationship can be sustained in the context of lies and mistrust. The strength of fellowship depends on a mutual agreement of what is true and right. *Reaction to truth* is the primary emphasis in 1 John that defines fellowship with Christ.

John further indicates what constitutes healthy fellowship with Christ: *reception of the brethren* and *rejection of the world.*

Reception of the Brethren

Once it is determined that a relationship will be based on being totally truthful, a discovery phase ensues; mutual likes and dislikes are established. In our relationship with Christ, His evaluation of what is good and bad is perfectly consistent with what will enhance or hinder joyful fellowship. So we are encouraged to love what He loves and to hate what He hates.

On the positive side, loving what He loves includes loving the brethren. In this epistle John repeatedly exhorts his readers to respond in a loving manner to all those who also love Christ. This theme occurs immediately after that of obeying the truth in chapter 2. Walking harmoniously with the Lord in the light definitely includes loving the brethren as Christ loves them (2:7–11). This is repeated again in 3:10–17, becomes a major emphasis in 4:7–21, and appears as an exclamation point at the end of the letter (5:16). Receiving the brethren emerges as a significant element of enjoying our fellowship with Christ.

Rejection of the World

Protecting a relationship from outside intrusions is another aspect of love. Love cannot survive in a competing environment, where the affections are torn between alternate allegiances. As Jesus said concerning the love of riches: "No servant can serve two masters, for either he will hate the one and love the other, or he will be devoted to the one and despise the other. You cannot serve God and money" (Luke 16:13).

This is a third theme of John's first epistle. Initially he warns against loving the world as a competing factor in our love for Christ (2:15–17). Like James (4:4), he sees the world as a competing lover and loving the world as an illicit relationship. To have joyful fellowship with Christ, faithfulness in our emotional commitment to Him is essential. Our Lord is serious about not tolerating any other affection that might siphon off any of the adoration that belongs only to Him.

Later John describes the world in terms of false spirits that vie for the readers' attention. Addressing the "beloved," he exhorts them, "do not believe every spirit" because there are false prophets that represent the "spirit of error" (4:1–6). For fellowship to be strong, one must guard the heart against alien affections. As *reception of the brethren* is the positive side of fellowship, so *rejection of the world* is the negative side.

Having engaged in this surface analysis of 1 John, let's graph the components, as we did with Ephesians.

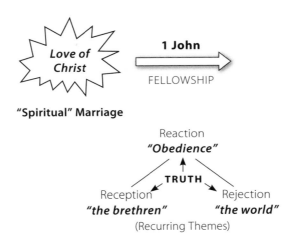

The remaining books in the "love set" of the Gentile Christian Epistles (Philippians and Colossians) and of the Jewish Christian Epistles (2 & 3 John) follow the push-pull pattern discussed in chapter 8. In this dual role, these books refine the positive and negative concepts of love set forth in the books of Ephesians and 1 John.

THE GENTILE PUSH-PULL "LOVE SET"

Having established our position in Christ (Ephesians 1–3) as the foundation of our *relationship* with Christ, Paul goes on in Ephesians to describe our *walk* with the Lord (4:1–6:9) and our *stand* against evil (6:10–24). The books of Philippians and Colossians, in turn, pick up those themes to expand on what it means to *walk* with Christ and to *stand* against evil, respectively.

Philippians

If you want to know how to walk with Christ in the full experience of His love, study the book of Philippians. This brief epistle is very attractive in the way it perceives our relationship with Christ. Here is love at its best. In Philippians divine love stoops to embrace our human experience, lifting us above the mundane into realms of unexpected spiritual fulfillment.

Although exhortations that encourage love abound in this little epistle, no accusations of moral failure or wrong doctrine are addressed. Of all Paul's epistles, Philippians is the most positive.

Paul's personal relationship with these people as reflected in the letter seems to be a mirror image of the more exalted union between Christ and the believer. Three times he calls them his "beloved"—even "dearly beloved and longed for, my joy and crown" (4:1 KJV). Such endearing expressions provide a fitting context for a treatise on Christ's love for His beloved and the beloved's response to Him.

Consumed by His Life (chap. 1)

To walk with Christ in love is to be totally wrapped up in who He is. Paul captures this sentiment when he says, "For to me to live is Christ" (v. 21). In fact, Paul says it really doesn't matter what other people do or say as long as Jesus Christ is made known (vv. 12–18). When Christ is our life, glorifying Him becomes the consuming passion of life—"whether by life or by death" (v. 20). No wonder Paul wrote, "My desire is to depart and be with Christ" (v. 23). When we walk with Christ, we are consumed by His life.

Absorbed in His Thoughts (chap. 2)

People who walk in love develop a common way of thinking. If there is going to be loving unity in the Philippian church, Paul exhorts them to think like Jesus—"Let this mind be in you which was also in Christ Jesus" (v. 5 KJV).

Jesus' approach to life is so different from ours. He had a servant spirit, a humble attitude, and a desire to obey the Father in all things (vv. 7–8). Having exhorted us to think that way (vv. 12–18), Paul concludes with two illustrations of the mind of Christ in action: Timothy (vv. 19–24) and Epaphroditus (vv. 25–30). When we walk with Christ, we are absorbed in His thoughts.

Enthralled with His Goals (chap. 3)

In a commitment of love, both parties are dedicated to the same purpose and goals. Paul is clear that his portfolio of accomplishments and assets are as nothing, when compared to the absolute joy of knowing and pursuing Christ (vv. 4–9). His whole purpose in life is to "press on toward the goal for the prize of the upward call of God in Christ Jesus" (v. 14). As a citizen of heaven (v. 20), his desire is that Christ would "subject all things to himself" (v. 21). When we walk with Christ we are enthralled with His goals.

Energized by His Strength (chap. 4)

Seeking to walk with Christ is a daunting aspiration. We are often plagued with conflicts of interest (v. 2), the need for help along the way (v. 3), and the weight of anxiety over all sorts of things (v. 6). But, through thankful prayer, we can enter into a lifestyle of rejoicing (v. 4), self-control (v. 5), incredible peace (v. 7), pleasant thoughts (vv. 8–9), and a spirit of contentment (vv. 10–12). As Paul so confidently says, "I can do all things through him who strengthens me" (v. 13). Furthermore, God supplies all our needs "according to his riches in glory in Christ Jesus" (v. 19). When we walk with Christ, we are energized by His strength and provision.

Colossians

The mood changes in Colossians. While Philippians expands on the idea of walking with Christ in love, Colossians delves more deeply into what it means to stand against the intrusion of evil influences. In the broad stroke, Philippians emphasizes positive exhortations toward unity with Christ, and Colossians gives specific warnings against destructive philosophies that can undermine that unity.

The message of Colossians, then, stresses a passionate fidelity to Christ in the midst of competing ideologies. An incipient gnosticism blended with a mystical Judaistic legalism had challenged the majesty of Christ in Colossae, so Paul was on high alert against this heretical teaching. With an emphasis on superior knowledge and emanations of angels, this hybrid Judaistic gnosticism reduced Christ to a mere creature, and salvation of the soul to a legalistic system of behavior. In answer, Paul simply exalts the preeminence of Christ as the means of repelling this seductive intruder.

As with many of Paul's letters, doctrinal issues precede practical applications. Thus the first two chapters of Colossians highlight the incredible fullness of Christ, while the last two chapters demonstrate the practical effects of Christ's supremacy upon Christian living.

Knowledge of Christ's Preeminence — Doctrinal (chaps. 1–2)

After expressing his love for the Colossian believers (1:1–14), Paul levels a lethal blow to the prevailing heresy by exalting Christ as (1) the Creator of all that exists (1:15–19) and (2) the only Savior from sin (1:20–23). The claim of superior knowledge by these mystery religions is dwarfed by the mystery of the gospel of Jesus Christ (1:24–29) and by the "treasures of wisdom and knowledge" that are in Christ (2:1–3).

Stern warnings flow from Paul's pen: "And this I say, lest any man should beguile you with enticing words" (2:4 KJV); "Beware lest any man spoil you through philosophy and vain deceit" (2:8 KJV); "Let no one pass judgment on you" (2:16); and "Let no man beguile you of your reward" (2:18 KJV). Paul is greatly concerned that the Colossians remain true in their allegiance to Christ. After all, nothing can compare to the preeminence and fullness that is in Him (1:18–19; 2:9–10).

Standing Firm with Christ — Practical (chaps. 3 – 4)

As believers in Christ, then, Paul exhorts us to set our affections on Christ as we resist earthly enticements (3:1–3). Furthermore, when Christ is our "life" (3:4), that relationship strengthens every area of life—*personal* (3:5–17), *marriage* (3:18–21), and *work* (3:22–4:1). Finally, prayer and godly living sustain us in our stand against evil influences (4:2–6), while other believers become the means of encouragement to remain faithful (4:7–17).

Grasping the Dynamics of a Loving Relationship

Notice how these three powerful epistles (Ephesians, Philippians, Colossians) unfold the full scope of our love relationship with Christ. Having established the core element of this relationship (*sit*—chaps. 1–3), Ephesians proceeds to clarify the two functional aspects that make the relationship work.

On the *positive side*, walking with Christ in unity and harmony is the joyful privilege of union with Him (*walk*—4:1–6:9). Expanding on this concept, Philippians delves more specifically into what it means to walk with Christ.

On the *negative side*, standing against the evil forces that seek to harm the relationship comes as an exclamation point at the end of Ephesians (*stand*—6:10–24). Protecting the relationship from disruptive influences, therefore, is an equally important function, and Colossians expands on this essential dynamic.

Do you see, then, how these three books function together as a trilogy of love? Their voices blend to establish what a meaningful *relationship* with Christ is intended to be.

THE JEWISH PUSH-PULL
"LOVE SET"

John's overriding concern in his first epistle is how the believer reacts to truth. Enjoying *fellowship* with Christ depends primarily on obedience to His voice of truth. Beyond that, fellowship involves accepting what He accepts and rejecting what He rejects. John's second and third epistles illustrate for us how these ideas of accepting and rejecting work.

Second John

The author of 2 John introduces himself as "the elder," whom tradition assures us was the apostle John. John had settled in Ephesus, and as an elder in the Ephesian church he wrote this letter to encourage a dear sister in Christ whom he calls the "elect lady" (v. 1). Her children reflect her deep love for the truth, and John devotes the first half of his letter to commending her for her obedience to God's Word (vv. 1–6).

This emphasis on truth as the core energizer of fellowship with Christ mirrors what we saw in John's first epistle. The word *truth* appears five times in the first four verses of 2 John, and *commandment* is prominent in verses 5–6. Furthermore, loving the Christian community is mentioned in verse 5, so that the two positive elements of the fellowship trilogy (obedience to truth and receiving the brethren) are rehearsed in these opening verses.

Then the elder, John, turns to the main focus of this second epistle — warning the lady to reject the advances of seducing error (vv. 7–11). "Many deceivers" (v. 7) were prowling about seeking to rob believers of their "full reward" (v. 8) by drawing them into false teachings.

The deceivers are called "antichrist" because they "do not confess the coming of Jesus Christ in the flesh" (v. 7). This means that they denied the incarnation of Christ — that Jesus was God in human form. This truth is fundamental to the gospel. In the words of John, anyone teaching otherwise should be totally rejected. "Do not receive him into your house or give him any greeting" (vv. 10–11).

So, as you can see, 2 John deals with *rejection of error* as an important element of fellowship with Christ.

Third John

This letter is addressed to a man named Gaius. Three other Gaiuses appear in the New Testament, and this seems to be a fourth. He is well known to John, though, who refers to himself again as "the elder" (v. 1).

As with 2 John, this brief epistle begins with a strong emphasis on the truth (vv. 1–4). Can there be any doubt that the main concern in fellowship with Christ is a radical commitment to the truth? John makes this abundantly clear in all three of his epistles.

The subject turns to receiving the brethren. Gaius is said to be "faithful" (v. 5) and loving (v. 6) because of his willingness to encourage the brethren by his hospitality. John concludes by saying, "We ought to support people like these that we may be fellow workers for the truth" (v. 8).

Using a stark contrast to drive home his point, John refers to an arrogant, prideful man in the church named Diotrephes, who "receives us not" (v. 9 New Scofield). Not only is this man hostile to John, but "he refuses to welcome the brothers, and also stops those who want to and puts them out of the church" (v. 10). Here John is comparing Gaius, who receives the brethren (vv. 5–8) with Diotrephes, who does not receive the brethren (vv. 9–10). What Gaius has done is good, but what Diotrephes has done is evil (v. 11).

Another man named Demetrius comes in for honorable mention at the end (v. 12), where John's emphasis again is on a commitment to truth. In contrast to 2 John, then, 3 John is about *reception of the brethren*.

Grasping the Dynamics of Loving Fellowship

Loving fellowship within a good relationship is a fluid dynamic, where three important elements are in constant flux. First John helps us understand this flowing trilogy by highlighting the prominent theme of obedience to the truth, while presenting the balancing factors of loving fellow Christians and rejecting the world.

The second and third epistles of John, in turn, are a "dynamic duo"— illustrating the two concepts of rejecting and receiving respectively by showing us how to implement these contrasting ideas in real-life situations. Rejecting the antichrist spirit of the world is the theme of 2 John, and receiving the brethren dominates the thrust of 3 John.

SEEING IT ALL AT A GLANCE

Having given a brief analysis of the six books in the Epistles of Love, it will be helpful to see them all in their relations to one another.

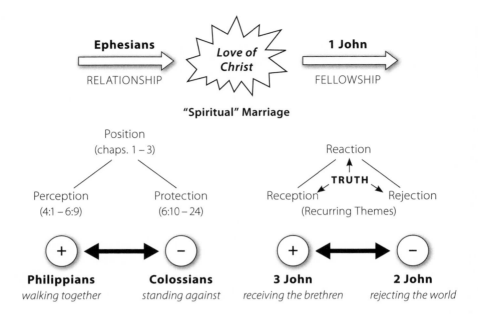

EMBRACING ARMS

Some people are huggers. They love to show their affection by wrapping their arms around you and squeezing, or patting you on the back. Embracing is a common way to express love.

God uses His metaphorical arms to do that with those whom He loves. Isaiah pictures the mighty arms of God tenderly embracing His people:

> Behold, the Lord GOD comes with might,
>   and his arm rules for him ...
>   he will gather the lambs in his arms;
> he will carry them in his bosom. (40:10–11)

Arms perform an important function in the demonstration of love. It should come as no surprise that the Epistles of Love are represented in our mosaic of Scripture by the arms in the embracing position. As with the Epistles of Faith, the arms are an apt illustration of the intricate interplay among the various Epistles of Love. Collectively, they picture the loving embrace of Christ and the believer.

First, notice the prominent books in each of the two "love sets": Ephesians (Gentile Christian Epistles) and 1 John (Jewish Christian Epistles). As the upper arm provides strength for all activities of the arm, these two epistles provide the muscle for meaningful love. Ephesians unveils the full scope of powerful elements that comprise a *relationship*, and 1 John unwraps the dynamic trilogy inherent in joyful *fellowship*. Here are the biceps of love —and love is never so strong as when the principles set forth in these books are implemented in experience.

Consider another observation. You will remember the unusual arrangement of the strength books of faith: Galatians appears after the Corinthian epistles, but James is positioned before Peter's epistles. I suggested in chapter 10 that this pattern could very well picture the walking posture of faith, where the arms swing in an opposite motion.

The activity is different when expressing love with an embrace. Look at your upper arms as you hug a loved one. The arms complement one another in parallel fashion—and the love epistles do the same. Ephesians comes before Philippians and Colossians, and 1 John precedes 2 & 3 John. The embracing function of the arms is accurately reflected in the arrangement of the Epistles of Love.

If it seems that I am straining at ideas here for the sake of the mosaic, perhaps you will at least concede that it is an interesting observation.

Continuing on with the analogy, however, I encourage you to review the end of chapter 8 to refresh your memory on the important rotation function of the forearms. The resultant push-pull scenario is definitely manifest in the four secondary love epistles.

In the Gentile love books, Philippians is a positive message of "pulling toward," while Colossians is a negative warning to push away. This pattern is seen in the Jewish love epistles as well, where 2 John is an exhortation to push away the antichrist spirit, and 3 John encourages a positive response to fellow Christians by pulling toward.

Look closer and you will see that the rotation in each set of epistles is opposite—as it was with the Epistles of Faith (see chap. 10). Hold your arms in an embracing fashion in front of you and rotate your forearms to push away an intruder, then again to draw a loving friend toward you. Notice that the rotations are opposite between the two forearms.

In our corollary, observe that Philippians comes first in the Gentile set, expressing a positive pull-toward idea, while the second book, Colossians, turns in a negative fashion to push away. The sequence is reversed in the Johannian Epistles (Jewish set). The negative comes first, with 2 John, followed by the positive in 3 John. Even rotational directions of these four epistles are accurately pictured by the movements of the forearms.

Also, remember that the overall purpose of the arms is to extend the hands to allow them to do what they do. The message of God's love abounds in Romans (the *work* of Christ) and Hebrews (the *person* of Christ), both of which function as hands in the biblical scheme. Since the Epistles of Love operate as arms, their purpose seems to be that of extending this message of God's love for us in Christ and our reciprocal love for Him.

So think of Ephesians, Philippians, and Colossians as expanding on the concept of a *relationship* with Christ in salvation, so beautifully set forth in the book of Romans. And then view the Johannine Epistles as an extension of *fellowship* with the Savior, expressed so enticingly in Hebrews. These two sets of love epistles (arms) are extensions of the scenario of spiritual love wrapped up in Romans and Hebrews (hands).

EMBRACING LOVE

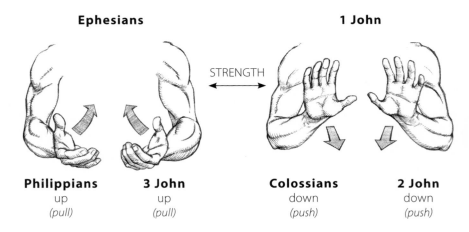

Ephesians			1 John
Philippians	**3 John**	**Colossians**	**2 John**
up	up	down	down
(pull)	(pull)	(push)	(push)

Well, there it is, the *love books*, functioning in the same manner as the arms extended in an embrace. Again, the similar pattern between the biblical books and the human anatomy is striking.

CHAPTER TWELVE

LIVING WITH HOPE

The Epistles of Hope

1 & 2 Thessalonian, Jude, Revelation

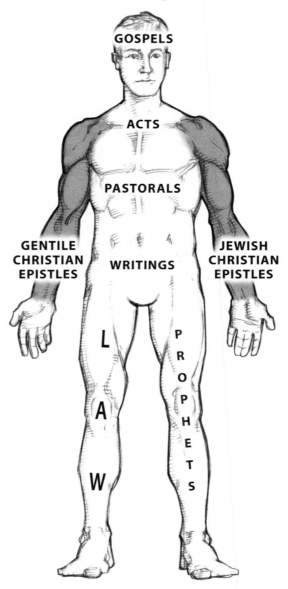

LIVING WITH HOPE

Loss of hope leads to discouragement, which can cause a person to slide into depression. In turn, the pit of depression is a slippery slope where hope can appear to be lost forever. This maddening cycle demonstrates how essential hope is to the human experience.

Like love, hope comes in various shapes and hues. Expressions of simple desire often elicit the word *hope*, as in, "I'm going to the beach tomorrow, so I *hope* it doesn't rain." Serious matters lean more heavily on hope to bolster the anticipation of a good result: "The tumor was contained, so there's *hope* for a full recovery." Hope is the silver lining in the dark clouds of life.

When it comes to eternal destiny, however, hope takes on its most serious dimension. To have the hope of eternal life, with its promise of celestial paradise, certainly trumps the threat of eternal death and damnation forever. The gospel of salvation in Christ comes wrapped in a package of hope that has always been an enticement to respond positively. In the midst of a depraved, hopeless world, Christ offers the bright hope of a glorious tomorrow.

> And not only the creation, but we ourselves, who have the firstfruits of the Spirit, groan inwardly as we wait eagerly for adoption as sons, the redemption of our bodies. For in this hope we were saved. Now hope that is seen is not hope. For who hopes for what he sees? But if we hope for what we do not see, we wait for it with patience. (Rom. 8:23–25)

Jonathan Edwards, the masterful theologian of the Great Awakening in eighteenth-century New England, preached a sermon that has since become famous—"Sinners in the Hands of an Angry God." In this sermon he pictured sinners hanging over the abyss of hell by a single thread, like a spider dangling in the air.

As the story goes, he read the sermon without emotion. The imagery was so vivid and devastating, however, that people began to weep and despair at their fearful situation, to the point where they clamored desperately for the hope of salvation offered to them by Jesus Christ. It was indeed a "great awakening," where people rose from a discouraged hopelessness to a euphoric realization of everlasting hope in Christ.

The gospel of Jesus Christ is truly a message of hope. But before people can realize the incredible quality of that hope, they must first come to grips with the horror of their lostness. The gospel really is all about hope in contrast to despair.

SETTING THE STAGE

Before we analyze the Epistles of Hope, perhaps it would be helpful to review the epistolary themes. Seeing these books in their context will aid us in our understanding of their message.

GENTILE CHRISTIAN EPISTLES	THEME*	JEWISH CHRISTIAN EPISTLES
1 Corinthians		James
2 Corinthians	**FAITH**	1 Peter
Galatians		2 Peter
Ephesians		1 John
Philippians	**LOVE**	2 John
Colossians		3 John
1 Thessalonians	**HOPE**	Jude
2 Thessalonians		Revelation

*See chapter 8: "A Trilogy of Motion"

Although the concept of hope is prominent throughout all the Epistles, four books are devoted specifically to that theme. In the Gentile Christian Epistles, 1 & 2 Thessalonians; in the Jewish Christian Epistles, Jude and Revelation.

The apostle Paul addresses two letters to the church in Thessalonica. The irony here is that these were the first letters to flow from the pen of Paul, but in the canonical order of Pauline Epistles, they appear last. Obviously *chronological development* was not the issue in arranging the order of biblical books (See Appendix 2: "Everything Is in Order: New Testament").

Theme seems to have been the driving force when it came to biblical sequence in aligning the Pauline Epistles (*faith*, then *love*, followed by *hope*). The books of *hope* crown the conclusion of the Gentile Christian Epistles, like an exclamation point at the end of a sentence. We walk by faith and we embrace love—but always in the all-encompassing aura of an ever-present and living hope.

The Jewish Christian Epistles exhibit the same pattern in a different way. Following the order of leadership in the Jerusalem church (see Gal. 2:9: James, Peter, John), James and Peter come first with their message of faith; John appears later with his Epistles of Love. John then lays the capstone of these general letters to Jewish believers with the Revelation of Jesus Christ and its crowning message of culminating hope.

Yet a surprise insertion greets us at the door of Revelation as the little Epistle of Jude sounds the first notes of hope's fulfillment: "Behold, the Lord cometh with ten thousands of his saints" (v. 14 KJV). Jude is the half brother of our Lord and a Jew, so it seems rather fitting that he should initiate this concluding message of realized hope for the Jewish Epistles.

ABSENCE OF PRIMARY BOOKS

The Epistles of Hope comprise four books, while the faith and love sets have six books each. The pattern changes with these books of hope for both the Gentile and Jewish epistles. And yet the marvelous symmetry continues. This anomaly of one less book exists on both sides. Is there any significance to this changing pattern?

An interesting correlation in this regard appears in the analogy of the arm function for hope. But let's save that for our discussion of the analogy itself. For now, it is sufficient to observe that the four hope books exhibit the rotational concept as we saw with 1 & 2 Corinthians, 1 & 2 Peter, Philippians and Colossians, and 2 & 3 John. In other words, the two books on each side of the Gentile and Jewish equation exhibit positive and negative elements.

First Thessalonians probes the positive consequences of a sure hope in the coming of Christ and is therefore a "pull-toward" book. A negative tone pervades 2 Thessalonians, however, as believers are told to push away wrong concepts related to the Lord's coming. This same rotational phenomenon can be observed with Jude and Revelation. Jude expresses a negative warning to "push away" the false teachers, while Revelation is a positive pull toward rejoicing in the Son of Man's victory over cosmic evil. The hope section, then, features rotational books.

Primary lead books are missing—those that develop the concept of hope, as Galatians and James did for faith, and Ephesians and 1 John did for love. Evidently the Spirit of God did not deem it necessary to include such books in developing the idea of hope—perhaps because hope anchors its assurance in the future, while faith and love are present challenges that require our participation. Not that hope isn't a present experience; but unlike faith and love, hope simply realizes that the future is secure. In other words, it does not appear to be a multifaceted concept like faith and love.

I realize that this explanation for the exclusion of lead books with the concept of hope is simplistic and premature to our study; we will return to this issue later in the chapter.

WHAT AND WHO

When Paul says that we are saved by hope in Romans 8:24, the context refers to a future redemptive event when Jesus Christ will return to gather His people and renovate the earth. This event is the foundation of the believer's hope. But the event is wrapped in a Person. You see, hope includes both a "what" (the event) and a "who" (the Person).

This is certainly in keeping with the dual emphasis found in Romans and Hebrews—the hands that function as the extension of the arms in the faith, love, and hope epistles. Remember that Romans articulates the full scope of salvation (the "what"), while Hebrews fleshes out the wonder of Christ as our Savior (the "who").

Years ago, while ministering at a year-round Christian camp in northern Wisconsin, I watched a fulfillment of hope that illustrates this twofold emphasis. A small boy wandered off into the woods, wide-eyed with wonder at the rabbits and squirrels and birds and bugs. Late afternoon turned to dusk, and the boy suddenly realized he was lost. Sitting on a fallen tree trunk, he began to cry as the darkness engulfed him—visions of bears and tigers prowling in his mind. He desperately wanted to be saved from his peril, but mostly his heart yearned for his dad to come and carry him back to camp.

A search party was organized as soon as the family realized the boy was missing, and for hours flashlights pierced the darkness of the forest. In the providence of God, the boy's dad was the one to find him, and the sense of relief for father and son was overwhelming. The boy's hope was fulfilled by the event of his rescue, but nothing could compare to the strong arms of his father carrying him back to safety.

In like fashion, we peer into the darkness of a corrupt world with eyes of hope, waiting (and sometimes crying) "for adoption as sons, the redemption of our bodies" (Rom. 8:23). You see, not only are we saved spiritually, but one day we will also be saved physically—and then redemption will be complete.

Yet our hope is more than a distant wish for rescue. Believing Jesus' promise that, having redeemed us from our sins, He will also redeem our bodies from corruption, we hold tenaciously to a "sure and steadfast" hope that serves as an "anchor of the soul" (Heb. 6:19). This culminating event of redemptive history, whereby all of creation is rescued from corruption at the appearing of our Savior, defines the believer's hope. One day Jesus is coming for us; when He does, all will be well. In this way, hope is the anticipation of both an event and a Person.

The Epistles of Hope give emphasis to this dual aspect of the believer's hope. In the Thessalonian epistles, the event looms paramount with all of its present and future benefits. The person of Christ is there, but understanding the ramifications of His coming is Paul's overarching concern. Paul also wants the Thessalonians to grasp the specific circumstances surrounding the future coming of Christ as he concludes the first letter and as he corrects their misconceptions in the second letter. First and 2 Thessalonians prepare us for the *event* of Christ's coming.

Jude and Revelation, on the other hand, emphasize the personal dimension of our hope. Jude contrasts the danger of false teachers with the powerful presence of Jesus Christ at His coming. In the Revelation, John begins by describing the awesome appearance of the Son of Man who opens the seals of judgment as the Lamb of God and divine Judge of the universe. Events involving seals, trumpets, and vials indicate the outpouring of the wrath of the Lamb (6:16–17). All eyes are on the person of the righteous King descending out of heaven as the victorious conqueror. Our hope is definitely consumed with the coming of this glorious Person.

An *event* and a *Person*—the elements of our hope. The Thessalonian epistles help us grasp the event, and Jude and Revelation magnify the wonder of the Person. What a magnificent study awaits us as we turn to these four concluding books—the Epistles of Hope!

THE "HOPE SET" OF THE GENTILE CHRISTIAN EPISTLES

In the absence of primary lead books for hope, we move immediately into the rotational sequence of the Thessalonian epistles. Paul wrote two letters to the believers in Thessalonica to encourage them in the midst of their suffering—one with a positive tone (1 Thessalonians) and another with a more negative bearing (2 Thessalonians).

To understand these Thessalonians letters, we must grasp the difficult dynamics of the Thessalonian context. As a result of the Diaspora, large populations of Jews lived in various cities of the Macedonian region. When Paul brought the gospel to Philippi, Thessalonica, and Berea, the reaction of these Jews to the claims of Christ exhibited the same hateful response as did the Jews in Jerusalem who conspired to crucify Jesus. They vehemently resisted the message of the gospel; this resulted in severe persecution toward any believers in Christ.

Beaten and imprisoned in Philippi, Paul and Silas moved on to Thessalonica, where they encountered the same vitriolic hatred from their Jewish persecutors. After a short time, threats against Paul and Silas's lives caused them to flee the area. Heading southwest, the Thessalonian radical Jews pursued them all the way to Berea, where they again stirred up strong opposition (Acts 16:11 – 17:15).

Upon reaching Corinth in Greece, Paul received word from Timothy that, although the Thessalonian believers remained faithful to the cause of Christ, the church continued to face a hostile environment. Out of deep concern for their welfare and spiritual stability, Paul wrote these two letters to the Thessalonians to encourage and sustain them with the message of hope in Christ's return. Reflecting upon this, D. Edmond Hiebert says,

> Having experienced the implacable hatred of the Thessalonian Jews even at Beroea, Paul was rightly concerned about the welfare of the Thessalonian believers. He could well imagine the kind of treatment they would receive from the enemy. And he had apparently heard that the persecution there was continuing. Hence he was filled with great concern for his Thessalonian converts, from whom he had been so suddenly and prematurely separated.[1]

1 Thessalonians

Before analyzing the content of this letter, it will help us to look more closely at Paul's specific purpose in writing it.

Jewish zealots in Thessalonica had previously targeted Paul as the troublemaker; their angry taunts had been aimed mostly at him. When Paul left the city, he probably hoped the trouble would subside so the church could grow without serious interference. Many months later, however, Timothy arrived in Corinth to give Paul an update on the church's situation (3:6), and Paul's worst fears for them were realized. Although the believers were still faithful to Christ (3:6–9), the community opposition to the ministry had been intense.

In fact, hatred for the gospel of Christ was every bit as hostile in Thessalonica as it had been in Jerusalem.

> For you, brothers, became imitators of the churches of God in Christ Jesus that are in Judea. For you suffered the same things from your own countrymen as they did from the Jews, who killed both the Lord Jesus and the prophets, and drove us out. (2:14–16)

Furthermore, in 2 Corinthians 8:2, Paul later referred to the Thessalonian believers as experiencing a "severe test of affliction" and "extreme poverty." Living and ministering under these conditions, the Thessalonians certainly needed a message of hope.

Understanding this, Paul concluded every chapter in 1 Thessalonians with an encouraging reminder of the coming of the Lord (1:10; 2:19; 3:13; 4:13–18; 5:23). In this way Paul wanted them to see all of their trials and concerns in the context of the sure and steadfast hope of Christ's return.

Paul's deep empathy for the Thessalonian believers, immersed in prolonged affliction and steady persecution, led him to write this impassioned letter. He wants to lift them above a fixation on their suffering into the encouraging hope of Christ's return.

Commitment to a worthwhile pursuit can strengthen resolve to persevere in times of difficulty. For this reason Paul doesn't raise false expectations for immediate relief from their plight. He draws their attention to the ultimate reward for which suffering is merely a process. In other words, eternal glory with Christ will outweigh the burden of temporary discomfort.

A careful analysis of 1 Thessalonians reveals a past-future pattern that leaves the reader with a present hope. In the first three chapters, Paul reminds the believers of their past to reassure them that their hope is valid. Then he takes them into the future, in chapters 4 and 5, to show them how hope in Christ's return can strengthen them in their current struggles.

1 THESSALONIANS		
PAST	**THEME**	**FUTURE**
BE CONFIDENT	HOPE	BE COMMITTED
Your hope is valid	in	*Your hope is vital*
(chaps. 1–3)	Christ's return	(chaps. 4–5)

Be Confident: Your Hope Is Valid (chaps. 1 – 3)

Confidence resulting from a genuine salvation (chap. 1). The entire first chapter rehearses the conversion experience of the Thessalonian believers. The evidences of their salvation were obvious (vv. 2 – 6), so that they had become living examples to all other believers in Macedonia (vv. 7 – 8). Their genuine faith, love, and hope (v. 3) were manifest in the trifold outworking of their salvation (vv. 9 – 10). They had every reason to be confident their hope was valid.

Confidence bolstered by a shared experience (chap. 2). Knowing that others have successfully endured the same trials can bolster a resolve to remain faithful. Paul first recounts his own journey of suffering in Philippi and Thessalonica for the cause of Christ (vv. 1 – 12). Reminding them again of their genuine response to the gospel, he commends them for their willingness to profess Christ in spite of similar persecution (vv. 13 – 16). Finally, he reassures them that, although absent for a time, his deep affection for them remained fervent. They were, in fact, his "crown of rejoicing" (vv. 19 – 20 KJV).

Confidence encouraged by a good report (chap. 3). Paul's concern for the Thessalonians' welfare had caused him to send his most trusted companion, Timothy, to encourage them and to assess their faith (vv. 1 – 5). Timothy's report of their faith and love was such "good news" (v. 6), Paul was filled with rejoicing and thanksgiving to God for them (vv. 6 – 11). He concludes this section with a prayer that God would sustain their love and holiness until the coming of Christ (vv. 12 – 13). They had every reason to embrace with confidence the hope that was set before them.

Be Committed: Your Hope Is Vital (chaps. 4 – 5)

Commitment to put everything in context (chap. 4). As we have seen, the overriding theme of 1 Thessalonians is living with hope in lieu of Christ's coming. In this section, Paul exhorts his readers to think of everything in the context of that hope. Even though the Thessalonian culture was base and immoral, believers looking forward to Christ's return were encouraged to conduct themselves with moral integrity (vv. 1 – 8). Having a reputation for love and compassion, as well as respect for others and a testimony of honesty, is also compatible with that hope (vv. 9 – 12). Finally, the catching up of the saints at Christ's coming is a truth that will replace despondent grief with temporary sorrow because of the expectation of future reunion (vv. 13 – 18). Living with the anticipation of the Lord's return changes everything.

Commitment to live as children of light (chap. 5). Paul's teaching about the Day of the Lord had confused the Thessalonian church. So Paul clarified their understanding that, although the world will be caught off guard by this occasion of God's global judgment, the Thessalonians will not be exposed to God's wrath (vv. 1–11). In the meantime, however, he exhorted them to respect church leadership, to help those in need, and to do the things that please Christ (vv. 12–22). Paul concludes the letter with a final reminder of the coming of the Lord Jesus Christ and an appeal for the Thessalonians to be totally set apart unto God (vv. 23–28).

2 Thessalonians

The Thessalonians thought they were experiencing the Great Tribulation because of the severe persecution they were enduring. Furthermore, the church had received a bogus letter, claiming to be from Paul, that insisted the final tribulation had come. Some had quit their jobs in anticipation of the Lord's imminent return and were expecting others to support them. This misunderstanding of end-time events had caused a serious problem within the believing community.

A few months after Paul wrote his First Epistle to the Thessalonians, this crucial situation warranted another communication. The second epistle expresses the same love and appreciation for these faithful believers as in the first letter, but the overall tone is more corrective. Doctrinal error had led to irresponsible behavior and Paul knew that if the problem was not corrected, it would produce serious consequences for the Thessalonian church.

In three short chapters, Paul readjusts their thinking and returns them to a realistic hope. First, he reminds them of their ultimate deliverance at the time of Christ's return. Then he realigns their understanding of the timing of the Day of the Lord before finally challenging them to live consistent, godly lives.

2 THESSALONIANS		
Living with realistic hope		
Chapter 1	**Chapter 2**	**Chapter 3**
DELIVERANCE	TIMING	LIVE
WILL COME	IS CRUCIAL	RESPONSIBLY

Deliverance Will Come (chap. 1)

After a brief salutation (vv. 1–2), Paul commends his readers for their steadfast faith in spite of the persecutions and afflictions they were enduring (vv. 3–4). This leads to a description of the awesome return of Christ, when they will be rescued from their tormentors who will face the destructive vengeance of the Lord (vv. 5–10). Paul ends with a prayer, encouraging the Thessalonians to always glorify the Lord Jesus by responding with good works (vv. 11–12).

Timing Is Crucial (chap. 2)

Paul had already taught the Thessalonians that the coming of the Lord would precede the day of the Lord's judgment (1 Thessalonians 5). Then they had been deceived by a fraudulent letter informing them that they were suffering because the Day of the Lord had already come (vv. 1–2). So Paul corrects their misconception by telling them that the Day of the Lord will not come until the Antichrist ("man of lawlessness" v. 3) appears, occupies the Temple, and deceives the world (vv. 3–12). Finally, he exhorts them to stand firm and hold on to what they had been taught (vv. 13–17).

Live Responsibly (chap. 3)

Knowing that the Thessalonians understood the disruptive effects of persecution upon the ministry of the gospel, Paul asks them to also pray for him to be delivered from wicked and evil men (vv. 1–5). He concludes the letter by addressing the problem of irresponsible actions on the part of some, while exhorting the whole church to not grow weary in doing good things (vv. 6–15). His final words are a benediction beseeching God for His peace to rest upon them (vv. 16–18).

THE "HOPE SET" OF THE JEWISH CHRISTIAN EPISTLES

We have finally come to the great capstone book of the New Testament: the book of Revelation. This final communication from the pen of the apostle John is a majestic treatise on the prophetic culmination of the ages. More than ever, people are turning to this book to satisfy their curiosity about global issues and future trends. Even though it is couched in symbolic language, the Revelation is a treasure chest of futuristic knowledge for those who will read it with a humble heart, a patient spirit, and spiritual discernment.

But we must not forget the little book of Jude in our hurry to grapple with the seals, trumpets, and vials of the Revelation. It too is an epistle of hope that functions as an essential introduction to the Jewish concept of hope. For the Jew, hope has always been about the Messiah—the One who would come and rescue them from oppression. Events for them have been wrapped in the glory of their deliverer. Before the thunderous apocalypse of John, therefore, Jude casts the spotlight on Jesus descending from heaven as the Judge of the universe.

As with the Gentile Epistles of Hope, Jude and Revelation stand alone without an initial, primary book to introduce the concept of Christian hope. Furthermore, the rotational principle is repeated with Jude (–) and Revelation (+). Jude challenges readers to contend for the faith; John in Revelation lays out the completion of God's plan. So let's begin with Jude as we seek to analyze these Jewish Epistles of Hope.

Jude

When Jude sat down to pen the book of Jude, he intended to write a treatise on the doctrine of salvation. Then he learned of a serious attempt by false teachers to undermine the gospel and pervert the faith of those to whom he was writing. So his short epistle became a polemic against false teaching rather than what he originally intended. When the circumstance changed, so did he. This is evident in verse 3: "Beloved, although I was very eager to write to you about our common salvation, I found it necessary to write appealing to you to contend for the faith."

Jude is one of five small, one-chapter books in the Bible. As with all the others, however, it is much in little. Like a stick of dynamite thrown into a nest of rattlesnakes, Jude decimates the false teachers with explosive illustrations and metaphors that leave no doubt about Jude's utter disgust with their venomous ways. For Jude, the return of the Lord accompanied by an overwhelming heavenly host will seal the ultimate demise of these renegades.

The book of Jude is like a brief outburst of righteous anger, setting the tone for the pouring out of God's wrath in the book of Revelation. In this way, Jude is indeed a fitting introduction to John's magnificent vision of the future.

Nothing stated in Jude identifies his intended readership. But, like his brother James (v. 1), who wrote to "the twelve tribes in the Dispersion," Jude seems to have an audience of Jewish Christians in mind. Hiebert notes:

> Some think that the intended readers were Jewish Christians. This is concluded from the fact that the author makes reference to himself as the brother of James who was highly esteemed by all Jewish Christians, from the Jewish tone of the epistle, as well as from the author's use of

Jewish illustrations and Jewish tradition. Those who accept this view are inclined to identify the readers with those addressed by his brother James.[2]

So there seems validity in identifying Jude as a Jewish Christian Epistle. And the hope of Christ's coming is the central focus of the book, making it a companion to the book of Revelation in the "hope set." As with Paul's purpose in the Thessalonian epistles, Jude seeks to encourage his readers with the realization that the return of the Lord is the final solution to the problems of life.

Jude seems to have structured his letter as an inverted parallel. He first addresses the readers. Then he describes the antagonists and proceeds to the central issue of Christ's return. The concluding thoughts are the same in reverse order: first, a further description of the antagonists, and finally challenging the readers again. An inverted parallel with a central climactic point is a *chiasm*. And the central thrust of a chiasm is always the main point of the discourse.

Inverted Parallel

Introduction (vv. 1 – 2)
The readers (vv. 3 – 4)
The antagonists (vv. 5 – 13)
Christ's Coming (vv. 14 – 15)   A Chiasm
The antagonists (vv. 16 – 19)
The readers (vv. 20 – 23)
Concluding benediction (vv. 24 – 25)

The Lead-in Section (vv. 1 – 13)

What an encouraging introduction for true believers: to know that they are "called, beloved in God the Father and kept for Jesus Christ" (vv. 1–2). Addressing the readers, Jude challenges them to "contend for the faith" against ungodly people who had infiltrated the assembly (vv. 3–4). A lengthy section unmasking the intruders follows with three illustrations of God's judgment (vv. 5–7) and a severe descriptive analysis of their perverted character (vv. 8–13).

Central Focus (vv. 14 – 15)

Using an extrabiblical prophecy of Enoch, Jude pictures the awesome return of the Lord accompanied by a massive angelic host to execute devastating judgment on these ungodly reprobates.

Lead-out Section (vv. 16 – 25)

A further description of the antagonists follows with a reminder that the apostles of Jesus Christ had predicted that scoffers would come (vv. 16–19). Jude then instructs the believers on how to respond by taking responsibility for their own spiritual welfare and by reaching out to those who were caught in the snare of false teaching (vv. 20–23). In conclusion, Jude pens one of the most celebrated benedictions in all of Christian literature, with emphasis on the glory of Christ and the preservation of the saints (vv. 24–25).

Revelation

Revelation is the only biblical book that promises a blessing to those who read it: "Blessed is the one who reads aloud the words of this prophecy" (1:3). This certainly implies that the book is, to a large extent, understandable. How can people be blessed if they don't comprehend what they're reading? Symbolisms and prophetic metaphors need to be clarified, of course, yet with patient reading and study, even they become clear.

Revelation follows a simple progressive pattern. The book begins with a series of messages to the churches and ends in the future kingdom with its subsequent eternal state. Between this beginning and ending are all the major events that will inaugurate the Kingdom Age. Seven seals followed by seven trumpets and seven bowls express the apocalyptic judgment of God whereby He cleanses the world from evil. All of this builds to a thunderous climax when Jesus Christ descends out of heaven to reclaim His dominion over the earth. What a dramatic conclusion to the biblical story!

The format of Revelation becomes clear when we make a simple observation: the main body of information (chaps. 6–19) is written in two parallel accounts. First, the entire scope of God's judgment is laid out in the sequential numbering of seals and trumpets (chaps. 6–11). The seventh trumpet brings us to the end with the coming of Christ to set up His kingdom on earth (11:15). Then the story is told again by expanding on the important details (chaps. 12–19). This section also ends with a reference to the awesome return of Jesus Christ (19:11–21). So there are two parallel accounts: first, the sequence, and second, the details. Grasp this design and the book will open as a masterpiece of future hope.

When we look at the big picture, the logical sequence of John's message appears to be as simple as it is profound. The complication is in the specifics. The basic plot, however, is a clear revelation of how all things will culminate in the glorious return of Christ in fulfillment of the believer's hope. Here is the promised blessing for those who will read the book.

Let's lay out the structure of the Revelation and its encouraging message involving the completion of God's plan.

Christ's Concern for the Church (chaps. 1 – 3)

The first words tell us that the entire book is a "revelation of Jesus Christ" (1:1). Many events and people pass across the prophetic stage, but Jesus Christ is the focal point of the book of Revelation. Introduced as the glorious "son of man" (1:13; a messianic title from Daniel 7), the qualities of Jesus' character and the wonder of His magnificent abilities form the opening fanfare of this prophetic magnum opus.

The book was addressed to seven first-century churches in Asia Minor (1:11). In chapters 2 – 3, each of these churches is singled out for a personal evaluation of its relationship to Christ. The churches were located in a geographical circle, which seems to picture a cycle of deteriorating love in the seven letters. Beginning in Ephesus, where the church had lost its first love (2:4), the cycle digresses to Thyatira, where the church was committing spiritual adultery (2:22), and concludes in Laodicea, where Christ is pictured on the outside, knocking on a door to get back in (3:20).

Before judgment is poured out upon the ungodly world, described in subsequent chapters, Jesus Christ wants the churches to know that the quality of their love for Him is His greatest concern. In turn, overcoming their wandering affections should become their greatest concern, as the letter to each church ends with an appeal to "overcome."

Christ's Judgment of the World (chaps. 4 – 19)

Preparation for judgment (chaps. 4–5). Chapter 4 opens with an invitation for John to step into the war chamber of heaven. There he sees the Son of Man preparing for His role as judge of the universe. A seven-sealed scroll, thought to be the title deed for dominion over the earth, emerges as the central focus. Jesus, as the Lamb of God, is the only Person with the authority to open the scroll. As chapter 5 closes, all preparations have been made for the judgment to begin.

Opening the seals and sounding the trumpets (chaps. 6–11). The first five seals express general conditions leading up to the day of the Lord's judgment, which is heralded in the sixth seal and enacted in the seventh seal. Before the seventh seal of judgment is opened, however, 144,000 Jewish men are branded as God's witnesses, and a great multitude of saints appears in heaven. Then the final seal unleashes seven successive angelic trumpets that announce the pouring forth of God's wrath. This period of judgment climaxes with the seventh trumpet, where "the kingdom of the world has become the kingdom of our Lord and of his Christ" (11:15).

Expanding on important details (chaps. 12–19). Israel experiences great persecution during this time, but God protects them from satanic annihilation (chap. 12). The activities of the Antichrist and False Prophet are highlighted next (chap. 13), followed by a further glimpse of the 144,000 Jewish witnesses and preparation for the final aspects of the day of the Lord's judgment (chap. 14). A final flurry of seven bowls of wrath is unleashed (chaps. 15–16), after which a detailed description of Babylon (the epicenter of Satan's evil system) and its ultimate demise is given (chaps. 17–18). The marriage of the Lamb and His majestic descent out of heaven emerges as the grand finale of God's judgment upon the earth (chap. 19). The earth is now ready for God's kingdom.

Christ's Provision for the Future (chaps. 20–22)

The Revelation concludes with a grand picture of the Kingdom Age and the eternal state. A new heaven and a new earth adorn the universe, and a beautiful city, the New Jerusalem, hovers in the sky. Hope for the reader has turned into reality as John lays down his pen. His parting words, "Come, Lord Jesus!" (22:20), continue to be echoed by every believer.

Seeing It at a Glance

Now that we have made our way through the Epistles of Hope, perhaps it will be helpful to graphically display the entire sequence.

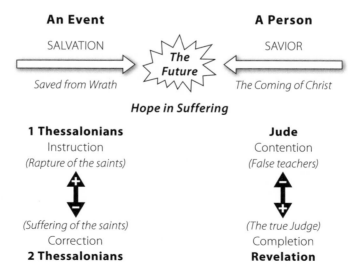

OUTSTRETCHED ARMS

We have been looking at the Epistles in terms of the arm function. The Epistles of Faith reflected the arms in a working mode. The Epistles of Love pictured an embracing action. As we come to the Epistles of Hope, we are looking for a movement of the arms that expresses help and encouragement. Is there anything in the Bible that helps us here? Yes.

Numerous times God can be seen in the Scriptures stretching out His arms to help the hopeless.

> Say therefore to the people of Israel, I am the LORD, and I will bring you out from under the burdens of the Egyptians, and I will deliver you from slavery to them, and I will redeem you with an *outstretched arm* and with great acts of judgment. (Exod. 6:6, emphasis mine)

Thirteen times this poignant picture of God's arms is used to reflect God's saving action.

We know that God doesn't really have arms. This is merely another anthropomorphism—where human physical traits are assigned to an activity of God. Yet the picture is profound and encouraging. The fact that the biblical God is a loving God gives credence to this function of the divine arms. In Christ's saving love, hope is personified.

So let's analyze the arms to see if they truly picture the Epistles of Hope in a stretched-out motion. First, notice that the biceps and triceps of the upper arms are totally relaxed when the arms are reaching out. This is reflected in our observation that there are no primary books for the hope epistles; they number four, not six as in the faith and love sets.

Second, what we have with the hope books is the rotational push-pull concept as in the forearms. On the Gentile side, 1 Thessalonians is the positive pull-toward concept of living with the hope of Christ's return. Second Thessalonians, on the other hand, expresses a negative push-away idea in the correcting of the Thessalonians' misconception of the Day of the Lord.

With the Jewish Christian Epistles, Jude is the negative push-away book, as he contends for the faith with false teachers in the light of Christ's coming. The positive pull-toward book is Revelation, where Christ is seen as judging the world for its evil and providing eternal rest for the saints.

So a positive and a negative book balance each other on both the Gentile and Jewish sides of the Epistles of Hope. But notice: as with the faith and love rotation books, the rotation in the hope books is opposite on the two sides. On the Gentile side, the positive comes first, and the negative is second. The opposite sequence exists on the Jewish side where the negative book comes first and the positive second.

Stretch your arms out in front of you and rotate them to push away and then to pull toward. Do you see that they rotate opposite to each other? The forearms in a reaching-out function do indeed picture the hope books, as God reaches out with a balanced message of hope.

EPISTLES OF HOPE — REACHING OUT

STRENGTH — *Throughout the whole arm*

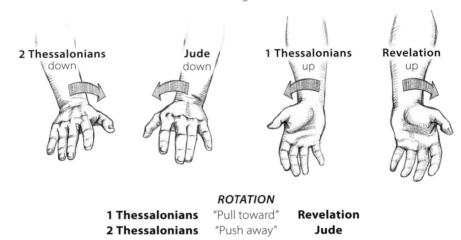

2 Thessalonians down	**Jude** down	**1 Thessalonians** up	**Revelation** up

ROTATION

1 Thessalonians	"Pull toward"	**Revelation**
2 Thessalonians	"Push away"	**Jude**

SUMMARY

It has taken us awhile to work through all the New Testament epistles, but the results have been rewarding. We have seen that Romans and Hebrews are accurately reflected in the human hands, and the remaining epistles function remarkably like arms in three basic ways—*faith* (working), *love* (embracing), and *hope* (reaching out).

As I have continued to investigate the legitimacy of observing the books of the Bible arranged according to the human form, I've been increasingly convinced that the similarity of the Inspiration (Bible) to the Incarnation (Jesus Christ) is more of a divine intention than a mere coincidence. It is at least a very intriguing possibility.

But let's press on to also consider the remaining books of the Old Testament. Here we encounter the feet and legs of the mosaic analogy.

PART 3

PILLARS
OF TRUTH

CHAPTER THIRTEEN

EXAMINING FOUNDATIONS

The Law and the Prophets

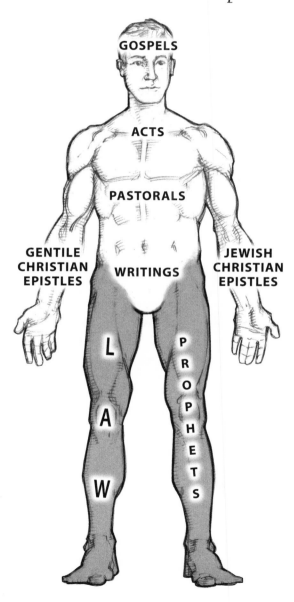

EXAMINING FOUNDATIONS

Foundations are important to the stability of any worthwhile endeavor.

Take education, for instance. A liberal arts education lays the basic groundwork for a well-rounded and successful life. Primary and secondary education, as well as most undergraduate collegiate experiences, has been based on that philosophy.

"Get a good liberal arts education, and you are more likely to succeed in whatever vocation you choose" is usually good advice. Conventional wisdom has understood that a broad base of knowledge lays a good foundation for life.

When building physical structures, the need for establishing good foundations becomes even more obvious. You can certainly get by in life without a liberal arts education. But try to erect a building on a poor foundation, and the results can be disastrous.

Remember the parable Jesus taught, where the foolish man built his house upon the sand, while the wise man anchored his house to a rock? When the storm came, the house on the sand collapsed, but the house on the rock stood firm. The whole parable is about foundations—not about types of houses. The foundation made the difference between a durable structure and a faulty one.

What is true for education and houses is also true for the Bible. This monumental sixty-six-piece mosaic stands on two pillars that, in turn, are anchored into a rocklike foundation. The Law (with its history of implementation) and the Prophets are the undergirding supports for the entire Word of God—just as the feet and legs provide support for the body.

To see the New Testament as a stand-alone document is a mistake. The beautiful architecture and exquisite construction of the New Testament edifice of truth rests firmly on the foundation of the Law and the Prophets. As the Old Testament needs the New Testament for its fulfillment, so the New Testament hangs in limbo without the solid support of the Old Testament. For instance, how can we understand the brutal death of Christ in the Gos-

pels apart from an awareness of the origin of sin in Genesis and the anticipation of messianic atonement in Isaiah? The roots of New Testament revelation
reach deep into the fertile ground of Old Testament truth. This is the reason
the New Testament continually quotes the Old Testament.

In our thematic overview of the Bible, we now come to the two foundational pillars of divine revelation: the Law and the Prophets. As a foundation
continues to be a relevant and sustaining part of a well-built house, so the
Old Testament Law and Prophets continue to provide stability and strength
for the New Testament. In fact, in the words of Jesus, the Law and the Prophets will always endure as a perpetual foundation for truth.

> Do not think that I have come to abolish the Law or the Prophets; I have
> not come to abolish them but to fulfill them. For truly, I say to you, until
> heaven and earth pass away, not an iota, not a dot, will pass from the Law
> until all is accomplished. (Matt. 5:17–18)

THE FOUNDATION OF TRUTH

As we observed in chapter 1, it seemed the sixty-six biblical books mirrored the form of a person. We have already seen how the Poetical Writings
appeared in the lower half of the torso, and were structured in the same
fashion as the stomach and viscera of the human body. What lies before
us now are the remaining thirty-four books of the Old Testament in two
complementary and symmetric columns of seventeen books each—the Law
(Historical Books) and the Prophets.

So let's begin by reviewing their symmetrical arrangement. First, each
sequence of the Law and the Prophets begins with five formative books that
lay the foundation for the historical and prophetic perspectives of Israel. The
Pentateuch establishes the framework for Israel's national life on the law/his-
tory side. In similar fashion, five Major Prophets set the tone for the prophetic
ministry as recorded in the prophecy column. These books are foundational
and basic to the entire biblical message and function in much the same way
as feet for the body.

The Pentateuch and Major Prophets also provide a balance between the
formation of divine law and the fulfillment of its purpose, respectively. The
Law is established as the basis of Israel's national life through the ministry of
Moses in the Pentateuch. On the balancing side, the Prophets articulate the
consequences of keeping or breaking that Law, as well as the future fulfillment of God's purposes. In this way the Law and the Prophets are again like

feet, which provide balance for the body. We will probe this concept more in the next chapter.

Second, growing out of the Pentateuch and Major Prophets are the Historical Books of Israel's national history and the Minor Prophets, with twelve books in each column. These Old Testament "pillars" provide a sense of fulfillment and destiny with regard to God's covenantal relationship with the nation of Israel. Firmly anchored in the Pentateuch and Major Prophets, these continuing books of history and prophecy carry us through the monarchy and captivity of Israel into the record of Israel's restoration and anticipation of the coming Messiah. In the end, they prepare us for the New Testament.

Notice the similarity in function to the legs of the human anatomy. Anchored firmly to the feet, the legs provide mobility and strength for the body. This analogy will be more completely developed in succeeding chapters.

For now, however, let's get this arrangement firmly fixed in our minds.

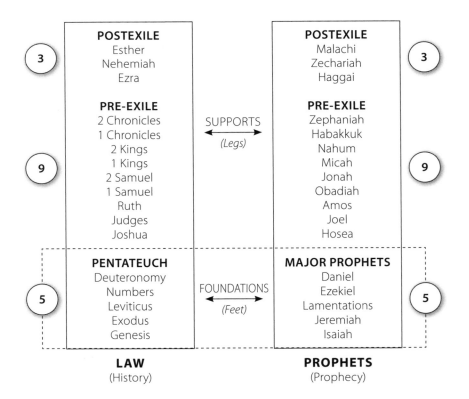

THE PENTATEUCH AND MAJOR PROPHETS

Years ago I worked building walls for a concrete construction company. Before we could carry the forms for the foundation into the excavated hole, concrete footings had to be established. If the area was sandy or unstable, concrete pylons would be drilled deep into the soil to create a solid base. These footings were the real foundation for the building upon which we would erect the concrete walls of the basement.

By way of analogy, the scriptural footings are the Pentateuch of Moses (Genesis, Exodus, Leviticus, Numbers, and Deuteronomy) and the Major Prophets (Isaiah, Jeremiah, Lamentations, Ezekiel, and Daniel). The foundational walls are the twelve books of continuing history and the twelve Minor Prophets. Good footings are essential for a building's stability, though both the footings and the walls are usually called the foundation. In the same way, all seventeen books in each Old Testament column are the foundation of Scripture, but the Pentateuch and Major Prophets are the footings that provide a firm base for the entire Word of God.

To change the analogy and get back to our investigation of the body mosaic, the Pentateuch and Major Prophets appear to be the feet upon which the body of truth rests. This will be our subject in the next chapter.

THE BIBLE HAS LEGS

We have noticed that two literary genres dominate the Old Testament — history and prophecy (along with the lesser genre of poetry in the Writings). In the providence of God, both of these pillars of truth have an initial set of five books and a continuing sequence of twelve books divided into two subcategories, nine pre-exile and three postexile. This symmetrical pattern appears to have been deliberate in the final formation of the scriptural canon.

Having made a few introductory observations concerning the Pentateuch and Major Prophets, we now turn to an analysis of the remaining twelve books in each column.

On the history side, the books of Joshua–Esther provide a record of the complete history of Israel's national life from the conquest under Joshua through the rise and fall of the monarchy to the concluding events of the restoration in the days of Ezra and Nehemiah. After laying the foundation of the Law with Moses (the Pentateuch), these twelve remaining books of history relate how the Law played out in the affairs of the nation.

Turning to the prophecy pillar, twelve Minor Prophets carry on the message of the Major Prophets. From Hosea to Malachi, the message is the same with a variety of settings and applications: obey God for blessing, but expect cursing for disobedience. All the prophetic seeds of messianic hope and kingdom living are sown in the Major Prophets and clarified in the Minor Prophets. These latter prophets are called "minor" because of the shorter length of the writings.

As we continue to think about the body analogy, these two sets of twelve books resemble foundational pillars and, in that sense, seem to fulfill the function of legs. But the analogy certainly needs to be looked at more closely. In fact, in my initial deliberations, these thirty-four Old Testament books seemed overwhelming, like a thousand-piece interlocking puzzle. The way to approach a puzzle, though, is one piece at a time — and that's how we need to approach these foundational books of God's Word.

A Pattern in the Historical Books

The sequence of twelve Historical Books of the Law shows a definite pattern of development, while the Minor Prophets as a group seem more aimless and independent. Taking a clue from the New Testament Epistles, where the arm segments reflected a parallel relationship, let's unravel the more obvious *historical leg* and see if a parallel idea exists in the *prophetic leg*.

The twelve Historical Books divide nicely into three easily identifiable segments. The first three books (Joshua, Judges, and Ruth) are premonarchy books that describe the conquest and occupation phase of Israel's national history. In the second segment, we find six books chronicling the rise and fall of Israel's kings, arranged in three couplets (1 & 2 Samuel, 1 & 2 Kings, and 1 & 2 Chronicles). Remember that these twin books were originally single units in the Jewish canon, so at times we will refer to them as Samuel, Kings, and Chronicles. Finally, three concluding books tell the story of Israel's return from captivity in Babylon (Ezra, Nehemiah, and Esther).

Notice carefully that there is a trilogy of trilogies — three segments composed of three books of the conquest, three double books of the monarchy, and three of the restoration.

CONQUEST	MONARCHY	RESTORATION
Joshua	1 & 2 Samuel	Ezra
Judges	1 & 2 Kings	Nehemiah
Ruth	1 & 2 Chronicles	Esther

But there is more to the pattern. All three segments (conquest, monarchy, and restoration) are arranged in the same fashion. The initial two books in each section reveal the historical sequence of that period; the final book dips back into that history to teach a spiritual lesson concerning trust and dependence on the Lord.

Joshua and Judges, for instance, give the account of Israel's conquest of the land under Joshua and the subsequent struggle for leadership in the period of the judges. This developmental period demonstrates the need for national organization and leadership. Finally, Ruth, which takes place during the time of the judges, explains the spiritual principle of trust and dependence on God for His blessings.

CONQUEST

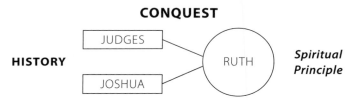

The books of Samuel and Kings follow the same pattern. From the early kingship of Saul and David in the books of Samuel, we digress to civil war in the days of Solomon, resulting in a split nation and a dual set of kings. The monarchy ends in 2 Kings, where Ephraim in the north is conquered by the Assyrians, and Judah in the south is taken captive by Babylon. The books of Chronicles repeat the same history from the perspective of the Temple rather than the throne. Dipping back into the tale of the monarchy in Samuel and Kings, the Chronicles stress the spiritual principle of trust and dependence on God (or the lack thereof) rather than reliance on the throne.

MONARCHY

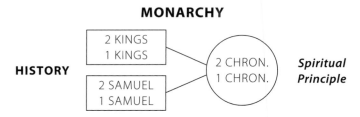

Again we see the pattern in the books of Restoration—Ezra, Nehemiah, and Esther. In Ezra and Nehemiah we read a sequential history of Israel's return to the land after the Babylonian captivity. Under Ezra's leadership the Temple is rebuilt, and through Nehemiah's leadership the walls of Jerusalem are restored. Then the book of Esther takes us back into the period of captivity in Persia to show us the importance of trust and dependence on God.

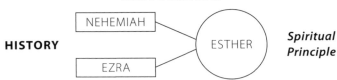

RESTORATION

HISTORY — NEHEMIAH / EZRA → ESTHER — *Spiritual Principle*

Notice that the two books in the Old Testament bearing the name of women (Ruth and Esther) are the books of trust and dependence manifest through the posture of submission and reliance—Ruth to Naomi and Boaz, and Esther to Mordecai and Ahasuerus. This is the biblical role for all women, and in the context of these Historical Books, God uses the stories of these two godly women to mirror how all God's people need to respond to God in a spirit of active submission. In the midst of male leadership for both the conquest and the restoration, it is women who teach us how to touch the heart of God. This too is part of the incredible design of the Old Testament Historical Books.

What about the Minor Prophets?

The Minor Prophets are admittedly harder to analyze in terms of a pattern. None of the prophets was related to the period of the conquest, so the same historical pattern described above is not evident here.

Furthermore, the historical settings vary among the prophets. Due to

LATER HISTORY

- NEHEMIAH / EZRA → ESTHER
- 2 KINGS / 1 KINGS / 2 SAMUEL / 1 SAMUEL → 2 CHRON. / 1 CHRON.
- JUDGES / JOSHUA → RUTH

MINOR PROPHETS

- MALACHI → ZECHARIAH / HAGGAI
- ZEPHANIAH / HABAKKUK → NAHUM / MICAH / JONAH / OBADIAH
- AMOS → JOEL / HOSEA

a split kingdom, three prophets prophesy in the north (Jonah, Amos, and Hosea), and six in the south (Obadiah, Joel, Micah, Nahum, Zephaniah, and Habakkuk). The only historical parallel seems to be with the last three (Haggai, Zechariah, and Malachi), who prophesied during the restoration period and were contemporaries with Ezra and Nehemiah. Historical orientation does not insert itself in a way that creates a sequential pattern.

Yet as I suggested earlier, there may be a thematic clue in the parallelism we observed with the Epistles. Remember how the concepts of *faith, love,* and *hope* were manifest in the same sequence for both the Gentile and Jewish epistles? Perhaps we might find a similar pattern of parallel concepts between the historical and prophetic books that reflect a mirror image of each other.

Before considering what these thematic concepts are, let's see what the mirror image parallelism would look like. Here are the two columns, side by side:

MAJOR THEMES

In the Epistles we discovered themes that easily expressed themselves in terms of the functions of human arms—working *faith,* embracing *love,* and reaching-out *hope.*

By way of the body analogy, perhaps the history and prophecy columns are three leg activities instead of two massive legs. Since we identified three Old Testament historical segments of conquest, monarchy, and restoration, I wondered if this might be a clue to discovering three leg functions.

Looking more closely at the three Old Testament segments from a religious perspective, I noted three variations of Israel's worship. During the first period of *conquest* with Joshua and the judges, the center of worship was the mobile Tabernacle. Wherever the nation went, the Tabernacle went with it. It was a scenario of movement.

As the throne was established in the period of the *monarchy,* the Tabernacle gave way to the Temple. In this second segment, we see a more permanent worship center. The nation was no longer on the move; it was now anchored in a stable setting. The Temple stood strong on Mount Moriah.

Eventually Nebuchadnezzar invaded Jerusalem, destroyed the Temple, and carried the Jews captive to Babylon. Seventy years later the *restoration* began as Ezra and Nehemiah led the people back home. Under Zerubbabel's leadership the Temple was rebuilt and a third segment of worship was introduced. Here the emphasis was in rebuilding what had been broken.

The worship center was the single most important structure in Israel. So grasp what's happening here. The three segments of the Law and the

Prophets are grouped in a way that reflects the three segments of Israel's worship experience. Could it be that there are three functions of the legs that reflect this pattern? Indeed there is!

THINKING ABOUT LEG FUNCTIONS

In part 2 we looked at three Christian graces that form the basis of our relationship with Christ: faith, love, and hope. In fact, Scripture groups together these three qualities as the essence of our spiritual life: "So now faith, hope, and love abide, these three" (1 Cor. 13:13). This became the pattern for our analysis of the Epistles as pictured in the functions of the arms.

As we come to the Old Testament and Israel's response to God, we ask: is there an appropriate trilogy in the Old Testament text that captures the ideals of Israel's relationship with God? *Absolutely!* Consider the opening verses of the Psalter:

> Blessed is the man
> who *walks* not in the counsel of the wicked,
> nor *stands* in the way of sinners,
>   nor *sits* in the seat of scoffers;
> but his delight is in the law of the LORD,
>   and on his law he meditates day and night.
>   (Ps. 1:1–2, emphasis mine)

The 150 psalms expressing the intimacy of our union with God open with this exhortation in Psalm 1. God wants His people to *walk* with Him, to *stand* firm on the truth, and to *sit* (or rest) in His provision for life. Here are three leg functions that capture the spiritual dynamic of Old Testament truth. Notice also how these three functions line up with the three segments of the Law and the Prophets and with the three scenarios of Israel's worship experience.

During the *conquest* Israel was on the move, walking wherever they went. The Tabernacle of that period also symbolized the motif of movement as it traveled with the walking nation. The word *walk* does seem to capture the mood of this segment.

The *monarchy* highlighted in the second segment established a nation firmly planted in the land. The permanent Temple stood as a symbol of Israel's commitment to God. The word *stand* seems highly appropriate for this period and this segment of books.

The *restoration* features the rebuilding of the Temple and the revitalization of the nation. How does the idea of sitting capture the significance of this period? Think about what happens when we sit. Sitting is the posture of rest and renewal. The body recuperates from its exhausting experiences and rebuilds its resources. This is certainly an apt picture of Israel as it rebuilt its Temple and reestablished its resources. After the exhausting experience of the captivity in Babylon, we see the people recouping their spiritual vitality. The word *sit* captures this idea perfectly.

Walk, stand, and sit are all functions of the legs. As we come to our study of the Historical Books and Minor Prophets, we will probe more closely how these twenty-four books can be represented by these three activities of the human leg.

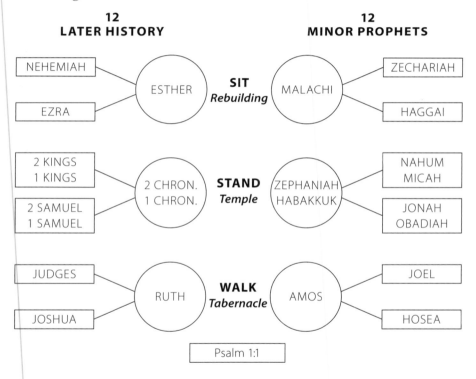

ANTICIPATING FEET & LEGS

With this brief orientation to the Law and the Prophets, we are ready to delve into an overview analysis of these thirty-four Old Testament books—twin pillars of truth.

We'll first consider the Pentateuch and Major Prophets with their balanced foundation. There is an amazing parallel design between these two sets of books, and the similarity of their construction is exactly how God created human feet.

In three concluding chapters, we will ponder the significance and arrangement of the Historical Books and the Minor Prophets. Each chapter will cover one of the three segments of conquest, monarchy, and restoration. Seeing how the books mirror the leg functions of *walk*, *stand*, and *sit* is a fascinating conclusion to the body analogy.

Analyzing most of the Old Testament books in just four chapters, we will be limited to a brief overview of each book, including how the books relate to one another. So turn the page and prepare yourself to enter the spectacular arena of the Pentateuch and Major Prophets.

CHAPTER FOURTEEN

BALANCING THE TRUTH

The Pentateuch and Major Prophets

Genesis – Deuteronomy and Isaiah – Daniel

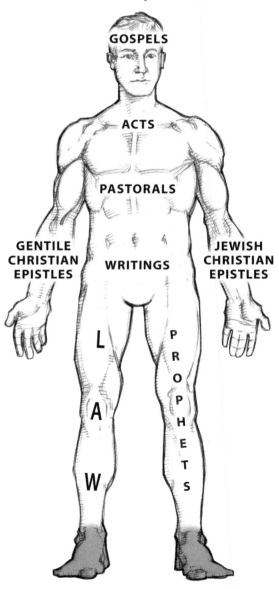

FOUNDATIONAL INFLUENCE

Foundations are not only important for stability; they also influence whatever is built upon them. Imagine attempting complicated mathematics like algebra, trigonometry, or calculus without a basic understanding of arithmetic. Trees need roots not only to give them stability, but also to provide nourishment from the ground to sustain them. What happens to people in childhood will have a profound effect on who they are as adults.

If you have ever watched a construction project develop, you have probably noticed tips of plumbing pipes sticking up out of the basement floor before the rest of the building is constructed. Plumbers lay a labyrinth of water and sewage conduits in the foundation before carpenters arrive on the scene. Eventually those pipes will reach up into every area of the building to service the structure for the life of the building. What is integrated into the foundation greatly influences what is built upon it.

Human feet are like that. Reflexology is a natural health-care alternative that applies pressure to the feet based on a system of reflex zones representing various areas of the body. The idea is that reflexes in the feet relate to every part of the upper body, and manipulating those reflex areas can effect changes in a person's health. Although reflexology has been practiced since ancient times in places like Egypt, China, India, and Japan, it wasn't brought to America until the early 1900s by Dr. William Fitzgerald, an ear-nose-throat specialist from Connecticut.

Wikipedia adds this historical note:

> Reflexology was further modified in the 1930s by Eunice D. Ingham (1889–1974), a nurse and physiotherapist. Ingham claimed that the feet and hands were especially sensitive, and mapped the entire body into "reflexes" on the feet. It was at this time that "zone therapy" was renamed reflexology.[1]

Whatever you might think of reflexology, the consistent age-old global belief that the feet possess zones that affect the rest of the body seems to have some validity. It certainly doesn't replace traditional medical treatment, but it strongly suggests that the body is greatly influenced by the feet.

I refer to this practice simply to illustrate the fact that the feet of Scripture (the Pentateuch and Major Prophets) have a pervasive and significant influence on the entire body of truth, the Word of God. Time after time the biblical authors quote or refer to something in the writings of Moses or the Major Prophets to substantiate or explain what they are writing.

I would go so far as to say that a person cannot truly understand the Bible without an awareness of what is taught in these foundational books. The foundations are indeed very influential to what is built upon them.

GETTING ACQUAINTED WITH THE BOOKS

As the feet have five toes on each foot, so the Pentateuch and Major Prophets comprise five books each. That is not to equate the books to the toes, but simply an easy way to remember how many books there are.

PENTATEUCH	MAJOR PROPHETS
Deuteronomy	Daniel
Numbers	Ezekiel
Leviticus	Lamentations
Exodus	Jeremiah
Genesis	Isaiah

Before analyzing how these books relate to one another, we will review the basic content of each book. We begin with the Pentateuch. Since we will obviously be dealing with an enormous amount of material, our examination of each book individually will concentrate primarily on central themes and basic structure. This will prepare us to see how the books relate to one another.

THE PENTATEUCH

Moses wrote five separate manuscripts, which became the first five books of the Bible: Genesis, Exodus, Leviticus, Numbers, and Deuteronomy. They are known as the Pentateuch, meaning "five books." From the creation of the world through the progressive development of the nation of Israel, these books reveal the foundation of world history from God's perspective.

Genesis

GENESIS

Becoming God's People

THE HUMAN RACE	THE HEBREW RACE
chaps. 1 – 11	chaps. 12 – 50

Beginning with the event of creation (chaps. 1–2), the first eleven chapters are a divine analysis of the roots of world history. Adam, the father of mankind, plunged the entire human race into sin (chaps. 3–5). This led to God's judgment on the early civilization in the flood of Noah (chaps. 6–10) and the rebellion of the repopulated earth at Babel (chap. 11).

Then God reached into this cauldron of evil and called Abraham through whom He would bless the world (chaps. 12–25). The rest of Genesis tracks the development of Abraham's family through Isaac (chaps. 25–26), Jacob (chaps. 27–36), and Joseph (chaps. 37–50). The emphasis in Genesis is clearly on "becoming God's people." Notice how the focus narrowed from the *human race* to the formation of the *Hebrew race*.

Exodus

EXODUS

Redemption from Egypt

THE EXODUS	THE LAW	THE TABERNACLE
chaps. 1 – 17	chaps. 18 – 24	chaps. 25 – 40

Exodus means "the way out," and the book chronicles how God brought Israel out of bondage in Egypt, demonstrating the spiritual principle of redemption.

The birth of Moses, the plight of the Hebrews, deliverance by way of ten plagues and a Passover sacrifice, crossing the Red Sea, and the journey to Mount Sinai—these are some of the greatest stories in human history (chaps. 1–17). Then God inscribed His Law on two tablets of stone, reflecting the moral code of the universe (chaps. 18–24). Worshiping God instead of the idols of Egypt required a special worship center that would teach the people how to approach their God. Almost half of the book of Exodus is devoted to the construction of this Tabernacle in preparation for its system of worship (chaps. 25–40).

Leviticus

LEVITICUS	
Making Fellowship	
SACRIFICE	SEPARATION
The Way	The Walk
chaps. 1 – 17	chaps. 18 – 27

For the Hebrew people to have fellowship with God, two things were paramount: sacrifice for sin and separation from the world system. The book of Leviticus expresses this theme.

Five specific sacrifices were required for God to have fellowship with His people (chaps. 1 – 7). In addition, special procedures were mandated for the priests who would administer the sacrificial system (chaps. 8 – 9). Laws of purity were also established for the nation (chaps. 11 – 15) and detailed instruction was given for the most holy day of all—the Day of Atonement (chaps. 16 – 17).

Various laws of separation were intended to keep the people from contamination with the ungodly world (chaps. 18 – 20), and the priests were given specific instruction in this regard (chaps. 21 – 22). Seven feasts were established as holy days (chaps. 23 – 24). Finally, Leviticus lays out God's promise for success if the people will keep the Sabbath of the land (chap. 25), understand the importance of obedience (chap. 26), and value their vows (chap. 27).

Numbers

NUMBERS		
Wandering in the Wilderness		
OLD	THE	NEW
GENERATION	WANDERING	GENERATION
chaps. 1 – 14	chaps. 15 – 20	chaps. 21 – 36

This book is called Numbers because Israel's men of war are numbered in chapters 1 – 4 and 26 – 27. The first numbering took place the second year after the nation had left Egypt (603,550 men), and the second census was taken thirty-eight years later when the new generation was about to enter Canaan (601,730 men).

In the first part of Numbers, the nation traveled north from Mount Sinai to the southern tip of the Promised Land at Kadesh-Barnea (chaps. 5 – 12). Twelve spies came back from scoping out the land, ten of whom gave a negative report. The nation decided not to trust God and refused to enter the land (chaps. 13–14).

God disciplined the nation for their unbelief and subjected them to thirty-eight years of wandering in the barren wilderness (chaps. 15–20). During this time the old generation responsible for the disobedience passed away.

The nation began to move again, making its way to the plains of Moab across from Jericho (chap. 21). There Balak the king of Moab tried to curse Israel through the prophet Balaam, finally succeeding by luring the men of Israel into acts of fornication with the women of Moab (chaps. 22–25). The new generation was then numbered (chaps. 26–27), the law of offerings and vows rehearsed (chaps. 28–30), and final preparations made to enter the land of Canaan (chaps. 31–36).

Deuteronomy

DEUTERONOMY

Preparation to Enter the Land

REVIEWING	ANTICIPATING
The Past	The Future
chaps. 1–11	chaps. 12–34

Deuteronomy means "the second giving of the law." Here the nation was camped on the plains of Moab waiting to enter the Promised Land. Before they could proceed, God prepared the new generation by reviewing the law (chaps. 1–11) and by expanding on the implications of that law for their future national life (chaps. 12–34).

First, the text reviews Israel's wanderings (chaps. 1–4) and rehearses the Mosaic Law received at Mount Sinai (chaps. 5–11). Second, the text gives specific laws related to their ceremonial, civil, and social responsibilities (chaps. 12–26). After this, God talks to the nation through Moses concerning their future (chaps. 27–30), ending with the death of Moses and the transfer of leadership to Joshua (chaps. 31–34).

THE MAJOR PROPHETS

The first five books in the *prophets* column are called "major" because of the extended content of their writings.

All the Old Testament prophets spoke to their times and challenged the culture. Yet Isaiah, Jeremiah, Lamentations, Ezekiel, and Daniel provide a scope of prophetic anticipation unrealized by the others. The Minor Prophets may fill in some of the details, but the Major Prophets plant the seeds and set the parameters of God's divine plan for the ages. In this way also, they are indeed the Major Prophets.

Isaiah

ISAIAH	
Being God's People	
CONDEMNATION	CONSOLATION
Law	Grace
chaps. 1–39	chaps. 40–66

Isaiah was a prophet of the Southern Kingdom of Judah about one hundred years before the Babylonian captivity. Assyria had conquered the Northern Kingdom and Isaiah warned the people of Judah that they were next if they didn't start being the people God intended them to be.

Many have noticed how the book of Isaiah is like a miniature Bible. It has sixty-six chapters; the Bible has sixty-six books. The first section of Isaiah has thirty-nine chapters, corresponding to the thirty-nine books of the Old Testament, both of which emphasize the Law and its consequences. The twenty-seven chapters of the second section mirror the twenty-seven books of the New Testament, with both stressing the grace of God.

Condemnation and judgment are the primary themes of Isaiah's opening chapters (chaps. 1–35). A historical interlude follows, describing King Hezekiah's salvation, sickness, and sin (chaps. 36–39). The tone changes in the second part, where Isaiah speaks of Israel's deliverance (chaps. 40–48), Messiah's gracious intervention (chaps. 49–57), and Israel's glorious future (chaps. 58–66).

Jeremiah

JEREMIAH		
Bondage to Babylon		
AGAINST	AFTER THE FALL	AGAINST
Judah & Jerusalem	of Jerusalem	The Nations
chaps. 1–39	chaps. 40–45	chaps. 46–52

Jeremiah was called the weeping prophet because of his great sorrow as he wrote of God's discipline upon Judah and the impending and then devastating fall of Jerusalem.

After his appointment to the prophetic office (chap. 1), Jeremiah accused

Judah of hypocrisy, idolatry, and listening to false prophets. He concluded with a prediction that Judah would endure seventy years of captivity (chaps. 2–25). He then revealed a number of personal conflicts God had with the nation and specific individuals (chaps. 26–29), before writing of Jerusalem's future restoration (chaps. 30–33). Finally, he chronicled the city's demise at the hands of the Babylonians (chaps. 34–35).

In a brief interlude, Jeremiah reflected on the aftermath of Jerusalem's fall (chaps. 36–39) and sought to minister to the remnant in Judah and to those who had fled to Egypt (chaps. 40–44). This was followed by a short message to his assistant, Baruch (chap. 45).

The remainder of the book is devoted to prophecies against various nations (chaps. 46–51). Jeremiah concludes his writing with a detailed description of the capture and destruction of Jerusalem with many exiled to Babylon (chap. 52).

Lamentations

LAMENTATIONS				
Breaking Fellowship				
		chap. 3		
	chap. 2	JEREMIAH	chap. 4	
chap. 1	JEHOVAH	66	JEHOVAH	chap. 5
JERUSALEM	22		22	JERUSALEM
22				22

Lamentations is included in the Major Prophets, even though it is a small book of five chapters, because it was written by Jeremiah, a major prophet. The book expresses Jeremiah's sorrowful lament over the fall of Jerusalem.

Though heavy with grief, this funeral dirge is wrapped in exquisite design. The five chapters are an inverted parallel, with Jeremiah's plea for mercy as the central focus in chapter 3. Furthermore, chapters 1, 2, 4, and 5 are acrostics of twenty-two verses, each beginning with the next letter of the twenty-two-letter Hebrew alphabet. Chapter 3 is three times as long, with units of three verses each devoted to the twenty-two letters of the alphabet. The book is like a beautiful bouquet of flowers gracing the sadness of death.

Jerusalem is devastated and forsaken in chapter 1, but Jeremiah ends with a prayer for restoration of the city in chapter 5. Jehovah's anger is described in chapter 2, and defended in chapter 4. The focal point of the book, however, is Jeremiah's confession of sin and prayer for mercy in chapter 3. Here we read that God's mercies are new every morning and that His faithfulness is great (3:22–23).

Ezekiel

EZEKIEL		
Confused in Captivity		
GLORY DEPARTING	FUTURE OF THE NATIONS	GLORY RETURNING
chaps. 1 – 24	chaps. 25 – 32	chaps. 33 – 48

As Ezekiel sat by the river Chebar in Babylon, God revealed Himself to Ezekiel in a fiery vision and commissioned him for his prophetic ministry (chaps. 1 – 3). Ezekiel's first message of judgment was against Judah as he witnessed the glory of God departing from the Temple (chaps. 4 – 24).

Although the surrounding nations were gloating over Judah's demise, Ezekiel revealed the full cycle of judgment that would come upon them as well (chaps. 25 – 28). A series of oracles specifically addressed to Egypt predicted her diminishing importance (chaps. 29 – 32).

Ten years after Ezekiel arrived in Babylon, Nebuchadnezzar finally destroyed Jerusalem and the Temple. Then Ezekiel began to write of consolation and comfort. He predicted that Judah would once again be returned to their homeland as the persecuting nations were destroyed by God (chaps. 33 – 39). Fourteen years later, Ezekiel was given a vision of the reconstruction of the Temple and city, with a spectacular return of the glory of the Lord to the Holy Place (chaps. 40 – 48).

Daniel

DANIEL		
Preparation to Return to the Land		
PROSPERITY among the nations	DELIVERANCE from affliction	PROTECTION from Gentile powers
chap. 1	chaps. 2 – 7	chaps. 8 – 12
(Hebrew)	*(Aramaic)*	*(Hebrew)*

Daniel was also taken captive to Babylon, but unlike Ezekiel, who lived among the captives, Daniel became a trainee for leadership in the Babylonian system. He and his Hebrew friends prospered and became a symbol for his people that they too would prosper during the times of Gentile rule (chap. 1).

Chapters 2 – 7 are written entirely in the Aramaic language of Babylon. Daniel used a Gentile language to express visions and stories that represented the conditions that would prevail during the Times of the Gentiles.

Returning to the Hebrew language, Daniel revealed major events and transitions during the period of Gentile domination. He predicted the conquest of Persia by Greece (chap. 8), gave the time framework for Israel's restoration (chap. 9), unveiled the spiritual nature of the conflict (chap. 10), revealed the final ruler who will unleash a time of great trouble (chap. 11), and answered final questions regarding the end of the age (chap. 12).

FINDING SPIRITUAL DIRECTION

Analyzing each of the ten books of the Pentateuch and Major Prophets is like examining trees without an awareness of the forest. If we truly want to understand the overall significance of these magnificent writings, we must discover how they all relate to one another. Grasping the big picture will enable us to see the divine design surrounding each nugget of truth.

Different Geographical Perspectives

First, notice the geographical difference between the two sets of books. Moses wrote the Pentateuch from the perspective of coming out of Egypt. In Genesis he described how God began His work on earth by choosing Abraham and his family. Then from Exodus through Deuteronomy, redemption out of Egypt became the dominant theme.

As we survey the Major Prophets, the geography shifts to Babylon. The emphasis is no longer on beginnings but on endings. Isaiah warned God's people that divine discipline was pending. The remaining Major Prophets, from Jeremiah to Daniel, tell the woeful tale of Judah's capture and enslavement by the Babylonians and future hope with God. God was continuing to pursue with His people what He had begun.

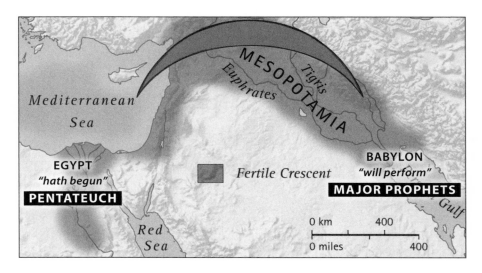

A spiritual principle confronts us here. As the children of God, we begin our spiritual journey when we are called by God and redeemed by the blood of the lamb (Pentateuch). At that point we become part of God's family, with all the privileges and responsibilities of a child in the Father's house. When we sin, we are disciplined—but only for a time. God has promised a glorious future for His children, and so He continues to perform what He began (Major Prophets). "And I am sure of this, that he who *began a good work* in you *will bring it to completion* at the day of Jesus Christ" (Phil. 1:6, emphasis mine).

Travel Routes

Second, an arid, barren condition exists in the central part of the Middle East, which forced ancient travel to follow the more fertile waterways along the Mediterranean coast and Mesopotamian rivers. When going from Egypt to Babylon, travelers would go north along the *Via Maris* (way of the sea) into Syria and Turkey before angling east along the Tigris and Euphrates valley down to Babylon—or vice versa. This route became known as the Fertile Crescent. Egypt was on one end and Babylon on the other, like a pot of gold on each end of a rainbow.

I pause here to share an interesting observation. We are considering the Pentateuch and Major Prophets in terms of feet. As an experiment, stand with your feet together and look down at your toes. Follow the little toe up to the big toe on the left, then the big toe down to the little toe on the right. It's like a miniature fertile crescent. (Use your imagination!)

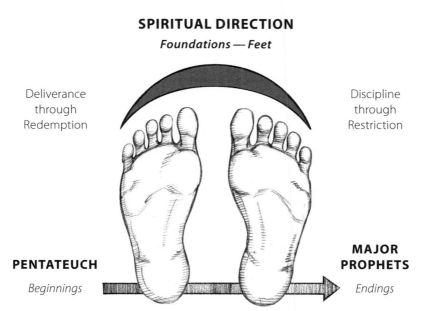

SPIRITUAL DIRECTION

Foundations — Feet

Deliverance through Redemption

Discipline through Restriction

PENTATEUCH

Beginnings

MAJOR PROPHETS

Endings

Consider this. The Pentateuch begins with one small family in Genesis and progresses to a large nation ready to enter the Promised Land in Deuteronomy. It goes from small to big. The Major Prophets are just the opposite. Isaiah begins by speaking to the entire nation, while Daniel reflects on the needs of a small remnant with hopes of returning home. The Prophets go from large to small.

I'm still pondering just how much to make of this observation, but at least it is a visual picture of spiritual direction for the people of God. We begin with *deliverance through redemption* (Pentateuch) and proceed to *discipline through restriction* (Major Prophets). All of Scripture is balanced on these two major concepts.

A PARALLEL PATTERN

In our study of the Epistles, we discovered parallel patterns between the Gentile Christian Epistles and the Jewish Christian Epistles. After all, the arms and hands are mirror images of each other. When we come to the feet and legs, the same is true in the human body. That simple deduction became a strong incentive to look for a parallel pattern between the books of the Pentateuch and the Major Prophets.

Even as the hands of Romans and Hebrews in our study are similar but different, reflecting a complementary pattern, perhaps we will find a complementary sequence in the foundational Old Testament books representing the feet. We have already seen the balancing spiritual concepts of *deliverance through redemption* (Pentateuch) and *discipline through restriction* (Major Prophets). Keeping that in mind as we review the content of these ten books, consider the pattern on page 219.

Referring to this schematic, let's consider these parallel relationships. Genesis and Isaiah, the first books of their respective sets, exhibit a complementary affinity for each other. "Becoming God's people," the theme of Genesis, correlates to Isaiah's theme, "being God's people." They are both mammoth books (the largest in their groups), and each sets the stage for all that follows. Historically, Exodus–Deuteronomy flow naturally out of Genesis, and Jeremiah–Daniel are the historical fulfillment of Isaiah's warning.

Exodus and Jeremiah are next in the order of books, and each performs the role of a sequel. Exodus takes place about four hundred years after the closing events of Genesis; Jeremiah writes about one hundred years after Isaiah. Each book completes the story of its predecessor. Exodus reveals how the posterity of Joseph at the end of Genesis became a people of bondage in need of redemption. Jeremiah, on the other hand, picks up the warnings of

PENTATEUCH *Deliverance through Redemption*		MAJOR PROPHETS *Discipline through Restriction*
GENESIS Becoming God's People *"Choosing"*		**ISAIAH** Being God's People *"Chastising"*
EXODUS Redemption from Egypt *"Old Covenant"*	**before**	**JEREMIAH** Bondage to Babylon *"New Covenant"*
LEVITICUS Making Fellowship *"Sacrifice"*		**LAMENTATIONS** Breaking Fellowship *"Suffering"*
NUMBERS Wandering in the Wilderness *"Tabernacle — Glory Remains"*	**after**	**EZEKIEL** Confused in Captivity *"Temple — Glory Departs"*
DEUTERONOMY Preparation to Enter the Promised Land		**DANIEL** Preparation to Return to the Promised Land

God's discipline in Isaiah and chronicles their fulfillment in the bondage to Babylon. Consider also this parallel between Exodus and Jeremiah: at the heart of Exodus (chap. 20) is the "Old Covenant" of the law, while central to Jeremiah's message (chap. 31) is the "New Covenant" of mercy and hope.

At this point we find a transition in each column. In terms of historical sequence, everything comes to a halt. Genesis and Exodus trace a continuous history of the children of Israel to their destiny at Mount Sinai, whereas the subsequent Leviticus takes a break from travel to ponder the elements of fellowship with God. In the Major Prophets, Isaiah and Jeremiah are a continuum of prophetic ministry from warning to fulfillment. Then time stands still as Jeremiah laments over the destruction of Jerusalem and the Temple in Lamentations. Leviticus and Lamentations are the bridges between what happened *before* and what is about to come *after*.

Finally, we come to the tandem books that complete the sections. Numbers continues the history of the new nation of Israel from Mount Sinai to the plains of Moab as they follow the cloud of God's glory. No progression occurs in Deuteronomy, only reflection. The new generation needed to understand the laws of God as they prepared to enter the Promised Land. Numbers and Deuteronomy go together as a unit.

In the Prophets, Ezekiel and Daniel address concerns of the exile—Ezekiel living among the captives and Daniel ruling with the captors. Ezekiel saw the glory of God departing from the Temple but ended with the realization that it would return. He wrote to encourage the people in exile. Daniel, writing as a contemporary of Ezekiel, spoke of the Gentile world and God's control over their destinies. He also sought to uplift the people in exile. Ezekiel and Daniel go together as a unit, like Numbers and Deuteronomy.

The sequence and arrangement of books between these two foundational sets, the Pentateuch and the Major Prophets, exhibit a complementary similarity that is a magnificent wonder of divine design. Whatever you may think of the subsequent application of these books to the body analogy of the feet, this study certainly enriches our understanding of God's creative genius in the crafting of His Word.

IT'S ALL IN THE BALANCE

Children learning to walk have trouble with their balance. Eventually, though, with enough trial and error, wobbly feet become more steady, confident walking becomes routine. It's simply a matter of adjusting to the inherent quality of balance programmed into the feet.

Design is critical to function, and the human foot is a grand example of that principle. Have you ever sat on a three-legged stool? How about a two-legged stool? We all know that a stool can balance on three legs but not on two. The same is true for the foot. To achieve balance, God designed the foot to function like a three-legged stool.

As the weight of the body filters down through the legs to the ankles, it is distributed to the feet in a way that achieves balance. Half of the weight of each leg goes to the heel. The other half is dispersed by means of an arch to the front of the foot, where it is spread in equal proportions to the two balls of the foot—one-quarter to the left and one-quarter to the right. This dispersal of weight to three critical points creates a three-legged-stool effect bringing balance to the body.

Here is another evidence of God's creative genius. The amazing design of the human foot is rivaled only by the equally amazing design of the hand.

THE FEET OF SCRIPTURE

In the parallel pattern observed between the Pentateuch and Major Prophets do we find any correspondence to the formation of the feet?

The Pentateuch

Coming first, like the two balls of the foot, Genesis and Exodus provide a historical continuum from one small family in Genesis to several million people in Exodus. We have already observed how the foot analogy seems to picture these books moving from the little toe on the left to the big toe on the right. These two books provide the foundational concept of "deliverance through redemption" that permeates the rest of Scripture. Genesis and Exodus are akin to one-quarter of the weight each at the front of the foot.

Skipping Leviticus momentarily, remember that Numbers and Deuteronomy function as a unit in a similar fashion to the heel's bearing of half of the body's weight. Four books (Genesis & Exodus and Numbers & Deuteronomy) seem to be the weight-bearing books of the Pentateuch.

Returning to Leviticus, we saw that it provides the bridge (or arch) connecting Genesis and Exodus with Numbers and Deuteronomy. Fellowship with God is the overarching connection between a redeemed people (Genesis and Exodus) and their beginning walk with the Lord (Numbers and Deuteronomy).

Can you see how the design of the Pentateuch and the structure of the human foot are amazingly similar?

The Major Prophets

The same foot pattern we just observed in the Pentateuch can also be seen in the Major Prophets. Isaiah and Jeremiah are historically sequential, providing two balance points at the front of the foot—warning of discipline in Isaiah and the carrying out of discipline in Jeremiah. Remember too that we have already seen the diminishing pattern from the whole nation in Isaiah (big toe) to a smaller group of exiles in Jeremiah (little toe). Each book is like one-quarter of the weight on each of the two balls of the foot.

Skipping to Ezekiel and Daniel, we noticed these books functioning as a prophets-in-exile unit. Coming at the end of the Major Prophets, they seem to share a likeness to the heel, together bearing half of the body's weight. These books complete the story of divine discipline and offer hope for future restoration.

Finally, like Leviticus, Lamentations functions like an arch between the pre-exilic prophets of Isaiah and Jeremiah, and the exile books of Ezekiel and Daniel. This lament over the destruction of Jerusalem and the Temple is the ideological bridge connecting the two sets of prophets.

SEEING IT ALL AT A GLANCE

When the books of the Major Prophets are set alongside the books of the Pentateuch, we are confronted with a foundation for the Holy Scriptures. As the feet provide a stable foundation for the body, so these books secure a solid base for the entire Word of God.

In all this, spiritual balance is achieved between the two major biblical themes of "deliverance through redemption" (Pentateuch) and "discipline through restriction" (Major Prophets). These twin truths are the feet upon which the Bible stands.

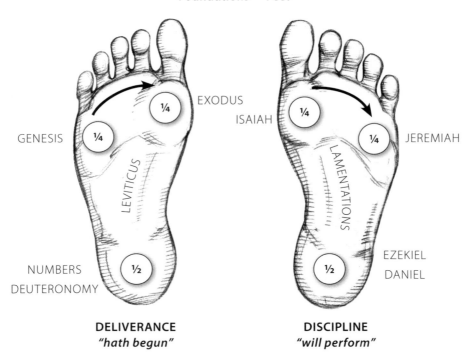

SPIRITUAL BALANCE
Foundations — Feet

DELIVERANCE
"hath begun"

DISCIPLINE
"will perform"

Philippians 1:6
CONFIDENCE

WHAT'S NEXT

Having analyzed the Pentateuch and the Major Prophets and probed the analogy to the feet, we now move to the twelve Historical Books and the twelve Minor Prophets. I suggest you review chapter 13 before continuing the study. With the big pictures in mind, you will be more equipped to ponder the great truths of the legs of Scripture.

CHAPTER FIFTEEN

WALKING WITH GOD

Joshua – Ruth and Hosea – Amos

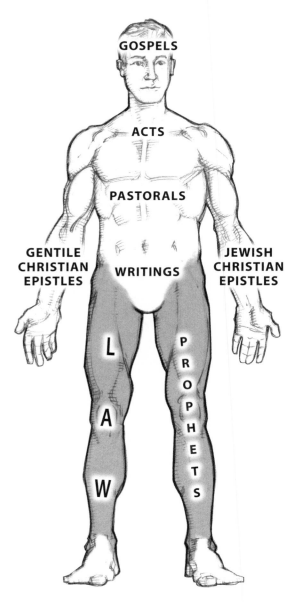

WALKING

Before the advent of motorized transportation, people walked more than they do today. Riding beasts of burden (or being carried in carts drawn by them) was the alternative, of course, but for the most part, people walked to their destinations.

The children of Israel walked—a lot! From Goshen in Egypt to Mount Sinai in Arabia was a long trek by foot. Two years after their arrival at Mount Sinai, they traveled north to Kadesh-Barnea. This was followed by thirty-eight years of wandering in the Sinai Peninsula before making their way north along the eastern edge of the Dead Sea to the Plains of Moab. That's a lot of walking. Especially when you're lugging everything you own.

Even in our mechanized society, walking is an important activity. For many, walking is exercise. Treadmills spin constantly at the gym as people walk, going nowhere. We can drive to the mall, but apart from scooters, we have to walk to do our shopping.

Perhaps that is why Ephesians 5:2 speaks of the Christian life as a walk: "And walk in love, as Christ loved us." Actually the Greek word for *walk* in this verse is a compound word meaning to walk around (*peripateo*—*peri* "around" + *pateo* "to walk"). All of life is pictured as a lot of walking around —going here and going there. As we walk through our days, God wants us to be like Christ.

Old Testament saints were also encouraged to see their spiritual life as a walk. The contrast to "walk not in the counsel of the wicked" is to walk in the counsel of God by obeying His Word (Ps. 1:1–3).

With this in mind, we now consider the Old Testament books that epitomize the idea of walking with God. The books of the conquest (Joshua, Judges, and Ruth) are books of action, as the children of Israel move into the Promised Land and begin to occupy what would become their national homeland. Joshua and Judges were written before a king was elevated to the throne.

Following the parallel concept, the first three books of the Minor Prophets (Hosea, Joel, and Amos) complement the idea of what it means to walk with God. In chapter 13 we saw that these prophetic books correlate with the books of historical conquest in an ideological rather than a historical manner. In other words, Hosea, Joel, and Amos were not contemporaries of Joshua, the judges, or Ruth. Yet the nature of their prophecies amazingly parallels the content of these books of conquest.

In this chapter we will focus on six books that rest on the sure footings of the Pentateuch and Major Prophets. Before analyzing the content of each book, however, let's become better acquainted with the historical and geographical settings.

WHERE ARE WE?

How does a girl from rural Minnesota get along with a boy from New York City? They are so different from each other because of their environmental conditioning. To understand why they think and act the way they do, one needs to become acquainted with their life situations.

This illustrates the importance of background study for the various books of the Bible. The Bible is unique in this way when compared to other religious writings. Philosophical meanderings of spiritualistic ideas in the Hindu Vedic Texts, for instance, differ radically from the real-life situations described in the time and space scenarios of the Bible. Bible study therefore begins with the question, *where are we?*

By the way, the girl from Minnesota and the boy from New York have gotten along quite well. We are happily in our forty-ninth year of marriage.

Books of the Conquest

Joshua, Judges, and Ruth are rooted in the formative years of Israel's national history. The wandering nomadic clans under Moses were emerging out of their wilderness incarceration, and Joshua had succeeded Moses as the leader of the children of Israel. As we open the pages of Joshua, everything is in place for Israel's conquest of the land promised to them by God. The people are still on the Plains of Moab east of the Jordan River, but they are clearly ready to forge an insertion into Canaan.

The book of Joshua chronicles the victorious battles of conquest and the apportionment of the land to the various tribes of Israel. This history continues in the book of Judges, where all of the events take place within the conquered land. Each tribe was to complete the conquest by subduing the

alien cultures with their pagan religions, but lack of commitment and dili-
gence left the Israelites vulnerable. This deplorable state of affairs required
a series of judges to deliver the people and clean up the mess. During this
period, Israel was in the land but struggling to occupy what they possessed.
No central government existed—only district judges.

In some ways the western frontier in early America resembles this time
period. Local sheriffs, like judges, attempted to enforce basic laws, but ren-
egade outlaws and Native American uprisings were a constant threat. Occupying the land of the Old West was not an easy task—just as it was not in
the days of the judges of Israel.

Times were tough, but God was still at work among His people. The book
of Ruth snuggles into this time of chaos as a bright spot on the darkened
landscape. Driven from the land by famine, a family of Judah faced further
tragedy in Moab. Out of the ashes of death, a young Moabite widow was
guided by the providence of God to find refuge and provision back in the
land of Judah. Thus this beautiful story of love and fulfillment is driven by a
paradoxical contrast. Looking for relief outside of God's crucible of hardship
led to despair. On the other hand, submitting to the discipline of divine trials yielded a sense of blessing and joy. That is the pivotal truth of the books
of conquest.

The First Trilogy of Minor Prophets

No cohesive history, like the story of conquest, binds together the prophetic writings of Hosea, Joel, and Amos. Yet historical provenance is crucial
to their message. The theme of each book looms as the prominent feature;
having said that, the cultural settings remain significant in comprehending
the themes.

We have already seen that although these three prophetic books are parallel to Joshua, Judges, and Ruth, in that both sets immediately follow their
pillars' "foundational five," they are not contemporaneous with the history of
the conquest. Historically, these prophets wrote during the times of the kings
after the division of the kingdom.

When King Solomon died, a struggle for power resulted in ten tribes
seceding from the union to form a second Hebrew nation. These tribes in
the north became known as the Kingdom of Israel (or Ephraim), while the
remaining two tribes of Judah and Benjamin were referred to as the Kingdom
of Judah. Out of that episode of civil strife came two sets of kings and two

spiritual scenarios. All the prophetic writings, including the Major Prophets, were divine messages to one or the other of these two competing factions.

The Major Prophets were consumed with the southern nation of Judah in the terminal years of the kingdom. Isaiah wrote about one hundred years before the Babylonian captivity, Jeremiah at the time of Nebuchadnezzar's invasion of Judah, and Ezekiel and Daniel during the exile of Judah in Babylon. The Minor Prophets, on the other hand, were scattered throughout both nations in the period of the kings; only the final three (Haggai, Zechariah, and Malachi) wrote subsequent to the monarchy and addressed the remnants of Judah who had returned from exile.

Hosea, Joel, and Amos were among the earliest of the writing prophets, preceded only by Obadiah. The message of Joel, the first of the three to write in 834 BC, was a warning of God's disciplinary action on Judah and Jerusalem. Amos wrote next in about 755. Although a citizen of Judah, his message concentrated on the wicked — yet prosperous — tribes of the Northern Kingdom. Thirty-five years later his prophecy was fulfilled when Assyria invaded the northern tribes.

Hosea, the only one of the three living in the Northern Kingdom, prophesied of God's unending love for Israel, even though the ten tribes would soon be dispersed by the conquering Assyrians. He concluded his writing around 725 BC, shortly before the Assyrians' invasion in 721.

Note that the order of books in the scriptural canon does not align with their historical occurrence. A sequential order would be Joel, Amos, and Hosea. In the Minor Prophets, themes are driving the arrangement of books, and we can expect that those themes will blend into a greater design.

Summary

So that's where we are. Joshua, Judges, and Ruth are books of *deliverance* set in the early history of Israel's conquest of the land. The initial Minor Prophets (Hosea, Joel, and Amos) deal with God's *discipline* of His people. Here the cultural settings are merely backdrops in the development of their prophetic messages.

We are now ready to look at the particular designs of individual books. The ancient writings of the Bible do not exhibit a primitive approach to literature. An unexpected sophistication in the structural design and communication techniques exhibited in these books argues for a divine involvement in the writings. In both the historic and prophetic books, the hand of God is evident — not only in the events recorded, but also in the way the story is told.

BOOKS OF CONQUEST

Joshua

Born a slave in Egypt, Joshua became the great conqueror of Canaan and the author of the book that bears his name. As the personal attendant to Moses, Joshua demonstrated leadership skills during Israel's wilderness wanderings and eventually emerged as Moses' successor. With a clear sense of order and logical sequence, he formatted his writing in two major divisions: first, all military endeavors related to *overcoming* the resistance; second, administrative details concerning the arrangement for *occupying* the land. The book divides neatly into these two halves.

BOOK OF JOSHUA

Victorious Living

OVERCOMING	OCCUPYING
chaps. 1 – 12	chaps. 13 – 24

In the *overcoming* section, Joshua describes the sequential accounts of Israel's progressive subjugation of their enemies. Beginning with their detailed preparation for battle, he discloses the secret work of the spies, the crossing of the Jordan, the renewal of their covenant with God through circumcision in Gilgal, and the celebration of Passover (chaps. 1 – 5). From the conquest of Jericho and Ai (chaps. 6 – 8) to the successful southern and northern campaigns (chaps. 9 – 12), he chronicles every move step by step like a general writing his memoirs.

Overcoming was a matter of military strategy and fighting prowess, but *occupying* (chaps. 13 – 24) demanded different skills. With diplomatic insight and divine enablement, Joshua proceeded to grant and assign portions of the land to the various tribes. This was done from two different locations: first, Gilgal (chaps. 13 – 17) and then Shiloh (chaps. 18 – 21). A controversial altar erected by the two-and-a-half tribes settled in the Transjordan area caused a measure of friction (chap. 22), but Joshua's farewell address to the elders (chap. 23) and to the people (chap. 24) solidified the divine perspective on their newly formed nation.

This simple overview of the book of Joshua demonstrates the careful design and meticulous order with which Joshua recorded the events of the conquest. Sprinkled with intriguing stories of courage and faith, along with candid admissions of failure and struggle, this book is a masterpiece of military history. When added to the Pentateuch, the roots of Israel's national existence are firmly established.

Rivaled only by the Epistle to the Ephesians in the New Testament, the book of Joshua emerges as the grand instruction in the Word of God as to what it means to walk with God by faith and to experience victory over sin and worldly opposition.

Judges

Joshua was now gone. Unlike at the death of Moses, no successor had been appointed to step in as the leader of the nation. The reason: Israel was a theocracy; God was their leader.

Tribal chieftains in conjunction with the ubiquitous Levites were expected to walk with the Lord as they governed the people. But as the old adage says: out of sight, out of mind. When God no longer had a physical presence in Israel like the pillar of fire in the wilderness, the various tribes drifted into spiritual apathy, giving their enemies advantage against them.

If we include the last judge, Samuel (probably the author of the book of Judges), this condition prevailed for about 360 years. It is not as though there was a continuous succession of judges or governors throughout this period. Rather, God raised up special leaders—judges—at various times to deliver the people from their oppressors.

An introductory explanation of conditions prevailing in the land subsequent to Joshua's death establishes the reason for Israel's cycle of failures during these early centuries (chaps. 1–2). Due to lack of commitment and obedience, the tribes failed repeatedly to drive out their enemies. This led to moral and spiritual compromise, which in turn resulted in blatant apostasy and ultimate subjugation to their Canaanite neighbors.

The main body of the book records particular cycles of deterioration, servitude, and deliverance (chaps. 3–16). Beginning with Othniel (the younger brother of Caleb) and ending with Samson, thirteen judges emerge at various times as divinely appointed saviors. In order of occurrence, we read of Othniel, Ehud, Shamgar, Deborah, Barak, Gideon, Tola, Jair, Jephthah, Ibzan, Elon, Abdon, and Samson.

The final section of the book (chaps. 17–21) clearly articulates the ultimate consequences of their willful disobedience. Both personal and tribal compromise led them into idolatry (chaps. 17–18) and immorality (chap. 19). This resulted not only in becoming prey to their enemies, but also in their beginning to turn on each other. A war with Benjamin (chap. 20), followed by men being murdered in Jabesh-gilead and women being kidnapped in Shiloh (chap. 21), concludes this tragic tale of the judges. The book ends with the statement "Everyone did what was right in his own eyes" (21:25).

The author records these cycles of enemy oppression and victorious judges in a well-crafted sequence highlighting the stories of certain judges (Othniel, Ehud, Deborah, Gideon, Jephthah, and Samson) for the purpose of teaching spiritual lessons. The book of Judges therefore is not simply a chronicling of Israel's premonarchy history. These individual lessons combine to forge a dominant theme: carnal compromise leads to failure and bondage, but spiritual obedience results in victory and freedom.

BOOK OF JUDGES		
A Mad Cycle of Failure & Victory		
DETERIORATING CONDITIONS chaps. 1 – 2	THE CYCLE OF JUDGES chaps. 3 – 16	DEVASTATING CONSEQUENCES chaps. 17 – 21

Ruth

Opening with "In the days when the judges ruled," the book of Ruth is a ray of light in a dark setting. As though to expand and emphasize the principle of walking with God by faith, the story of a Gentile woman is chosen as the example.

Israel had difficulty trusting God during the times of the judges, but Ruth puts the nation to shame. Not only is she a Moabite; she is also a woman. Not only does she trust God; she does it in dire circumstances. How humiliating for the Hebrew males that she should be the one chosen to model trusting faith.

In four short chapters, Ruth's faith blossoms and is rewarded by God through the means of a kinsman-redeemer. Boaz is Ruth's kinsman by marriage, and he is the one who redeems her from her desperate situation. Here we find a beautiful picture of Messiah redeeming His people. The book of Ruth, undoubtedly also written by Samuel, is a magnificent example of the blessings that come with trusting God.

Written as a romantic short story, the plot plays out in two parts:

BOOK OF RUTH	
Kinsman — Redeemer	
PREPARATION FOR BLESSING chaps. 1 – 2	PROVISION OF BLESSING chaps. 3 – 4

Preparation for the Blessing of God by Faith (chaps. 1 – 2)

Initial decisions are made by Naomi and Ruth after the death of their husbands to place their lives in God's care in a time of famine by returning to Bethlehem (chap. 1). As Ruth seeks God's provision among the poor in the fields of Boaz, he shows her special kindness by granting her extra measures of grain (chap. 2).

Provision of Blessing by the Kinsman-Redeemer through Faith (chaps. 3 – 4)

Learning that Boaz is a family kinsman, Ruth appeals to him to save her according to the custom of the land (chap. 3). Boaz agrees to pay the redemption price, takes Ruth to be his wife, and blesses her with a son. In the genealogy that concludes this book, we discover that Ruth has become the great-grandmother of King David (chap. 4).

Why did Boaz condescend to love and marry a Gentile woman? Perhaps he learned the principle of God's unbiased mercy and grace from his mother, Rahab—the Gentile harlot from Jericho. This ancestry is confirmed in the genealogy of Jesus (Matt. 1:5), where both Rahab and Ruth appear. We are thus assured that the principle of trusting God for blessings as we walk by faith is for all people—not just the Hebrews.

BOOKS OF THE MINOR PROPHETS

Hosea

Prophesying at a time when the ten northern tribes of Israel had declined to the point of ultimate chastisement, Hosea writes of God's persevering love in the midst of His severe discipline. The Assyrians are perched to invade and capture the Northern Kingdom, but trumping this menacing harbinger of doom are Hosea's words that God will not abandon them forever. One day God will restore them to His favor because of His unfailing love.

The impact of Hosea's prophecy is bolstered by the tragic story of his own marriage. In fact, the first three chapters describing Hosea's disappointing relationship with his wife form an illustrative introduction to the rest of the book. Hosea's wife, Gomer, went beyond adultery to engage in harlotry, which Hosea compares to Israel's spiritual harlotry against God. Hosea can understand the gut-wrenching revulsion expressed by God in the prophecy he was writing as recorded in chapters 4 – 14.

BOOK OF HOSEA

God's Unfailing Love

HOSEA'S	GOD'S
STORY	INDICTMENT
Unfaithful Love	Undeserved Love
chaps. 1 – 3	chaps. 4 – 14

An overriding theme of love permeates the book, however. Hosea is encouraged by God to restore and forgive his wife as a picture of God's persevering love for Israel. The Assyrian captivity looms as the disciplining hardship incurred by Israel's grievous sins, but God will ultimately restore and forgive them because of His infinite, pursuing love. This is the grand theme of the book of Hosea.

Joel

Writing almost a century earlier than Hosea, Joel sees a devastating locust plague covering the Southern Kingdom as a harbinger of spiritual doom. Targeting Jerusalem and Judah with his message, the prophet swings from bad news (coming judgment) to good news (future blessing for the faithful). In simplistic terms, this dual message comprises the two parts of the book.

BOOK OF JOEL

Barrenness to Fruitfulness

LOCUST PLAGUE	RESTORATION
Barrenness & Discipline	Fruitfulness & Restoration
chap. 1	chaps. 2 – 3

"The day of the LORD," an apocalyptic term for God's ultimate judgment on sinful humanity, is foundational to Joel's prophecy: "Let all the inhabitants of the land tremble; for the day of the LORD is coming; it is near" (2:1); and, "For the day of the LORD is great and very awesome; who can endure it?" (2:11).

A definite sign of celestial disturbances will herald the advent of the day of the LORD (2:30 – 31), which historically is still future to our day (see Rev. 6:12 – 17; the sixth seal judgment). So saying that it was "near" (2:1) did not necessarily mean that it was imminent. Actually Joel along with Obadiah (v. 15) were indicating that in God's reckoning of time (1,000 years = 1 day; 2 Pet. 3:8), the Day of the Lord is indeed near.

Grasping the divine perspective of time is crucial to many prophetic scenarios. The pouring out of God's Spirit (2:28) happened on the day of Pentecost a millennium later, according to Peter's sermon (Acts 2:17). And the judgment of the nations in the Valley of Jehoshaphat (Joel 3:12) will eventually take place at least two millennia after Pentecost at the second coming of Christ (Matt. 25:31–46; sheep and goats judgment). The final period of incredible blessing from God that concludes Joel's prophecy (3:18) will climax subsequent to the Day of the Lord in the Kingdom Age.

So catch the impact of Joel's prophecy. He begins by describing a destructive locust plague denuding the earth of every green thing as a grotesque fore view of what the day of the Lord's judgment will do to the earth (chap. 1). Yet, through the provision of God's Spirit, a seed of hope is sown that God will one day restore the years the locust has eaten (chap. 2). Following all of this, Joel indicates that the nations will be judged and the earth will once again be green (chap. 3).

Amos

Though living in Tekoa, south of Bethlehem, Amos prophesied in Bethel against the Northern Kingdom of Israel. The king of Israel resided in Bethel, which had become a center of idolatry, so Amos delivered his message at the core of the Northern Kingdom. He denounced Israel's indifference to spiritual things even as they enjoyed a time of cultural prosperity.

As a humble herdsman from southern Judah, he excoriated Israel for its blatant immorality. His prophecies were rejected with a warning to flee for his life and return to Judah. Just thirty years later, Hosea would prophesy to the same people informing them of their imminent peril as Assyria gathered its forces on the border.

The book of Amos consists of three parts, corresponding to the prophet's threefold communication approach. He begins with eight prophecies (or "burdens") against the surrounding nations—Damascus, Gaza, Tyre, Edom, Ammon, Moab, and Judah—forming a spiraling effect that finally zeroes in on the nation of Israel (chaps. 1–2). Then he delivers three sermons emphasizing Israel's past, present, and future sins. In each sermon he stresses the fact that their judgment is deserved (chaps. 3–6). Finally, he reveals five visions involving various metaphors of judgment: grasshoppers, fire, a plumb line, summer fruit, and God over the altar (chaps. 7–9). In the last five verses of the book, Amos adds a softening touch by recording promises from God of a future restoration of Israel to divine blessing.

BOOK OF AMOS		
Kinsman — Restorer		
8	3	5
BURDENS	SERMONS	VISIONS
chaps. 1 – 2	chaps. 3 – 6	chaps. 7 – 9

Amid all these harsh words, Amos reminds the people of Israel that the severity of their discipline was commensurate with the extent of their disobedience. They had enjoyed the blessings of being part of God's family but had seriously abused that privilege. As Amos began his three sermons of judgment therefore, he quoted God as saying,

> You only have I known
> of all the families of the earth;
> therefore I will punish you
> for all your iniquities. (3:2)

The point here is that the scope of violated privilege determined the extent of the punishment. This principle is at the core of God's disciplinary action.

PARALLEL RELATIONSHIPS

The fact that a carefully constructed design is evident within the Historical Books and the Minor Prophets encourages us to look for further parallel comparisons between the individual books.

Before we pursue this comparative thinking however, it is imperative that we reestablish the overall themes developed in the Pentateuch and Major Prophets, which are the foundations of these later Historical Books and Minor Prophets. As extensions of these books, the subsequent twelve books of history and twelve books of prophecy will most certainly expand on those themes.

The Pentateuch, you will remember, emphasized the ideas of *deliverance* and *redemption* as Israel became the people of God. The Historical Books of the conquest, monarchy, and the restoration demonstrate how God fulfilled the intent of this theme. The Major Prophets, on the other hand, stressed the concepts of *discipline* and *restriction* for those who had abused the privilege of being God's people. In similar fashion therefore, the Minor Prophets unfold these very themes in greater detail.

With this in mind we can examine more closely any parallel design that may exist between the books of the conquest and the first set of Minor Prophets. Perhaps it will help us to lay all of this out in a graphic perspective.

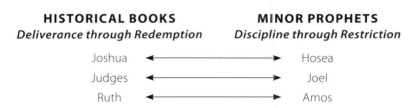

HISTORICAL BOOKS
Deliverance through Redemption

MINOR PROPHETS
Discipline through Restriction

Joshua	←——————→	Hosea
Judges	←——————→	Joel
Ruth	←——————→	Amos

Joshua and Hosea

As the first books in their respective columns, Joshua and Hosea share an initial prominence as being books of strength and unwavering pursuit of God's will.

The book of Joshua highlights the importance of consistent faith in the provisions of God for victory over the world. Here we see the victorious life of faith lived out in simple trust and complete obedience. As one of the most positive books in the Bible, its message is clearly that of the *power of faith*.

Because of the tragic story of unfaithful love as illustrated by Hosea's wife, Gomer, and the nation of Israel, the book of Hosea has often been viewed as a negative prophetic writing. That evaluation misses the mark. The powerful backstory wraps itself around the unrelenting love of God for His wayward people as reflected in the pursuing love of Hosea for his adulterous wife.

Actually, the book of Hosea is as strong on the *power of love* as the book of Joshua is on the power of faith. In the end, both are messages of victory over evil. The negative storyline in Hosea merely serves to strengthen the positive resolve of pursuing love.

Consider also that the book of Hosea is given special treatment by being placed first in this trilogy of prophets. Chronologically Hosea prophesied after Joel and Amos, yet it precedes those books in the biblical order. This seems to indicate that Hosea's message of persistent love is intended by God to lead the sequence of thoughts in this series of books.

Joshua and Hosea are indeed parallel messages balancing the importance of faith in the matter of deliverance and the necessity of love as a crucial ingredient of discipline.

Deliverance through Redemption	*Discipline through Restriction*
JOSHUA	**HOSEA**
The Power of FAITH	The Power of LOVE

Judges and Joel

Vacillating from burdensome hardship to liberating freedom, Judges and Joel exhibit a similar cycle of judgment to deliverance. In Judges we see a repeating cycle as the people fall prey to the dominating influence of pagan cultures only to be rescued by regional judges. Joel, on the other hand, describes a single cycle of locust devastation followed by divine recovery to be duplicated in the eschatological Day of the Lord.

In both of these books the message is the same. Obedience to the Word of God brings blessing; disobedience results in judgment. Whether in the days of the premonarchy (Judges) or of the kings of Judah (Joel), the divine principle of obedience for blessing and disobedience for cursing was inviolable. God was serious about the practical implementation of His law in the lives of His people. Unfortunately the people of Israel were inconsistent in this matter of obedience. Consequently they bounced between blessing and judgment, victory and failure, bondage and deliverance.

Deliverance through Redemption	*Discipline through Restriction*
JUDGES	**JOEL**
Vacillating FAITH	Inconsistent OBEDIENCE

Ruth and Amos

The explicit trust for divine blessing as exhibited by Ruth in her darkest hour forms a fitting connection between the faith of Joshua to overcome Israel's enemies and the obedient responses of the judges under difficult circumstances.

In Joshua, faith is the victory that overcomes the Canaanite world of opposition as the means of establishing Israel in the land of promise. The story of Ruth, then, broadens the application of this faith principle to include righteous Gentiles, in that Ruth was a Moabitess. Unwavering faith in the Lord was the issue for both Joshua and Ruth.

Yet a connection to the book of Judges is evident also. The events of the book of Ruth began in a famine-ravaged Bethlehem. Similar scenarios of hardship plagued Israel from time to time throughout the sequence of the judges. Ruth exemplified the faith of the judges, not the disobedience and lack of trust in the people. In this way, the book of Ruth connects the book of Joshua to the book of Judges.

Amos is like Ruth in many ways. The prophet himself came from Tekoa, just seven miles south of Bethlehem, the setting for the book of Ruth. Furthermore, Amos was a farmer like Boaz, not a professional prophet. He raised a special breed of sheep and grew pomegranate fruit in the same Judean area where Boaz had a field of barley.

Canonically Amos comes after Hosea and Joel (even as Ruth came after Joshua and Judges), but in real life he came between them. Joel's prophecy to the southern tribes can be dated around 835 BC, while Hosea wrote just prior to the Assyrian invasion of Israel in 721. Amos, on the other hand, prophesied against the same northern tribes as Hosea, about thirty-four years earlier in 755. Historically then, Amos forms a fitting connection between Hosea and Joel.

Consider yet another way in which Amos bridges these two other prophets. Joel lived and prophesied in the Southern Kingdom of Judah, where he lived. Amos lived in Judah but prophesied in the royal city of Bethel in Israel. With one foot in each kingdom, he connects the concerns of Joel in Judah with the burden of Hosea for Israel.

But these two considerations—that historically Amos comes between Hosea and Joel and geographically he identified with both Judah and Israel—do not in themselves prove that Amos is the conceptual link between the other two prophets. They do, however, position his book within the trilogy of prophets in a similar fashion to Ruth among the books of the conquest.

More to the point: the theme of Amos's writing could be described as a variation on the subject of rescue from dilemma, mirroring the plot in Ruth. Amos writes that God calls Israel His family, which explains the reason for His disciplinary action (3:2). And Amos concludes with the encouraging promise that God will one day restore His children to a place of great blessing (9:13–15). In a significant way then, God is the Kinsman-Restorer for Amos, even as Boaz was the kinsman-redeemer for Ruth. The books of Amos and Ruth do seem to have an affinity for each other as bridge books in these two trilogies.

Deliverance through Redemption	*Discipline through Restriction*
RUTH	**AMOS**
Kinsman — Redeemer	Kinsman — Restorer

PULLING IT TOGETHER

Having gone through all six books in these two initial trilogies of history and prophecy, let's put it all together to see the big picture. As we do, remember the balancing concept of truth, as reflected in the foundational books of the Pentateuch and the Major Prophets: Historical Books—*deliverance through redemption*; Prophets—*discipline through restriction*.

WALKING WITH GOD

"Blessed is the man who walks not in the counsel of the wicked" (Ps. 1:1).

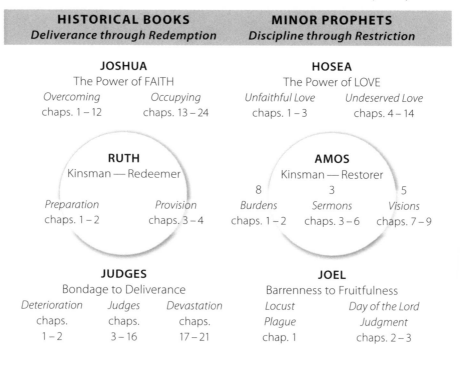

HISTORICAL BOOKS	MINOR PROPHETS
Deliverance through Redemption	*Discipline through Restriction*

JOSHUA
The Power of FAITH
Overcoming — *Occupying*
chaps. 1–12 — chaps. 13–24

HOSEA
The Power of LOVE
Unfaithful Love — *Undeserved Love*
chaps. 1–3 — chaps. 4–14

RUTH
Kinsman — Redeemer
Preparation — *Provision*
chaps. 1–2 — chaps. 3–4

AMOS
Kinsman — Restorer
8 — 3 — 5
Burdens — *Sermons* — *Visions*
chaps. 1–2 — chaps. 3–6 — chaps. 7–9

JUDGES
Bondage to Deliverance
Deterioration — *Judges* — *Devastation*
chaps. 1–2 — chaps. 3–16 — chaps. 17–21

JOEL
Barrenness to Fruitfulness
Locust Plague — *Day of the Lord Judgment*
chap. 1 — chaps. 2–3

THE BODY ANALOGY

How is all of this pictured by the concept of the legs in a walking action? As we have seen, the Historical Books and the Minor Prophets serve as the legs of God's Word, and the first three books in each column (if indeed the Historical Books set the pattern) present Israel as a mobile people with a movable worship center (the Tabernacle). The children of Israel were learning to walk with God.

The ability to walk adds the wonderful quality of mobility to the human experience. We can come and go because of the way our legs are structured. But have you ever scrutinized the walking process to understand how walking works? It's really quite interesting—with a few surprises.

The legs are composed of three major components: the thigh, the calf, and the knee joint that connects them. Let's compare the three books in the two pillars (Historical Books and Minor Prophets) to these three parts of the leg.

The Thigh

The thigh provides strength for the leg with a massive complex of muscles packed around the single large femur bone. The quads and hamstring muscles serve as powerful sources for motion to propel us along in the walking process. But it may be surprising to observe that the thigh provides only forward motion—a strong thrusting action (unless you're walking backward, of course). While walking, the thigh provides no backward motion.

Take a few steps, looking at your legs. Notice that as one thigh moves forward, it waits for the other thigh to catch up and thrust ahead before repeating the same forward action. The strength of walking is in the thighs' forward motion.

Joshua and Hosea stand out as the books of strength in these two sets of trilogies. On the historical side, Joshua kept moving forward by exhibiting the power of faith for divine deliverance. On the prophetic side, the power of love as illustrated by Hosea himself demonstrated God's unwavering love even in matters of discipline. Working side by side, Joshua and Hosea show us how to walk in strength with God through faith in His provision and steady confidence in His love.

The Calf

The calf portion of the leg is different. Although it can twist from side to side, the calf essentially performs a swing motion, allowing the foot to leave the ground and move to a new forward location. First, an initial backward motion permits the foot to elevate. Then a forward swing moves the foot ahead. First, back; then, forward. This pendulum sequence is repeated over and over in the activity of walking.

Isn't it interesting that this back-and-forth motion captures the mood of both Judges and Joel? Remember that the first movement of the calf is backward, which reflects the initial stroke of each book. Before the judges appear, Israel deteriorates to a backward state. In Joel the first motion is backward, as locusts devour the land.

Then a forward thrust occurs as the first judge appears in the book of

Judges, and as the Spirit descends in Joel. This back-and-forth swing repeats itself in Judges through deliverance from six servitudes, and in a single occurrence in Joel as the nations are destroyed in the Day of the Lord while Israel is restored to divine favor.

Even the structure of the calf, with its smaller tibia and fibula bones that allow for the twisting motion, pictures the weakened condition of the people in both Judges and Joel. We are confronted in these books with a back-and-forth, vacillating scenario in the life of a struggling nation.

The Knee

The knee joint bridges the thigh to the calf, bringing the strength of the upper leg to bear upon the swing motion of the lower extremity, with a solid cap to protect the ligaments and tendons that facilitate the smooth functioning of this very special hinge. The knee joint is an intricate mechanism serving a simple operation.

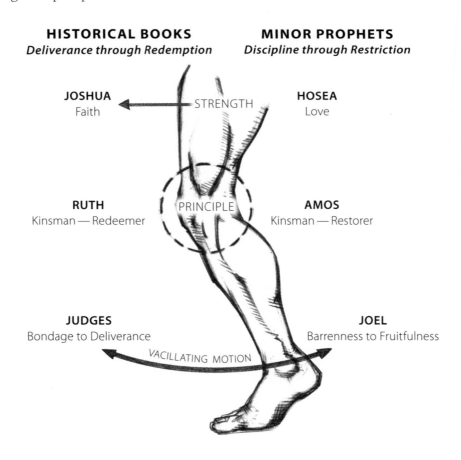

HISTORICAL BOOKS
Deliverance through Redemption

MINOR PROPHETS
Discipline through Restriction

JOSHUA
Faith

STRENGTH

HOSEA
Love

PRINCIPLE

RUTH
Kinsman — Redeemer

AMOS
Kinsman — Restorer

JUDGES
Bondage to Deliverance

JOEL
Barrenness to Fruitfulness

VACILLATING MOTION

As a connection that makes it all work, the knee beautifully illustrates the books of Ruth and Amos, which establish spiritual principles that bind the other books together. The faith principle exemplified in Ruth, of ultimate trust in the Kinsman-Redeemer, enables the walking-with-God motion manifested in deliverance in Joshua and Judges. The love of the Kinsman-Restorer for His children in Amos puts the disciplinary work of God into perspective for Hosea and Joel.

The functioning principles in the books of Ruth and Amos do seem to bridge the gap between the other books—providing a necessary hinge to the truth of walking with God.

WRAPPING IT UP

This study has given special attention to interrelational ideas, which has spawned the observations in this chapter. Most of what I have seen and read isolates these books to studies of the individual content, with little attempt to relate their themes to the books around them. I admit looking specifically for the body analogy—but, quite frankly, the parallels seem to fall in line naturally. Our study of the legs has only begun however. Historically, we now come to the three sets of double books describing the monarchy of Israel; prophetically, to the next six books of the Minor Prophets. Prepare yourself for an amazing journey into the realm of kings.

CHAPTER SIXTEEN

STANDING FOR TRUTH

1 Samuel – 2 Chronicles and Obadiah – Zephaniah

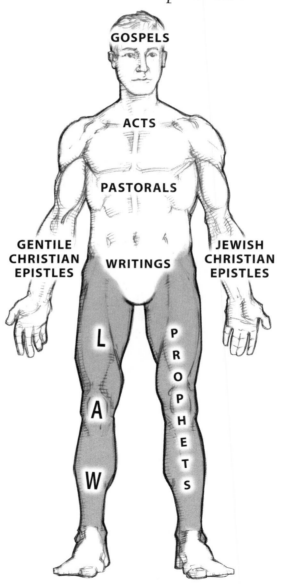

STANDING FIRM

If you don't stand for something, you'll fall for anything. My dad used to say that, and I've heard it repeated many times over the years. Standing for the truth has always been an admirable quality. Conversely, distortions of what is good and right elicit disdain among the righteous.

"Standing firm" expresses the idea of planting your physical or ideological feet in an immovable position. It brings to mind soldiers or athletes defending themselves against aggressors; or lawyers and pastors not willing to compromise. These are the people applauded by those who stand up for what is right.

God also uses the standing position to describe our relationship to the truth. When speaking of the spiritual conflict, Paul wrote, "Put on the whole armor of God, that you may be able to *stand* against the schemes of the devil ... and having done all, to *stand* firm. *Stand* therefore ..." (Eph. 6:11, 13–14, emphasis mine). As the enemy of righteousness assails the fortress of truth, God tells us to stand firm to repel the attack.

Israel also knew the importance of standing firm against the enemies of God. The psalmist specifically warned the children of Israel, "Blessed is the man / who walks not in the counsel of the wicked, / nor *stands* in the way of sinners" (Ps. 1:1, emphasis mine). That is simply the negative way of exhorting them to stand with those who honor what is good.

Having the courage to stand for truth and righteousness has always been a crucial aspect of the redeemed life. God wants His people to walk with Him, but He also wants them to stand firm against evil and error.

In the next series of Historical Books and Prophets, the standing analogy is paramount. Historically this is the period of the kings, where the mobile Tabernacle has transitioned into the permanent Temple. Having occupied the land (the books of conquest), Israel is now ready to establish its national roots as recorded in the books of the monarchy. Walking with God has led to a place of standing firm among the nations of the world as the people of God.

As for the parallel books in the Minor Prophets, these prophets all ministered during the time of the kings. Again we read of prophets to the Northern Kingdom of Israel and prophets to the Southern Kingdom of Judah, but it is their thematic content that provides the parallel concepts along with the books of history.

KINGS AND PROPHETS

If kings were mighty steeds to give power and strength to the nation, then prophets were the reins to steer them. Most of those who occupied the throne were headstrong and unruly, however, turning the prophetic reins into whips of chastisement. Instead of a stellar history, as might be expected from the chosen people of God, the era of Israel's kings exhibited the same deteriorating pattern of willful governance that led to the demise of other nations.

We read of good kings, but mostly bad kings—all in need of choleric prophets to instill the voice of God into their self-serving ways. When Israel exchanged a theocracy under the judges for a monarchy ruled by kings, they soon discovered that sinful men in the grip of power were more of a bane than a blessing.

Samuel, the last of the judges and the first of the prophets, became the anointer of Israel's first kings. Against his own inclinations, but with the permission of God, he yielded to the people's wishes by anointing Saul as their first national ruler. As the people's choice, however, Saul failed miserably. Then in a secret ceremony, Samuel anointed David as God's choice to be the future king of Israel. The period of the monarchy had begun.

Kings were never meant to replace God's theocratic rule over the nation. They were to obey God's Word and lead the people as a royal representative of the divine presence. They all struggled with this responsibility.

David and his son Solomon began well, but even they fell prey to their own fleshly inclinations, causing mayhem for the nation. In David's day we see palace intrigue with split familial loyalties. After Solomon's death, civil war divided the nation. Moments of glory were replaced by patterns of conflict and national crisis. Israel's monarchy began poorly under Saul, experienced a brief golden age with David and Solomon, and plummeted downhill from there.

A boundary divided the kingdom when the northern tribes withdrew from the nation to form their own separate entity. Twenty kings would come and go in this Northern Kingdom before God terminated it. All of these kings were evil, flaunting their personal agenda in the face of God. Conquered by the Assyrians in 721 BC, these tribes faded into the landscape of other nations.

The Davidic dynasty continued in the southern tribes of Judah and Benjamin, however, where another twenty kings would extend the rule of David. Some were good, leading the nation in the ways of God, but most were bad like their counterparts in the north. God extended the national life of this southern kingdom until 586 BC, when it too met its demise. After seventy years of captivity in Babylon, the Persians allowed the Hebrews to return to the land of Israel. But never again would there be a throne in Judah.

During the time of the northern and southern kings, God raised up prophets to call the people and kings to repentance and humble obedience. They expressed the voice of God with words of exhortation and warning. Some were prophets of action, like Elijah and Elisha; others committed their proclamations to writing. Eventually their written messages became Holy Scripture, now known as the Major and Minor Prophets.

With this brief synopsis of the kings and prophets in mind, we turn to the books that record these events. Historically the double books of Samuel, Kings, and Chronicles give us the political and cultural understanding of the times. The entire scope of Israel's monarchy streams through the books of Samuel and Kings, while the Chronicles retell that same story through the eyes of the priests.

Prophetically the six parallel Minor Prophets performed their ministries during this period and were counselors to the kings. The task before us in this study is to investigate the parallel relationship that might exist between these books of history and prophecy to see if there is a complementary pattern. Are the themes of Obadiah and Jonah parallel to 1 & 2 Samuel? Can a similar flow of ideas be found in Micah and Nahum that complement the books of Kings? And what affinity do Habakkuk and Zephaniah have with the books of Chronicles?

BOOKS OF THE MONARCHY

Following our established method, let's first examine each of these twelve books in terms of structure and message. Then we will compare their themes, looking for any natural parallels between the two columns of books. Finally, we will probe the body analogy to see if the legs in a standing position reflect how these books work together.

HISTORICAL BOOKS OF THE MONARCHY

The six books following the books of Joshua, Judges, and Ruth record the entire history of Israel's kings. Originally these were three books—Samuel, Kings, and Chronicles. When the Jewish Scriptures were translated into Greek, however, the interpreters divided this massive trilogy into two books each: 1 & 2 Samuel, 1 & 2 Kings, and 1 & 2 Chronicles.

This separation of the three larger books actually makes it easier to find and reference the wealth of material included in these national records. Whatever the reason for this human action, divine providence undoubtedly had a hand in altering the structure of these significant writings.

Books of Samuel

King Saul, Israel's first royal ruler, dies in battle at the end of 1 Samuel, which provides the natural break for the division of the two books. The reigns of Saul in 1 Samuel and of David in 2 Samuel provide a contrastive study in the spiritual dimension of the kingdom.

1 SAMUEL		
Conflict between the Flesh & the Spirit		
SAMUEL	SAUL	DAVID
chaps. 1–7	chaps. 8–15	chaps. 16–31

Three individuals rise to prominence in this first book of the monarchy. As the last judge and the first prophet, Samuel bridges the gap between provincial leaders in the time of the judges and national rulers in the monarchy. After anointing Israel's first king, Samuel gives way to the dominant presence of Saul, who rules the kingdom as a man of fleshly indulgence. Then David, anointed in his youth to be king (again by Samuel), quickly emerges as a man with divine favor to become King Saul's successor.

The second half of 1 Samuel pits the fleshly oriented Saul against the spiritually minded David. The youthful David handles the conflict in a spiritual manner, while King Saul's fleshly ways become the means of his own demise.

This struggle between the flesh and the spirit seems to be the overriding theme running through the historical development of 1 Samuel. The flesh is dominant in Saul, and the spirit struggles in David. In the end God vindicates David and abandons Saul.

2 SAMUEL

Triumph of the Spirit

DAVID'S SUCCESS	DAVID'S LAPSE	DAVID'S TRIUMPH
chaps. 1 – 10	chap. 11	chaps. 12 – 24

Second Samuel is the book of David's forty-year kingship. After tracing the ascension of David from Hebron to the throne in Jerusalem, the writer proceeds to unveil David's great sin involving adultery, which leads to overwhelming consequences for his family and the nation. The fact that God eventually restores him to his throne simply highlights the amazing mercy and grace of God.

This story of great success, a serious fall, and repentance that leads to forgiveness and restoration is the oft-repeated scenario of the triumph of the spirit. Second Samuel provides a sequel to the conflict of flesh and spirit in 1 Samuel by extending the ultimate hope of spiritual victory in this titanic struggle to those who will humble themselves before God.

Books of Kings

Talmudic tradition ascribes the books of the Kings to the prophet Jeremiah. In all, forty kings occupied the two thrones of Israel and Judah before Assyria and Babylon respectively terminated the Jewish monarchy.

As a united kingdom, Israel rose to its greatest heights of prosperity and power. The division of the nation into northern and southern factions in 931 BC was the beginning of Israel's demise. As the two kingdoms of Israel and Judah eventually fell to their enemies, Israel's monarchy ceased, never to rise again until the future kingdom of the Messiah.

1 KINGS

A Deteriorating Nation

SOLOMON'S REIGN	CIVIL WAR	DIVIDED KINGDOM
chaps. 1 – 11	chap. 12	chaps. 13 – 22

As King David lay dying, Solomon became his choice for succession to the throne. In the first three chapters of 1 Kings, Solomon is anointed and acknowledged as God's choice to replace his father. Solomon was famous for his wisdom, but as chapters 4 – 10 make clear, his wealth was just as impressive. Without question, building the Temple of God stands as his greatest achievement (chaps. 5 – 8). Just as Solomon reached the height of his regal glory, his heart succumbed to the seduction of immorality and idolatry (chap. 11). In the end, his shame was as renowned as his fame.

At the death of Solomon, ten northern tribes pulled away from the nation in a rebellious move to establish their own kingdom (chap. 12). From this point on, there existed two kingdoms and two sets of kings. Idolatry and immorality emerged as the norm for eight successive kings in the north; occasionally more godly kings appeared in Judah — specifically, Asa and Jehoshaphat (chaps. 12 – 22). Countering the evil in the north that rose to new heights under Ahab and Jezebel, the prophet Elijah thundered across the scene as God's voice of judgment (chaps. 17 – 19).

2 KINGS		
Terminated Nations		
PARALLEL KINGDOMS	ASSYRIAN	THE FINAL KINGDOM
Israel & Judah	CAPTIVITY	Judah
chaps. 1 – 16	chap. 17	chaps. 18 – 25

The Northern Kingdom endured for another 131 years (853 – 722 BC) through the successive reigns of twelve more wicked kings from Ahaziah to Hoshea (chaps. 1 – 16). The prophet Elisha repeatedly called the nation to repentance; like Elijah in 1 Kings, his ministry was rejected. Finally the Northern Kingdom fell to the Assyrians in 721 BC and ceased to exist (chap. 17).

In these same early chapters (1 – 16), eight additional kings from Jehoram to Ahaz ruled in the Southern Kingdom of Judah. Half of them ignored the God of heaven, while a few (Joash, Amaziah, Azariah [Uzziah], and Jotham) turned their hearts toward the Lord. During this period the earliest of the writing prophets, Obadiah and Joel, began to write.

Following the Assyrian captivity, God extended the life of Judah for another 136 years (722 – 586 BC). Hezekiah, a righteous man, was the next king to reign, but Manasseh and Amon who followed him were both evil (chaps. 18 – 21). Then King Josiah tried to right the nation once more by ruling according to God's Word, only to be followed by four more wicked monarchs (chaps. 22 – 24). This brought Judah to its tragic end as Babylon destroyed Jerusalem and carried the people into captivity (chap. 25).

Books of Chronicles

The books of Samuel and Kings reveal the history of Israel's monarchy from the political view of the kings with emphasis on the throne. In the fifth century BC, after the Babylonian Captivity (450 – 430 BC), God moved Ezra the priest-scribe to record the significant aspects of this period from a priestly perspective, focusing on the centrality of the Temple. The Chronicles are the resulting product.

1 CHRONICLES

A Spiritual Perspective

| GENEALOGICAL RECORD
OF GOD'S PEOPLE
chaps. 1 – 9 | BIOGRAPHICAL RECORD
OF KING DAVID
chaps. 10 – 29 |

Long genealogies are hard to read, but they serve as significant records to establish family relationship and legal rights. Beginning with Adam to the time of King David (chaps. 1 – 2), this initial portion of 1 Chronicles affirms the patriarchal lineage of God's people. The remaining genealogies cover all the tribes of Israel but give a disproportionate emphasis to the line of David and the family of Levi (chaps. 3-9). The ten northern tribes are only briefly mentioned.

Two-thirds of the book is devoted to the reign of King David (chaps. 10 – 29). First Chronicles unfolds the more positive spiritual perspective of the books of Samuel by omitting David's struggle with Saul, his seven-year reign in Hebron, his sin with Bathsheba, and Absalom's rebellion. Instead, we read of David's ascent to the throne and recovery of the ark (chaps. 10 – 17), as well as his many victories and preparation for the building of the Temple (chaps. 18 – 27). The conclusion of the book highlights David's final exhortation to the people and provision for the Temple. At the end Solomon is crowned as the next king, and David dies.

2 CHRONICLES

A Temple Perspective

| TEMPLE GLORY
UNDER SOLOMON
chaps. 1 – 9 | TEMPLE HISTORY
OF THE KINGDOM
chaps. 10 – 36 |

Beginning with the inauguration of Solomon as King of Israel (chap. 1), the spotlight quickly turns to the completion of the Temple (chaps. 2 – 9). Six of these nine chapters detail the construction and dedication of this grand center of worship. After observing the Temple and its sacrificial system, Ezra tells us that the visiting queen of Sheba was left speechless. We then read of the death of Solomon.

The remaining chapters peel back the spiritual veil of the divided kingdoms (chaps. 10 – 36). This parallel account of the book of 2 Kings deals mostly with the Southern Kingdom from a priestly and temple perspective. The apostasy of the Northern Kingdom and their separation from the temple service is dealt with in two short chapters (10 – 11). Then all twenty kings of the Southern Kingdom are reviewed with respect to their loyalty to the Lord and His Temple. Special emphasis is given to the eight good kings (chaps. 12–36).

PROPHETIC BOOKS OF THE MONARCHY

The six Minor Prophets in this study are positioned parallel to the histories of the monarchy and were written by prophets who ministered during the divided kingdom. They understood the turbulent conditions surrounding the kings and wrote courageously of significant issues plaguing the two kingdoms.

Of these six, only Jonah wrote to the ten northern tribes, having lived in the lower Galilee before going to Nineveh. The prophetic emphasis in the other five books is clearly on the Southern Kingdom of Judah, where the only remnant of righteousness could still be found.

Obadiah

OBADIAH	
The End Is Near	
DEMISE OF EDOM	DELIVERANCE OF ISRAEL
vv. 1–14	vv. 15–21

The conflict between Edom and the Israelites described by Obadiah was a continuation of the struggle between Esau and Jacob. These twins represented two distinct contrary forces in the womb of Rebekah—the spirit (Jacob) and the flesh (Esau). As the descendants of Esau, the Edomites' hatred for Israel personified the warring antagonism of the flesh against the spirit. Obadiah, thought to be the first of the writing prophets, predicted the utter destruction of Edom because of its violence against Israel (vv. 1–14).

In Obadiah's prophecy, Edom is symbolic of all the ungodly nations of the world that will meet their demise in the judgment at the Day of the Lord (vv. 15–16). Israel, on the other hand, will be delivered in that day (vv. 17–20) to joyously participate in the kingdom of the Lord (v. 21).

Jonah

JONAH	
Overcoming through Repentance	
REBELLION	OBEDIENCE
(The Flesh)	(The Spirit)
chaps. 1–2	chaps. 3–4

After running from God, Jonah wrote his story of personal repentance as a living illustration of Israel's condition and need. Also guilty of rebellion against God, Israel was desperately in need of repentance from their fleshly ways. If God could be merciful to Jonah and the vile Ninevites, He would certainly extend His mercy to Israel if they would repent.

Jonah's rebellious heart and the severe consequences of his actions are graphically described in the first half of the book. He was thrown into the sea and swallowed by a great fish (chap. 1). In the place of death (the fish's belly), Jonah cried out to the Lord and repented of his rebellious heart. He was then delivered from his bondage by the God of second chances (chap. 2).

The remaining part of the book is devoted to Jonah's successful evangelistic ministry among the people of Nineveh. Obedience by the prophet led to God's blessing on his life; he had overcome in the spirit (chap. 3). As Jonah struggled to comprehend the incredible mercy of God, the message became clear that God forgives even the worst of sinners who will repent and turn to Him (chap. 4).

Unfortunately Israel never got the point and would eventually experience God's judgment at the hands of these very Assyrians from Nineveh.

Micah

MICAH		
Discipline of Judah		
DISCIPLINE DESERVED	RESTORATION PROMISED	REPENTANCE REQUIRED
chaps. 1 – 3	chaps. 4 – 5	chaps. 6 – 7

Living just twenty-five miles southwest of Jerusalem, Micah's greatest concern was for the people of the Southern Kingdom. Declining social and moral conditions led him to chastise Judah's corrupt leaders—the evil rulers, false prophets, and self-serving priests. Although Micah begins the book by mentioning the sins of the Northern Kingdom and its capital, Samaria, he concentrates on warning Judah that they are in danger of God's discipline (chaps. 1–3).

Micah's prophecy then turns to a more positive challenge to consider the goodness of God. He delivers a message of hope concerning the coming kingdom, which will be ruled by God's anointed. Then he challenges them to live in the light of that hope (chaps. 4–5). Finally he shares two major grievances God has with the nation and pleads with the leaders to repent before it's too late (chaps. 6–7).

Nahum

NAHUM		
Destruction of Nineveh		
DECLARED	DESCRIBED	DESERVED
chap. 1	chap. 2	chap. 3

Writing about eighty years after the fall of the Northern Kingdom and more than one hundred years after the ministry of Jonah, Nahum anticipates the destruction of Nineveh by the Babylonians in 612 BC. As a prophet of Judah, his prophecy demonstrates the sovereign authority of God over the nations. The wheels of divine justice may move slowly, but they are sure. Assyria destroyed the Northern Kingdom, but then God destroyed Assyria.

The demise of Nineveh is decreed by God, who has condemned the Ninevites because of their sin (chap. 1). The prophet then gives a graphic description of the plundering of the city (chap. 2), after which he justifies the actions of God (chap. 3). There had been a brief reprieve in the days of Jonah, but Nineveh had quickly reverted to its former ways. The fact that God is holy and will punish the wicked is the nail in Nineveh's coffin.

Habakkuk

HABAKKUK		
The Life of Faith		
PUZZLED BY GOD'S WAYS	TRUST IN GOD'S WISDOM	PRAISE FOR GOD'S CARE
chap. 1	chap. 2	chap. 3

Habakkuk was a Judean prophet, a contemporary of Jeremiah in the final years of the Southern Kingdom. Reacting to the unbridled corruption in the land, Habakkuk questioned God's seeming indifference. God assured the prophet that the Babylonians would be His rod of correction upon Judah —which troubled Habakkuk even more. God seemed to be out of touch with Habakkuk's concept of justice and propriety (chap. 1).

Habakkuk went to a private place to wait for God's answer to his dilemma. God did not explain His actions but told the prophet that the just simply had to live by faith. They needed to trust in the wisdom of God (chap. 2). Habakkuk accepted God's response and concluded his prophecy with words of praise for God's providential care (chap. 3).

Zephaniah

ZEPHANIAH		
God's Final Judgment		
DISCIPLINE UPON JUDAH	DESTRUCTION OF THE NATIONS	DELIVERANCE OF THE FAITHFUL
chap. 1	chap. 2	chap. 3

Zephaniah appears to have come from the royal line of King Hezekiah. Prophesying after the evil reigns of Manassah and Amon in Judah, he predicted a time of final judgment called the Day of the Lord. Judah would be disciplined by God, but the whole earth would be affected (chap. 1).

Specific nations surrounding Israel are singled out as deserving of God's wrath in the Day of the Lord (chap. 2). After including Jerusalem in God's final discipline of Judah, Zephaniah concludes with an encouraging message of restoration for Israel. The Day of the Lord will usher in a time of great blessing for the faithful (chap. 3).

PROBING PARALLEL CONCEPTS

We are now ready to probe the possibility that parallel concepts exist between the two columns of these twelve books, similar to the schema of the books of the conquest (Joshua, Judges, Ruth and Hosea, Joel, Amos). The trilogy pattern is definitely manifest on the historical side, where the Samuels and the Kings give the entire scope of the kings, while the Chronicles dip back into the same period to consider the monarchy from another point of view.

The question before us, then, is whether the same pattern can be seen on the prophetic side. Since the Minor Prophets are not a chronological history, our investigation will concentrate on overall themes between the two sets of books.

Obadiah was actually written before any of the other Prophets, including Hosea, Joel, and Amos. Yet it is positioned fourth in the biblical collection. Although Jonah canonically comes directly after Obadiah, it is historically positioned between Joel and Hosea. Micah and Nahum appear to be in their correct place in terms of historical sequence, but Habakkuk and Zephaniah are reversed.

The main thing to note here is that the chronology of writing is not driving the biblical order of the books. Unless we are willing to accept the idea of random order, which seems incongruous with divine providential oversight, the more important criteria for each book's position must be thematic content. If this is true, a study of the themes becomes imperative for grasping the canonical order of these Minor Prophet books.

1 & 2 Samuel and Obadiah & Jonah

Following the sequence of books within the history and prophecy pillars, 1 Samuel is parallel to Obadiah, and 2 Samuel is positioned across from Jonah. Do the themes of these four books reflect similar and parallel messages?

The spiritual lesson in 1 Samuel seems to involve contrastive personalities. Early in the book Eli the priest, an indulgent man, is compared to Samuel, a person with a godly spirit. Then a major conflict develops between Saul, a man of the flesh, and David, a man of the Spirit. These lessons inherent in these flesh-versus-spirit scenarios drive the story line.

Turning to Obadiah we see the same emphasis in the fleshly excesses of Edom compared to the spiritual bent of Israel.

In both books note another similarity. In 1 Samuel God, not David, eliminates King Saul (the flesh). In Obadiah God, not Israel, terminates Edom (the flesh). As the flesh weakens, the spirit gets stronger to eventually triumph in both books.

This then is the lesson that binds these books together. It is not by natural ability and human prowess that we prosper with God, but by spiritual dependence upon the Spirit of God.

In 2 Samuel we see the journey of a spiritual man (King David) who begins with God's blessing but then falls into sin through disobedience. His humble, contrite response, however, leads to restoration with God and eventual triumph.

This same scenario confronts us in the book of Jonah. As a prophet blessed of God, he too disobeys and exhibits a rebellious attitude. Due to Jonah's humble response in the fish's belly, God restores him to his prophetic calling and helps him to overcome in the spirit.

These two pairs of historical and prophetic books certainly seem to mirror each other in the progression of conflict to triumph in the spirit over the flesh.

1 SAMUEL	Flesh vs. Spirit	**OBADIAH**
(Saul & David)		*(Edom & Israel)*
2 SAMUEL	Triumph	**JONAH**
(David)	of the Spirit	*(Jonah)*

1 & 2 Kings and Micah & Nahum

The books of the Kings provide a lesson in deteriorating patterns of spirituality as both the Northern Kingdom and Southern Kingdom spiral out of control.

In 1 Kings the united kingdom begins strong with Solomon, as the newly constructed Temple rises on Mount Moriah. But Solomon's spiritual decline at the end of his life graphically anticipates the future decline of the nation through civil war and spiritual neglect. The Southern Kingdom emerges stronger with the Davidic dynasty, the Temple, and occasional good kings —but the Northern Kingdom plunges immediately into the abyss of spiritual degradation and chaos.

Micah, the parallel prophet to 1 Kings, reflects the divine evaluation of this declining pattern. With warnings of judgment and an appeal to repentance, he mirrors the message of 1 Kings. Writing specifically to Judah, though, he includes an encouraging promise of eventual restoration.

Second Kings completes the picture of sliding decline, inevitably followed by divine judgment. First, the Northern Kingdom is conquered by the Assyrians, whose capital is Nineveh. Then Babylon invades the Southern Kingdom, taking its citizens captive. Kings are deposed, the throne is terminated, and the nation enters into servitude. The monarchy is no more.

Looking across to the prophetic column, we see that Nahum provides a similar scenario of demise with the destruction of Nineveh. The Assyrians had been Israel's nemesis, but now the searing wrath of divine justice levels their magnificent city. Nahum completes the message of 2 Kings by showing the full extent of God's judgment, not only on Israel, but also on the ungodly nations.

1 KINGS	Kingdoms	**MICAH**
A Deteriorating	in	*Discipline*
Nation	Decline	*of Israel*
2 KINGS	Kingdoms	**NAHUM**
A Terminated	in	*Destruction*
Nation	Judgment	*of Nineveh*

1 & 2 Chronicles and Habakkuk & Zephaniah

As we have seen, the Chronicles repeat the history of the monarchy by revealing another point of view of the same period. Concentrating on the reign of David in 1 Chronicles, the author crafts a spiritual analysis of David's life. As King David walked with God and lived by faith, both he and the nation were blessed.

The parallel prophetic book is Habakkuk, and he, like David, had to learn to trust God by faith in the midst of life's greatest challenges. When he wrote, "The righteous shall live by his faith" (2:4), he articulated a primary spiritual principle that would eventually be repeated three times in the New Testament. Both Habakkuk and David exemplified this principle.

The theme of 2 Chronicles shifts to the Temple and the importance of worshiping the Lord. As the heart and soul of the nation, the Temple represented a God-centered life. As kings honored the Temple, their reigns were blessed by God. This is the author's thrust.

Zephaniah is the book that corresponds to 2 Chronicles. This prophet lays out the disastrous effects of neglecting the central focus of God and the Temple. Writing toward the end of the evil reigns of Manassah and Amon, Zephaniah prepared the way for Josiah's reforms as this righteous king rediscovered the Word of God in the Temple. Zephaniah concludes his prophecy by assuring the nation that those who trust in the Lord will be delivered.

1 CHRONICLES		HABAKKUK
Life of faith	A	*Principle of faith*
	Spiritual	
2 CHRONICLES	Perspective	ZEPHANIAH
Temple worship		*Focus on the Lord*

The parallel concept between the Historical Books of the monarchy and the corresponding six Minor Prophets does seem to be a valid observation. So how do these twelve books reflect the legs in a standing position?

THE BODY ANALOGY

Israel not only had to stand courageously against their enemies, they also were responsible to stand firm for the truth of God. When the psalmist said that the blessed man does not stand in the way of sinners, he contrasted that with meditating on the Word of God day and night (Ps. 1:1–3). Knowing how to stand with God is a crucial aspect of the spiritual journey.

The books we've been studying in this chapter group together in a way that beautifully illustrates the standing function of the legs. As Israel's throne and Temple gave them a permanent position in the land, so the books that reflect this period teach us how to stand strong in the Lord.

The Thighs

The strength of standing is in the thighs, with their single femur bone and massive quadriceps and hamstring muscles. For a warrior, the upper legs are the strongest parts of the body and, when well-toned, make him an immovable force. King David in the books of Samuel epitomized this formidable warrior.

The "thigh books" in the body analogy of Scripture for the standing function are 1 & 2 Samuel in one leg and Obadiah and Jonah in the other. The powerful message in each of these pairs centers on how the spirit can have victory over the flesh. Is there anything more essential in effectively standing for the truth than a strong spirit over the indulgence of the flesh? The spirit's victory over the flesh is the key to standing strong.

The Calves

The weaker portion of the legs while standing is the lower section. Two smaller bones, the tibia and fibula encased in the less muscular calf, taper down toward the ankle giving a diminishing effect. This is exactly what happens in the books of 1 & 2 Kings. In 1 Kings the nation is divided into two kingdoms and the deteriorating condition in each kingdom causes it to taper off into captivity in 2 Kings. Micah and Nahum also exhibit a declining pattern for Judah, as well as the thorough demise of Nineveh. The lower legs are a fitting picture of this scenario.

This message reveals the core issue of spiritual standing. When the spirit divides its focus with the flesh the eventual result is a diminishing strength and effectiveness. The tibia is a larger and stronger bone than the fibula, even as Judah was spiritually superior over northern Israel. Yet they both declined and came to their end, because they both were more given to the flesh than the spirit. When we attempt to mix some interest in spiritual things (e.g., going to church) with a lot of involvement in fleshly things (e.g., indulgence in the world), the unfortunate consequence will always be a weaker spiritual condition.

The Knees

Connecting the two segments of the legs is the all-important knee joint. This structure aptly portrays the function provided by 1 & 2 Chronicles, as well as Habakkuk and Zephaniah. Serving the books of Samuel and Kings, the Chronicles provide the essential spiritual principles that governed the monarchy—walking with God by faith and a consuming focus on worship (the Temple). On the prophetic side, Habakkuk and Zephaniah serve the same function with an emphasis on faith in Habakkuk and on the Day of the Lord in Zephaniah. Like the knees, these four books function as connecting principles in the process of standing for the truth.

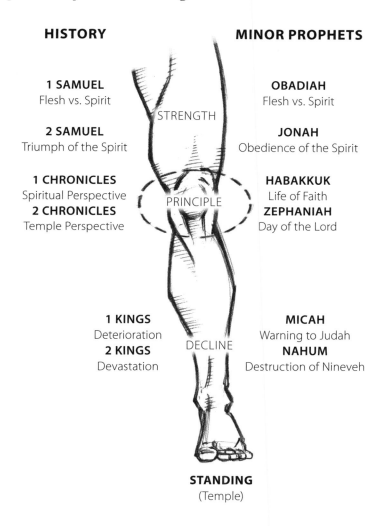

HISTORY   **MINOR PROPHETS**

1 SAMUEL   **OBADIAH**
Flesh vs. Spirit   Flesh vs. Spirit

            STRENGTH

2 SAMUEL   **JONAH**
Triumph of the Spirit   Obedience of the Spirit

1 CHRONICLES   **HABAKKUK**
Spiritual Perspective   Life of Faith
PRINCIPLE
2 CHRONICLES   **ZEPHANIAH**
Temple Perspective   Day of the Lord

1 KINGS   **MICAH**
Deterioration   Warning to Judah
        DECLINE
2 KINGS   **NAHUM**
Devastation   Destruction of Nineveh

STANDING
(Temple)

We turn now to our next study to encounter the fascinating books of *restoration* — Ezra, Nehemiah, Esther and Haggai, Zechariah, and Malachi. Here are six concluding books with a positive message on how to rest in the Lord.

CHAPTER SEVENTEEN

RESTING IN THE LORD

Ezra – Esther and Haggai – Malachi

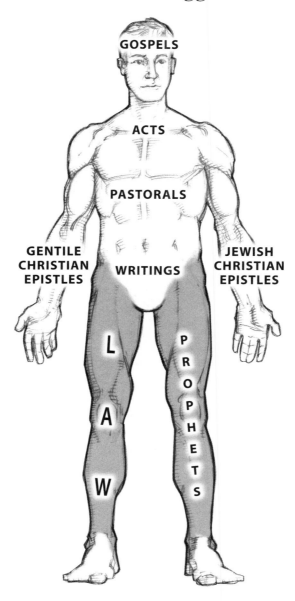

SITTING DOWN TO REST

Sitting down after a long time of being on your feet can be a refreshing experience. In sitting, we can relax and regain our strength. Kicking the shoes off and putting the feet up feels so good after a day of walking and standing.

Apparently God made knees and hips to flex and bend for this very purpose. The ability to sit is a fundamental human experience that provides a welcome change of pace for our tired bodies.

Yet sitting too long can present problems — which is why someone invented the "intermission" for long plays and concerts. An old quip concerning ponderous lectures and sermons states it well: "The mind can only absorb what the seat can endure." The ability to sit does not nullify the joy of walking and standing.

In the spiritual sense, God uses the sitting experience to picture the believer's rest in the finished work of Christ.

> But God, being rich in mercy, because of the great love with which he loved us, even when we were dead in our trespasses, made us alive together with Christ — by grace you have been saved — and raised us up with him and seated us with him in the heavenly places in Christ Jesus. (Eph. 2:4–6)

It is interesting to note that in the Tabernacle and Temple of Israel, no seats were provided for the officiating priests. They never sat down, because their work was never completed. The sacrifices had to be repeated over and over, day after day, year after year. Sitting down to rest was a foreign idea to the tabernacle and temple systems.

According to the author of the book of Hebrews, this deliberate arrangement demonstrated that only the sacrificial death of Christ could provide final atonement for sin and ultimate rest with God (10:11–12). Unlike any priest in the history of Israel, Jesus Christ sat down when He had completed the work of redemption. Salvation had been accomplished and the work was done. On the cross Jesus said, "It is finished" (John 19:30), and after His ascension, He sat down with the Father (Heb. 12:2). That is why the apostle Paul encourages us to realize that we also sit with Him.

Everything has been done by Christ to procure our eternal salvation. When we place our faith in Him to receive His salvation, we no longer have to labor for God's forgiveness and acceptance. We simply sit down with Christ and rest—forever.

Walking with the Lord and standing for truth are still important functions of the Christian life, but sitting with Christ provides the rest that continually rejuvenates the soul. These thoughts seem to capture the essence of the *restoration* books.

As we turn to the histories that record Israel's return to Jerusalem from exile in Babylon, notice the emphasis on rebuilding. After the destruction of their city and Temple and having faced the stress of displacement in captivity, the returning remnant became wholly dependent on the Lord to resurrect their national life.

As recorded in Ezra, the Temple in Jerusalem was rebuilt under Zerubbabel with the encouragement of Haggai the prophet; later with Ezra the emphasis is on spiritual renewal and a recommitment to the Word of God.

Rebuilding the walls of Jerusalem under the leadership of Nehemiah involved considerable labor for several months, but the book is clearly about trusting God to reestablish the city's security.

Finally, we see Esther, who was powerless to rescue the Jewish people from persecution in the kingdom of Persia; but here we see God's sovereign intervention spare them from annihilation. Although He elevated Esther and used this Jewish queen as an instrument of His providence, God did all the work and the Jews simply benefitted from His care.

The analogy of sitting seems to express the themes of these books. Resting in the Lord as the means of revitalizing the nation captures the substance of their collective message. However, before plunging into the instructive content of these last books, let's look at the monumental shifts in political power that form the background of these classic stories.

KINGDOMS IN TRANSITION

History can be boring if it is just names and dates. Yet the flow of the ages becomes more intriguing with the discovery that history is God's story—or His-story. The kaleidoscope of people and places throughout the course of time form the cultural and geographical backdrop for the superstory of redemption, which expresses the divine theme running through the human experience.

This becomes apparent when observing the transition of empires in the biblical lands during Israel's captivity and restoration. After serving God's purpose in the grand plan of Israel's destiny, each empire gave way to the next.

The Assyrians of Nineveh swept in first, only to succumb to the rising star of Babylon. Yet in a mere seventy years—long enough to fulfill Jeremiah's prophecy (25:11) of Israel's discipline by God—the light of national supremacy darkened in Babylon and turned to Persia. This allowed for Israel's return to Jerusalem to begin the essential projects of restoration.

The Assyrians

As the Northern Kingdom of Israel approached her final years, the Assyrian Empire reigned supreme in the Middle East. The Assyrians had a long history of ebb and flow until Tiglath-Pileser III assumed control in 745 BC, elevating the kingdom to regional prominence. This cruel usurper, along with his five successors, became the nemesis of the ten northern tribes of Israel.

In 721 BC, Sargon of Assyria conquered Samaria and scattered the northern Jews throughout the Assyrian Empire. At that point the Assyrians became an imminent threat to the Southern Kingdom of Judah until Nabopolassar of Babylon (Nebuchadnezzar's father) destroyed Nineveh in 612 BC. After about 130 years of cruel domination, the Assyrians were out and the Babylonians were in.

The Babylonians

Shortly after conquering the Assyrians, Nabopolassar died, leaving control of the Babylonian kingdom to his son Nebuchadnezzar. In 606 BC, Egypt decided to challenge the ascending power of the Babylonians and their young ruler by engaging Nebuchadnezzar in battle at Carchemish, north of Judah. The Babylonians overpowered the Egyptians, who fled south to the borders of Egypt with Nebuchadnezzar on their heels. Along the way the Babylonians easily squashed Judah, adding the Jews to their growing collection of conquered nations.

Having carried the royal family (including Daniel and his friends) into exile in Babylon, Nebuchadnezzar tried to control Judah for the next twenty years through appointed Jewish vassals. He found them unreliable and disloyal, however, so he invaded Jerusalem again, destroyed the Temple, and took additional captives back to Babylon.

For the next fifty years, the Jews were a displaced people in Babylon, until Darius the Mede, in league with Cyrus the Persian, conquered Babylon in 536 BC. The second transition of Middle-East powers, from Babylon to Medo-Persia, was complete. Babylon had fulfilled its God-ordained purpose as the rod of chastisement for the discipline of God's people, and so they were eliminated.

The Persians

In keeping with Isaiah's prophecy written two hundred years earlier (44:24–45:6), Cyrus the Persian absorbed all the kingdoms of the Middle East and established the Persian Empire. The Jews in Babylon were then under his authority. Having a policy that permitted subject peoples to return to their homelands, Cyrus gave the decree for the first of two returns of Jewish exiles from Babylon to Jerusalem. About fifty thousand Jews participated in the first wave of the restoration (536 BC) under the leadership of Zerubbabel as recorded in the book of *Ezra*.

Eighty years later, by the decree of the Persian king Artaxerxes in 456 BC, Ezra led another group of about three thousand exiles to return to Jerusalem. Between these two returns, the events of *Esther* took place in the Persian capital of Susa during the reign of Ahasuerus, whose Greek name was Xerxes (485–464 BC). Thus a great number of Jews had already returned to Jerusalem when the story of Esther occurred.

Finally, *Nehemiah* felt God's prodding to assist the returned exiles in rebuilding the walls of Jerusalem just ten years after Ezra arrived with the second wave of returnees. The same Artaxerxes commissioned Nehemiah for his task.

Thus two Persian kings (Cyrus and Artaxerxes) were used of God to reestablish the Jewish people back in the land of Judah, effectively ending the years of exile in Babylonian captivity. As the story of Esther illustrates, not all of the Jews returned; the majority had become accustomed to living in Babylon. And the new generation born during the seventy years of captivity had no recollection of living in Jerusalem. Babylon had become their home.

The three concluding Minor Prophets lived and ministered in Jerusalem as an integral part of the restoration history. *Haggai* and *Zechariah* prophesied as contemporaries shortly after Zerubbabel initiated the construction of the Temple. Haggai's message encouraged the people to finish the temple project, which lay in a partially completed state. Zechariah added a future perspective for the nation. Darius I ruled as king of Persia during this time.

A hundred years later, Malachi wrote as an eyewitness of the deplorable spiritual condition of the nation. Writing between Nehemiah's first and second visits to Jerusalem, he prophesied during the reign of Artaxerxes in Persia.

PREPARING FOR STUDY

So let's put this historical backstory of the restoration books into a visual form.

BOOKS OF THE RESTORATION

As we have seen, the Old Testament Law and Prophets divide neatly into these divisions: the conquest, the monarchy, and the restoration. The Jews had lived in exile in Babylon for seventy years before Cyrus the Persian allowed them to return to Jerusalem. That's when the Israelites began to rebuild their Temple and restore their Hebrew ways of life. Thus this segment of Israel's history is called the period of restoration.

Six biblical books record the historical events and prophetic challenges surrounding the return of the exiles to their homeland. Ezra, Nehemiah, and Esther cap the historical pillar of books to give us the history of the restoration. Haggai, Zechariah, and Malachi conclude the prophetic writings as the prophets of the restoration. With these books, the Old Testament writings come to an end.

Ezra

Doing first things first is always a good idea. Israel had lost its kingdom because it had neglected its spiritual priority. Understanding this, the first order of business for the returning remnant was to build the Temple. Putting God first was uppermost in their minds.

In the first six chapters of Ezra, Zerubbabel emerges as the leader and principal character of the story. As the great-grandson of King Jeconiah, Zerubbabel was a political figure in the royal line of King David. In other words, if Judah had not lost its throne, Zerubbabel would have been king of Judah. Ezra the priest would come and lead a movement of spiritual renewal eighty years later, but first the Temple had to be rebuilt. God put it in the heart of the king (Zerubbabel), not the priest (Ezra), to do that.

These two ideas—rebuilding the Temple (Zerubbabel) and spiritual reform (Ezra)—form the two segments of the book.

EZRA	
Rebuilding the Temple	
REBUILDING	REFORM
(Zerubbabel)	*(Ezra)*
chaps. 1–6	chaps. 7–10

At the decree of Cyrus the Persian, about fifty thousand Jewish captives returned to Jerusalem under the leadership of Zerubabbel (chaps. 1–2). Construction on the Temple began (chap. 3) but was interrupted by opposition and a growing apathy among the people (chap. 4). Even though the rebuilding project was eventually resumed, further delays continued to stall their efforts (chap. 5). Finally the rebuilding effort came to completion (chap. 6).

Zerubbabel returned to Jerusalem in 536 BC, but it wasn't until eighty years later in 456 that Ezra led a second smaller group of about three thousand (including women and children) back to their Jewish homeland. This return began with the decree of Artaxerxes (chap. 7), resulting in another group of exiles arriving in Jerusalem, where they offered a sacrifice of thanksgiving to God in the Temple (chap. 8). Soon the returnees began to intermarry with local pagans, creating a spiritual crisis for which Ezra interceded on behalf of the people before God (chap. 9). A great revival took place as the people separated themselves from their sinful relationships and made a covenant with God to follow His ways (chap. 10).

Nehemiah

Events in the book of Nehemiah follow a similar pattern to that of Ezra; the first half of each book describes the building process (the Temple in Ezra, the walls in Nehemiah), while the second half is devoted to spiritual reforms.

BOOK OF NEHEMIAH
Rebuilding the Temple

WALLS	SPIRITUAL
Rebuilt	Reform
(Nehemiah)	*(Ezra)*
chaps. 1 – 6	chaps. 7 – 13

Nehemiah arrived in Jerusalem around 445 BC, about twelve years after Ezra, so the two men were contemporaries. Although the Temple had been rebuilt, the walls of the city remained in disrepair. This troubled Nehemiah, who obtained an edict from King Artaxerxes (chaps. 1 – 2) to return to Jerusalem to organize a rebuilding project.

With God's enabling, the walls were repaired in fifty-two days (chaps. 2 – 6). Within six months of Nehemiah's receiving the commission from Artaxerxes, the people were organized and functioning as a fortified city. The first priority had been the Temple, but God was also faithful to give them their city.

Then Ezra the priest led a revival (chaps. 7 – 13), as he had done after the rebuilding of the Temple. The Word of God was restored to its rightful place of authority and adoration. Soon after (432 BC) Nehemiah returned to Persia and seven years later made a second trip to Jerusalem. Further reforms were needed as he cleansed the Temple, emphasized the importance of the Sabbath, and dealt again with the issue of foreign wives.

Esther

Not all of the Jews returned to Jerusalem from captivity. The story of Esther takes place in Persia among those remaining Jews.

Between the first return under Zerubbabel and the second return under Ezra, a sinister plot to exterminate all Jews from Persia led to the events of this book. God's providential care of His people wraps itself around this heroic tale of one Jewish family (Mordecai and Esther) standing in the gap to save thousands of their people. The Jewish Feast of Purim still celebrates this great victory.

ESTHER
God's Providential Care

ANTICIPATION	RESOLUTION
OF THE CRISIS	OF THE CONFLICT
chaps. 1 – 4	chaps. 5 – 10

The book of Esther divides neatly into two dramatic movements. First, the crisis is anticipated—as God prepares Esther, and Haman hatches his nefarious plot (chaps. 1–4). Second, the conflict is resolved by the courageous action of Esther (chaps. 5–10). Through the means of two banquets, Esther reveals Haman's wicked plans, he is hung on his own gallows, and the Jews end up prospering in the kingdom.

Haggai

Haggai was the voice of God at a crucial time in the history of the restoration. Prophesying as a contemporary of Zechariah, he was concerned that the rebuilding of the Temple had stalled. Sixteen years after Zerubbabel had laid the foundation the Temple remained unfinished due to opposition and apathy.

In four brief messages precisely dated, Haggai chastised and prodded the remnant to finish what they had started. He assured them that present and future blessings would follow the completion of the Temple.

HAGGAI			
Rebuilding the Temple			
1	2	3	4
REPROOF	GLORY	BLESSING	PROMISE
chap. 1		chap. 2	

The book lays out four messages in two chapters. First, Haggai reproves the people for not following through with the priority of the Lord's Temple (1:1–15). Second, he assures them that the glory of the rebuilt Temple will one day surpass Solomon's Temple (2:1–9). Third, God's blessing on their national and personal lives was inextricably tied to the completion of the Temple (2:10–14). Fourth, Zerubbabel is promised that God will ultimately destroy the oppressing nations and once again exalt the throne of David (2:20–23).

Zechariah

Like Ezra, Zechariah was a priest. According to tradition, he belonged to the Great Synagogue that collected and preserved the Holy Scriptures of Israel. Unlike his contemporary, Haggai, Zechariah's prophecy went far beyond concern for the Temple to embrace visions of the messianic hope.

Five months after the rebuilding of the Temple resumed at the prodding

ZECHARIAH

Realizing the Future

| RESTORATION OF THE NATION
chaps. 1–8 | RETURN OF THE KING
chaps. 9–14 |

of Haggai, Zechariah experienced a seven-part vision graphically displaying Israel's future among the nations. The overall impact of this vision assured the nation that once again God's favor rested upon them, and He would judge the nations who oppressed them (chaps. 1–6). In response to a question, Zechariah then laid out four messages concerning empty ritualism, past disobedience, restoration of the nation, and future kingdom joy (chaps. 7–8).

In the final section of Zechariah's prophecy, he turns his attention to the future in the form of two burdens. First, he laments that when their messianic King arrives they will reject Him (chaps. 9–11). He then reassures them that their King will come again, at which time they will receive Him. The book ends with a majestic view of Christ's second coming and the beginning of the Kingdom Age (chaps. 12–14).

Malachi

Not long after Nehemiah finished his work, the restored remnant once again fell into spiritual decline. In spite of the Temple and rebuilt walls, they had drifted into ritualistic formalism and blatant hypocrisy. The promises of God for a Savior seemed unfulfilled and distant, causing them to be apathetic and insincere in their worship of the Lord. As the last voice of God to the nation, Malachi stepped into this spiritual void to rebuke them for their sin and remind them that God's promises are sure.

MALACHI

Confidence in God's Promise

| SIN OF THE PRIESTS AND PEOPLE
chaps. 1–2 | SURETY OF THE PROMISE OF A SAVIOR
chaps. 3–4 |

The priority and centrality of the Temple was intended by God to keep the nation's focus on the divine presence. Responsibility for this lay with the priests who had allowed their temple service to become mere religious duty. Thus they were the biggest culprits in a national scandal. This is why Malachi begins his prophecy with a divine reprimand of the priests (1:1–2:9). Only then did the prophet chastise the people for their sinfulness, appealing for their repentance.

In the second section, the prophecy turns to the coming of the Lord to the Temple. Malachi begins (3:1) and ends (4:5) with a reference to the messengers who will prepare the way of the Lord. When Messiah comes, He will judge the wicked (3:1–15) and bless the godly (3:16–4:6). In this way, Malachi provides an incentive for the nation to repent of their sins and to renew their confidence in God's providence.

GRAPPLING WITH PARALLELS

As we come to this final set of trilogies, the question arises once more: are there parallels between these historical and prophetic books?

The arrangement of parallel books is determined by their canonical sequence. Thus we are not looking for random parallels, but for similarities between specific books — Ezra and Haggai, Nehemiah and Zechariah, and Esther and Malachi. As we have done before, let's probe these books to see if common threads do indeed exist.

Ezra and Haggai

Here the similarities are obvious. Both books emphasize the Temple as the central focus of the nation. Ezra informs us that the first concern of the returning remnant was to rebuild the Temple. Zerubbabel initiated the rebuilding effort, recorded in the book of Ezra, but it took the prophetic ministry of Haggai (fifteen years later) to get them to finish what they had started.

Haggai's pleas wrapped in four messages and Ezra's reforms in the second half of his book blend together as divine proddings for the people to take seriously the Temple and the Word of God. As the remnant began their new lives, they demonstrated that spiritual things must come first.

Nehemiah and Zechariah

The emphasis in the book of Nehemiah rests clearly on the city of Jerusalem as the place of God's blessing. Rebuilding the city walls, rather than the Temple, consumed his attention. Spiritual reform became an issue only after the walls were finished and the city was secure.

As Nehemiah spoke of restoring the city, Zechariah prophesied about restoring the nation. When Zechariah wrote his prophecy, the Persians dominated the Middle East, including Israel. Looking into the future, Zechariah reminded the Jews that God would one day deliver them from their enemies by sending the Messiah who would be their Shepherd-King. Though they would initially reject Him as their Shepherd, He would return to bless them as their King. The place of His return would be their beloved Jerusalem.

What binds Nehemiah and Zechariah together is their concern for the secular aspects of God's blessing. In these books the Temple fades into the background (as an assumed priority), while the city of Jerusalem and the future of the nation take center stage. In the book bearing his name, Nehemiah himself stands as an example of the Messiah providing leadership and security for the people. Zechariah, on the other hand, presents the fulfillment of the messianic hope as Messiah Himself descends upon Jerusalem to judge the nations and bless His people.

Esther and Malachi

The majority of Jews remained in the land of their captivity. Settled throughout Babylon and Persia, these Jews became the target of Persia's anti-Semitic purge. The story of Esther penetrates this scenario with a strong lesson on God's providential care of His people. Through courage and trust in the Lord, Esther and her uncle Mordecai are used of God to avert the pending tragedy. This book lays down the principle of *divine protection through faith in the Lord.*

Malachi is not so much about protection as provision. The sins of the priests and people had caused a spiritual crisis for the nation. Malachi first rebukes them and then assures them that the promise of God to send a messianic Savior remained true and sure. Messiah would come, and their national discipline would turn to kingdom deliverance. Here we see the principle of *relief from divine discipline through faith in the Lord.*

Like Esther, the book of Malachi has two parts. First, the problem is introduced. In Esther the sins of Persia created a crisis for the Jews and in Malachi the sins of the Jews created a crisis for the nation. The second halves of the books demonstrate God's answer to each dilemma. By providential care the crisis is overruled in Esther, and by divine promise the hope of Israel will be realized in Malachi.

Furthermore, a thematic complement can be observed between Esther and Malachi. Notice the balancing principles. God will not only protect His people as they live among the Gentiles (Esther); He will also preserve His people and provide for their ultimate destiny (Malachi). In both of these scenarios *faith is the guiding principle and hope is the grand consequence.*

HERE IS WHAT IT LOOKS LIKE

HISTORICAL BOOKS	MINOR PROPHETS
Deliverance	*Discipline*
EZRA Rebuilding the Temple	HAGGAI Pleas for the Temple
ESTHER Protection through Faith	MALACHI Provision through Faith
NEHEMIAH Security for the City	ZECHARIAH Promises for the City

These books of the restoration do seem to line up in a specific pattern. The priority of the Temple representing the spiritual dimension of the nation is clear in Ezra and Haggai. The more secular concerns for the city of Jerusalem are addressed in Nehemiah and Zechariah. Finally, the connection principle of faith for protection and provision completes God's picture of this period in Israel's history.

THINK ABOUT SITTING

Sitting is the posture of rest for the purpose of rebuilding resources. In this way the legs in a sitting position picture the Historical Books and Prophets of the restoration. Restoring and rebuilding certainly express the message of these books. Rebuilding the Temple and the city were primary functions, but restoring the nation's covenantal relationship with God as a spiritually blessed people streams through all six of the books.

To understand how these books mirror the legs as they bend to sit, observe your legs as you sit. Notice your thighs are horizontal as your posterior bears the weight of your body—with your quads and hamstrings in a state of relaxation. The lower parts of your legs hang down with relaxed calves as your feet rest on the floor. Fulfilling their function as connecting hinges between the upper and lower legs, your knees remain flexed for rest. In fact, as you sit there with your legs in this position, your whole body experiences relief. What a wonderful provision our Creator gave us—the ability for the human body to sit!

As we have done previously, let's insert the books at hand into the anatomical framework to see if this sitting function of the legs is pictured by the thematic arrangement of the books.

The Thighs

The first pair of books, assuming the position of the thighs, is Ezra and Haggai. Remember that these books center on the reconstruction of the Temple, the ultimate symbol of the spiritual dimension of the nation. As the thighs are the largest portion of the legs, so the spiritual quality of the people loomed as the most significant area of their lives.

Furthermore, the thighs are at rest in a horizontal position, and resting in Christ is the essence of worship. As the remnant went through the process of restoring and rebuilding their resources, their first commitment was to worship God and trust in His provision.

Notice that again in the sitting position the thighs top the rest of the legs and are therefore primary and foremost. Ezra and Haggai, first in order for their respective restoration groupings, demonstrate that their emphasis on the Temple and worship is primary and foremost. The thighs in a sitting posture do graphically picture the books of Ezra and Haggai.

The Calves

The next two books, Nehemiah and Zechariah, occupy the calf position of the legs. In these books we read of the physical concerns of the Israelites for their city, their land, and their nation. These blessings hang on a vital connection to God. It's as though the spiritual dimension is a strong horizontal beam as pictured in the thigh, while the physical dimension is a dangling cable attached to the beam as represented by the calf. A spiritual connection to God is primary, and physical blessing flows down from that spiritual union. Coming second in the biblical order of restoration books, Nehemiah and Zechariah appear to be dedicated to communicating this truth.

Here is one of the great principles of life with God: recognize the primary place of God in your worship and trust, and He will provide for your mundane needs.

Psalm 37:4: Delight yourself in the LORD, and he will give you the desires of your heart.

Matthew 6:33: But seek first the kingdom of God and his righteousness,
and all these things will be added to you.

We often want God to bless us with comfortable living, satisfactory relationships, and physical possessions without a strong commitment to His purpose
and righteousness. Though He may bless us in spite of ourselves, the normal
pattern is for us to build the temple of God in our hearts first—and then He
will enable us to build walls of security and to receive blessing from heaven.

How do we do that? The answer is simple: live by faith and trust God
with your life.

The Knees

Again the knees form the connection between the thighs and the calves.
Esther and Malachi form this connection as books of principle. Esther faced
adversity with courageous faith. Malachi exhorted the people of Israel to put
away their sin and live righteous lives in anticipation of the Messiah.

SUMMARY

So there it is—the restoration books as a mirror image of the legs in the bent
posture of sitting. Ezra and Haggai function as the thighs. Nehemiah and
Zechariah fulfill the role of the calves. And Esther and Malachi are beautifully illustrated by the knees. (See figure on next page.)

THAT'S NOT ALL

Having analyzed the restoration books, we have now completed our thematic
survey of the entire Bible. My purpose has been to demonstrate that God has
crafted His Word in a way that every book and segment of Scripture functions in a coordinated harmony similar to the design of the human body. The
Word of God is both written (the Bible) and living (Jesus Christ)—and these
two special revelations of God are truly mirror images of each other.

But that's not all. The books of the Bible are woven together by systems
that tie all the parts into a single whole in similar fashion to the systems that
unify the entire human body from head to toe.

The sixty-six books of the Bible not only bind together in collective units,
where each book plays a vital role within each of the units (Gospels, Pastorals, Writings, Pentateuch, etc.), as we have seen; the units themselves are
seamed together. Exquisitely crafted by the master Designer, the Bible is not
just a random volume of writings collected over the centuries.

HISTORICAL BOOKS
Deliverance

MINOR PROPHETS
Discipline

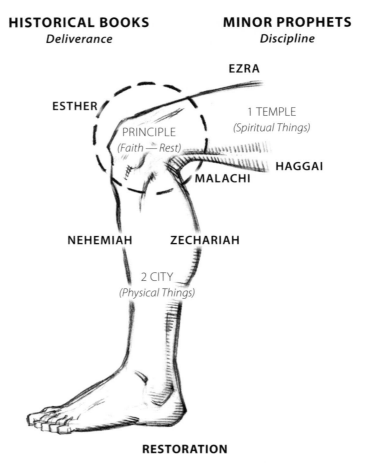

RESTORATION

"They who wait for the Lord shall renew their strength." (Isaiah 40:31)

So let's consider these systems as we conclude our study of the biblical mosaic of the body. The Bible has two *fundamental systems* and three *functional systems*, just like the human body of our Lord. In my opinion, these systems add a convincing climax to the body analogy of Scripture.

PART 4

UNIFYING SYSTEMS

CHAPTER EIGHTEEN

FUNDAMENTAL SYSTEMS

Skin and Bones

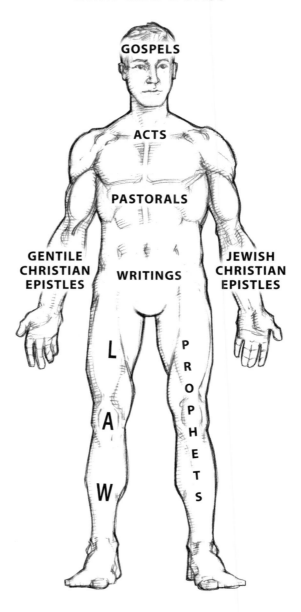

GOSPELS

ACTS

PASTORALS

GENTILE CHRISTIAN EPISTLES   WRITINGS   JEWISH CHRISTIAN EPISTLES

LAW

PROPHETS

A FUNCTIONING UNIT

The Bible is more than a random collection of books. Rather than an anthology of disconnected pieces, the sixty-six books of the Bible present a unified plan of God for the human race that is a carefully crafted product.

From Genesis to Revelation, the Bible claims to be a divine communication to mankind. God's words flow through all the books in a steady stream of developing ideas, with each book adding to the collective whole. Everything is tied together and intricately woven into an exquisite masterpiece of divine revelation.

The human body is like that too (including the body of Jesus Christ). Instead of a pile of independent parts, every segment functions in coordinated harmony with the rest of the body. Unifying systems permeate the human anatomy so that every single aspect of the body makes a meaningful contribution to the whole. Like a well-conceived state-of-the-art machine, the body exhibits a flawless design that can accomplish complicated functions controlled by an amazing computer (the brain). The body is one phenomenal unit, not a jerry-built collection of organs and limbs.

Both the Bible and the body have unifying systems, and our study of the body design of Scripture would be incomplete without a brief consideration of these systemic functions. In fact, the mirror-image correspondence between the systems of the body and of the Bible add another dimension of credibility to the overall impact of this study.

TWO FUNDAMENTAL SYSTEMS

Although many auxiliary systems add to the complexity of the body (e.g., endocrine, digestive, reproductive), five systems stand out as comprehensive to the body's existence (epidermal, skeletal, muscular, circulatory, and nervous). These systems, covering the body from head to toe, provide basic support for the auxiliary systems and make it possible for the body to exist and function.

Two of these systems are fundamental to the structure and identity of the human form. First, the *skeletal system* ensures that the body is more than a useless blob on the floor. Everything within the body depends on the bones to give it a proper place within the complicated mix of organs and appendages. Second, the *epidermal system* of skin (or flesh), which covers the body, wraps all the parts into a single unit. The body is a complete package because it is covered with skin.

The skeletal system (bones) and the epidermal system (skin) are the *fundamental* systems. The other comprehensive systems (muscular, circulatory, and nervous) are contained within the skin and bone structure and therefore will be referred to as *functional* systems. We will observe the importance of these three systems in the next chapter.

Can you imagine what life would be like without skin and bones? Lying helpless in a heap of "stuff," we would not be able to go anywhere or do anything except throb and pulsate as a living mass of parts. That's pretty gross, but it does illustrate how essential skin and bones are to the human body. In fact, the Bible sometimes refers to the human condition in terms of these two fundamental systems.

Genesis 2:23: Then the man said,

> "This at last is *bone* of my *bones*
> and *flesh* of my *flesh*;
> she shall be called Woman,
> because she was taken out of Man." (emphasis mine)

Luke 24:39: [Jesus said,] "See my hands and my feet, that it is I myself. Touch me, and see. For a spirit does not have *flesh* and *bones* as you see that I have." (emphasis mine)

When life is reduced to its minimal existence in a prolonged illness or anorexic state, we often say someone is "nothing but skin and bones." That is the fundamental condition of the human form; apart from these systems we would cease to exist. Skin and bones—the fundamental systems.

FOLLOW THE CLUES

So how do skin and bones factor into the biblical mosaic of books? Is there a scriptural symbolism here to guide us in our analysis? Where do we look for clues?

The Pageantry of Passover

The last of the ten plagues used by God to extract the Jewish people from Egypt was the death of every firstborn son. Firstborn fathers, brothers, and sons died that night in homes throughout Egypt, even in the palace.

As the grim death angel passed through the land, however, Jewish dwellings with the blood of a lamb smeared on the lintel and doorposts were passed over. Jewish firstborn sons lived to see another day. Since that time, Jews all over the world have celebrated the Passover.

One of the peculiar features of the Passover concerned the manner in which the Passover meal was to be eaten in each home. Moses chronicled God's instructions: "It shall be eaten in one house; you shall not take any of the flesh outside the house, and you shall not break any of its bones" (Exod. 12:46).

Moses then established the Passover celebration for future generations with the same instructions.

> In the second month on the fourteenth day at twilight they shall keep it. They shall eat it with unleavened bread and bitter herbs. They shall leave none of it until the morning, nor break any of its bones; according to all the statute for the Passover they shall keep it. (Num. 9:11–12)

Notice the reference in Exodus to the flesh and the bones. Special care was to be taken in guarding the procedure for these two elements. The flesh of the lamb had to be eaten in its entirety with nothing left in the morning (Num. 9:12). In this way the flesh of the lamb became part of those consuming it. It identified with their humanity.

The bones followed a different pattern. Normally bones are discarded as irrelevant after a meal. But in the Passover, God wanted special attention given to the bones. As noted above, in the original event and in later celebrations, no bones could be broken. This seems to be a strange request, but God does nothing without purpose and significance.

The unbroken bones are clearly symbolic of something that had special meaning to God. If the flesh of the lamb became identified with the Israelites' humanity, what do the unbroken bones signify? Our first clue has given rise to an interesting question.

Anticipating Fulfillment

The New Testament is clear in associating the Jewish Passover with the death of Jesus Christ hundreds of years later. As the Passover bespoke redemption from bondage in Egypt by the shed blood of the sacrificial lamb, so the shedding of Christ's blood on the cross accomplished redemption from sin for those who put their faith in Him. In the Christian gospel, the Passover is a recognized symbolic type of the cross of Christ. "For Christ, our Passover lamb, has been sacrificed. Let us therefore celebrate the festival, not with the old leaven, the leaven of malice and evil, but with the unleavened bread of sincerity and truth" (1 Cor. 5:7–8).

This helps explain the connection in Psalm 34:19–20 between a poignant allusion to the Passover lamb and the righteous One whom the Lord will deliver from affliction.

> Many are the afflictions of the righteous,
>> but the LORD delivers him out of them all.
> He keeps all his bones;
>> not one of them is broken.

The fact that this psalm is said to be fulfilled in the crucifixion experience of Christ (John 19:36) makes the unbroken bones of the Passover lamb symbolically significant.

Here is our second clue. Bones that are unbroken in Psalm 34 have something to do with a righteous character of life. But only God is perfectly righteous (without sin) – which was certainly true of Jesus Christ. Therefore it seems that the solid nature of unbroken bones is a picture of the unbroken character of God. As the consumed flesh was associated with humanity, so the unbroken bones seem to be symbolic of deity.

Let's test this observation by comparing it with John's description of Christ's crucifixion.

The Drama of Redemption

The Jewish day begins at sundown. So when Jesus and His disciples met in the Upper Room, Passover had just begun. They ate the evening Passover meal and then went to the Garden of Gethsemane where Jesus was arrested. Six mock trials ensued throughout the night; by nine o'clock in the morning Jesus was already on the cross. Six hours later Jesus died, and by sundown He had been laid in the grave. The Lamb of God (John 1:29) had shed His blood for the remission of sins on the very day the Jews were celebrating Passover.

This connection of the death of Christ with Passover shows the prophetic intent and symbolism of the Passover feast. The lamb of Passover foreshadowed the true Lamb of God, whose perfect blood would provide final deliverance. That is why Jesus' flesh and bones were noted in the crucifixion account.

Jesus' flesh was cut and pierced by the whip, the nails, and the thorns. His humanity was torn apart in the same manner as the Passover lamb. In fact, Jesus told His disciples that the broken bread of the Passover meal was a symbol of His body, which they were to eat in the same way the Jews ate the flesh of the Passover lamb. "Now as they were eating, Jesus took bread, and after blessing it broke it and gave it to the disciples, and said, 'Take, eat; this is my body'" (Matt. 26:26).

The apostle John (an eyewitness of the event) noted this about the crucifixion:

> So the soldiers came and broke the legs of the first, and of the other who had been crucified with him. But when they came to Jesus and saw that he was already dead, they did not break his legs ... For these things took place that the Scripture might be fulfilled: "Not one of his bones will be broken." (John 19:32–33, 36)

There is no doubt that not breaking the bones of Jesus was significant. But why? What was there about the bones that made them so important? Remember that the emphasis on righteousness in Psalm 34 provided a clue that the bones were associated with a likeness to God. John is the only gospel writer who tells us that they did not break Jesus' bones and, as we have seen, his gospel is dedicated to the theme that Jesus is God.

"But these are written so that you may believe that Jesus is the Christ, the Son of God" (John 20:31). For John, the unbroken bones of Jesus became another piece of evidence that Jesus is truly God.

The fact that Jesus Christ is both human and divine does seem to be reflected in the flesh and bones symbolisms. His flesh represented His humanity, which could be broken, and the bones at the core of His being pictured His deity, which could not be broken. Here is the mystery of flesh and bones as highlighted in the Passover and fulfilled by Christ in the crucifixion.

Connection to the Body Analogy

Now the question arises: Is there any likeness of the flesh and bones symbolism of Jesus' body in the body analogy of Scripture? In other words, are there flesh and bones systems encompassing the entire Bible?

To begin answering these questions, notice what Jesus said to the Jews who threatened Him because He claimed to be God.

Jesus answered them, "Is it not written in your Law, 'I said, you are gods'? If he called them gods to whom the word of God came—and Scripture cannot be broken—do you say of him whom the Father consecrated and sent into the world, 'You are blaspheming,' because I said, 'I am the Son of God'"? (John 10:34–36)

Jesus answered His critics by quoting Psalm 82:6, where God called the judges of Israel gods (with a small g) because they spoke for God among the people. This was an indisputable fact because Scripture is absolutely reliable; it cannot be broken. So here's the point: the Jews should have had no problem with Jesus calling Himself the Son of God, because the Scriptures are indelibly clear that the judges were called gods.

Our purpose at present is not to probe this interaction of Jesus with the Jews and the impact of this argument, but only to observe that "Scripture cannot be broken." The reason of course is that the Bible was not written only by men, but also by God—who cannot be broken.

This is our next clue. The divine nature of the Written Word is spoken of in similar terms to the bones of Christ, the Living Word. At the core of each there exists a divine nature that cannot be broken.

MIRROR IMAGE

The theological term *hypostatic union* represents the foundational perspective of who Christ is, as a person. The word *hypostatic* comes from a Greek word that literally means "to stand under"; it refers to the basic essence of something. Thus hypostatic union captures the idea that the core essence of Jesus Christ is a union of two natures: the human and the divine.

The realization that Jesus Christ is both perfect humanity and undiminished deity has remained a fundamental belief of the Christian church from the very beginning. He is truly a hypostatic union. But what we also need to understand is that the Bible is also both human and divine. It too is a hypostatic union.

Consider a comparison of the following two verses, which explain how the Bible and Jesus Christ each came to us from God.

The Bible: For no prophecy was ever produced by the will of man, but men spoke from God as they were carried along by the Holy Spirit. (2 Pet. 1:21)

Jesus Christ: And the angel answered her, "The Holy Spirit will come

upon you, and the power of the Most High will overshadow you; therefore the child to be born will be called holy — the Son of God." (Luke
1:35)

Notice the similarities. The acting agent in both was the Holy Spirit, who
is divine. He impregnated Mary, and He inspired the Scriptures. The instrument He used in each case was human: Mary gave birth to Jesus, and men
wrote the Bible. In both situations, the product was divine and human. The
Holy Spirit and Mary produced the God-man Person; the Holy Spirit and
men produced the God-man Book.

	Luke 1:35	**2 Peter 1:21**
Agent	Holy Spirit/divine	Holy Spirit/divine
Instrument	Mary/human	men/human
Product	God-man Person	God-man Book

Human and divine components combined to produce the Living Word
(Christ) and the Written Word (Scripture). In previous pages we saw how
flesh and bones symbolized these two essential aspects of Jesus' nature. As
visible flesh (or skin) covered His entire frame, so His humanity was the
visible manifestation of who He was. Jesus' bones, on the other hand, were
inward and invisible, representing the fact that He was also God. The Jews
had a hard time seeing His deity, corresponding to the fact that they could
not see His bones. Skin and bones were the foundational systems of Jesus,
symbolizing His two foundational natures — human and divine.

This symbolism is also mirrored in the Bible as the Body of Truth. The
Bible first of all is totally human. Each book was written by a human person
and reflects the unique vocabulary and writing style of that person. In a
sense, the Bible is covered with skin from Genesis to Revelation. The human
element is obvious from beginning to end.

The divine quality of Scripture is not so obvious. Yet abundant evidence
argues that the biblical text is inspired of God in its entirety. This is what the
apostle Paul was saying when he wrote, "All scripture is given by inspiration
of God ..." (2 Tim. 3:16 KJV). The Bible is not only pervasively human; it is
also intrinsically divine.

In a real sense the Bible also has a comprehensive skeletal system, a symbol of deity. At the core of every book of the Bible, we find the solid bone of
divine presence giving support and structure to the entire collection of biblical revelation. This is what Jesus said "cannot be broken."

The body of Scripture is a mirror image of Jesus in that it is also fully human and fully divine. Using the symbolic imagery, they both have epidermal (skin) and skeletal (bones) systems.

CRUCIAL CONTRASTS

The hypostatic unions—a human and divine nature—of Jesus Christ and the Bible is unique in the world. To be totally human and also fully God is something only hinted at with the fictional character Superman.

This union of God and man is so unusual because the two natures are so remarkably different from each other. Although the human and the divine have certain things in common because man was made in the image of God (Gen. 1:27), there are characteristics of each that defy the other. These radical differences are pictured in the contrast between skin and bones. Let's consider two of these contrasts.

Visible versus Unseen

Skin provides the outward manifestation of a person's identity and is visible to other people. Skin, with its identifying features, helps us to differentiate one person from another; each person is unique.

Jesus' flesh made Him an identifiable person. The Bible is like that too. More than forty different human authors contributed to the writing of Scripture, and each exhibits distinguishable characteristics. Biblical scholars analyze and critique the various books of the Bible by scrutinizing the authors' circumstance of life, occupational background, writing style, and vocabulary. This is the visible aspect of Scripture that adds to the intrigue of Bible study.

Bones are altogether different. Anytime we can see our bones, we've got a problem. We know the bones are there, but the skin hides them. Yet evidence of bone structure is obvious. A protruding chin, high cheek bones, tall versus short, knobby knees—all are indicators of the presence of bone. We believe in bones by faith, but not without compelling evidence.

The divinity of Jesus was that way, and so is the divine nature of the Bible. As skin covers the bones, so Jesus' humanity veiled His deity—and human authorship of the Bible obscures the view of its divine nature. The skin and bone symbolism helps us grasp this tension between the human and the divine with both Jesus and the Bible.

The Jews had trouble believing in Jesus' deity because they couldn't see it. Critics deny the divine inspiration of Scripture because the divine presence is not obvious to them. But all that is like denying the existence of bones because they are not outwardly visible.

Pliable versus Rigid

Take a piece of skin and a piece of bone and try to manipulate them. The skin will bend and twist; the bone won't. In terms of their basic nature, skin is pliable and bone is rigid. Could any two elements be more different? Yet both are necessary to the body's function and each complements the other. What is true of skin and bone is analogous to the difference between the human and divine natures of Jesus and the Bible.

The humanity of Jesus bent and flexed to meet the needs of life. Physically He walked, slept, ate, talked, and used His hands to minister to people. He was pliable emotionally as well. He felt compassion for the woman caught in adultery, and He wept at the tomb of Lazarus. Jesus was no extraterrestrial. His humanity reflected the same qualities as ours. Dr. Luke the physician examined Jesus and wrote a gospel to demonstrate that Jesus was a true man. He possessed genuine humanity.

The deity of Jesus was not so flexible. Truth and righteousness were non-negotiable. Though He had compassion on people in need, His righteous anger drove the money changers and animal sellers out of the Temple. Jesus was not about to tolerate evil men making God's house of prayer into a den of thieves. Even when He was tempted by Satan, though His flesh was severely tested, His deity was rigid and unmovable. His deity gave Him unbreakable strength.

The Bible reflects the same qualities of a pliable outer nature and a rigid inward nature. Outwardly every man used of God to write Scripture was humanly frail. Moses disobeyed God and thus was not permitted to enter the Promised Land. King David committed adultery and murder, and Peter denied the Lord three times. The human element of Scripture is certainly suspect and potentially fallible.

Yet the divine presence in the process, as well as in the final product, strengthened any human weaknesses. Pliable faults in the writers were not allowed to transfer into the inspired text. God superintended the process of writing so that the product was exactly what He wanted to say. Like bones at the center of the body keeping the skin from collapsing, the divine nature at the core of Scripture upholds the pliable human contribution. That is why Jesus could say, "Scripture cannot be broken" (John 10:35).

The pliable consistency of flesh and the rigid quality of bones seem to be an apt picture of the pliable humanity and rigid deity of both Jesus Christ and the Bible.

SEEING IT AT A GLANCE

As the body has two fundamental systems holding the frame together (skin and bone), the Bible as two components that correspond to those systems (the human and the divine). Perhaps it will help to see these systems in graphic form.

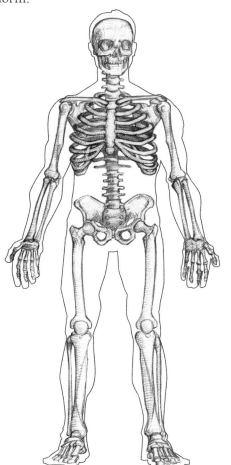

UNIFYING SYSTEMS
Fundamental Systems
Skin & Bone

SKIN
Outward Surface
Man
(Humanity)
Visible & Pliable
Broken

Holy men spoke (2 Pet. 1:21)

BONE
Inward Core
God
(Deity)
Unseen & Rigid
Unbroken

Holy Spirit moved (2 Pet. 1:21)

THERE'S MORE

Skin and bones are the two *fundamental systems* that tie the body together as a unit. But other systems also aid in this process. The muscular system, the circulatory system, and the nervous system all serve as *functional systems* to provide unity for the body. This leads us to our final study on how these functional systems picture three biblical systems that unify the Scriptures.

CHAPTER NINETEEN

FUNCTIONAL SYSTEMS

Muscular, Circulatory, Nervous

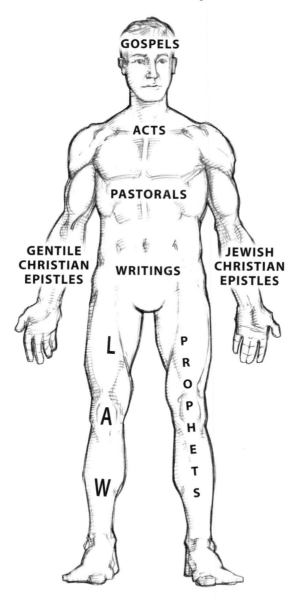

OBSERVING SYSTEMS

We readily understand the need for functional systems in our contemporary society. A house may set on a solid foundation and be perfectly framed with a beautiful cosmetic finish, but if it doesn't have an electrical system, a plumbing system, and some sort of AC/heating system, living conditions will resemble those of a pioneer in a log cabin. Every time we flip a switch, adjust a thermostat, or turn on a faucet, we acknowledge our dependence upon functional systems to give us the conveniences we enjoy.

Twenty-first-century cars operate with computerized electrical systems that synchronize the engine and spread power from the headlights to the taillights. Computers work with systemic functions that allow software programs to do their magic. Life as we know it depends on the pervasive influence of systems.

When God created the human body, He programmed it with holistic systems that service all the functioning parts. As mentioned in the previous chapter, some systems are specialized (e.g., digestive, reproductive, endocrine). Yet three basic systems provide the essential features that support the entire body: the muscular, circulatory, and nervous systems. These are what I have called the *functional systems*.

The Bible has functioning systems that parallel these major systems of the body and service the entire biblical record from Genesis to Revelation. Here is another confirmation that the body design of Scripture is more than a coincidence.

THE MUSCULAR SYSTEM

Imagine the human body without muscles. It would simply be a stationary masterpiece of skin draped over bone. Muscles not only provide motion for every activity, they also flesh out the anatomy, giving form to the body.

More than 640 muscles acting in bilateral pairs enable the body to work, wink, write—accomplish every conceivable function of life. From the head to the feet and toes, muscles blanket the entire human frame. Muscles turn energy into motion so that the body can do all that it does.

Two Basic Kinds of Muscles

Not all muscles are the same, because unique muscular abilities are required for different bodily functions, some consciously controlled and others more automatic. In God's design of the human body, He fashioned two basic types of muscles, differentiating between one's conscious effort to move and unconscious support of life. The muscles of the heart are an exception, featuring a very specialized third kind of cardiac muscle. Other than that one anomaly, all muscular functions fall within one of the two basic types.

Striated or voluntary muscles are attached to the skeletal frame (and sometimes called skeletal muscles). Every conscious act is performed by these voluntary muscles. When a decision is made to reach out the arm, circle the fingers around a cup and raise it to the lips, every motion in that process results from the action of voluntary muscles activated by a voluntary decision.

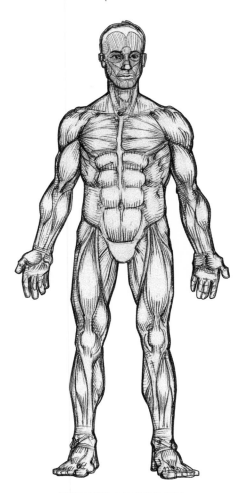

MUSCULAR SYSTEM

The second type of muscle is called smooth or involuntary. Smooth muscles act independently of the thought process and keep the central core of who we are operational. The viscera of our abdominal area (stomach, urinary bladder, intestinal track, etc.) constitute most of the smooth muscle system, but other areas also feature smooth muscles (e.g., esophagus, uterus, blood vessels). How fortunate we are that these organs or vessels continue to function without our having to think about it.

So here is another evidence of God's creative genius. The muscular system enables the body to engage in motion that preserves and interacts with life. This is accomplished in two ways—with voluntary (striated) muscles and with involuntary (smooth) muscles. The entire body from head to toe is served by these muscles.

Observing the Muscles of Scripture

As we turn to the body analogy of the Bible, we ask: is there any aspect of Scripture that mirrors the muscular system? What element of biblical revelation spans all sixty-six books and provides the ability to live and move in the spiritual realm? The answer stares us in the face when we consider the covenants that God made with mankind.

God's Covenants with Man

That the sovereign, almighty God of the universe would enter into binding agreements with finite human beings is one of the wonders of the world. But that is exactly what the Bible says God did. He entered into covenantal relationships with men.

A covenant is a contractual agreement between two or more parties that provides for certain benefits in lieu of particular responsibilities. According to the Bible, God made numerous covenants with a variety of people. These contracts were the muscle of spiritual life with God and became the source of divine blessing (or cursing) for the human race. In this way the covenants of God fleshed out human life.

The impact of divine covenants reaches into every area of recorded Scripture, just as muscles serve the entire human body. Spiritual prosperity and strength with God was energized by these covenantal relationships. Similar to muscles, covenants turned divine energy into human motion. A variety of divine covenants grace the biblical text from the Theological Covenants of creation in Genesis (Covenant of Redemption, Covenant of Works, and Covenant of Grace) to the New Covenant blessings of eternal life as pictured in the New Testament.

In addition to the three Theological Covenants associated with creation, six covenants emerge as Biblical Covenants because the word *covenant* is used to describe them. God made a covenant of life with Noah after the Flood (Noahic Covenant) and a covenant of law with Moses after the Exodus (Mosaic Covenant). But the most far reaching covenant of all was with Abraham (Abrahamic Covenant) because of its three extensive provisions that spawned three additional covenants.

The Abrahamic Covenant is repeated four times in Genesis (12:1–3;

13:14–17; 15:1–7; 17:1–8), indicating the importance God attached to this unilateral agreement with Abraham. As it is first expressed in Genesis 12, three promises were made to Abraham; these involved extensive ramifications—promises for a land and a nation, plus an assurance that the whole world would be blessed by his seed. Later each of these stipulations was ratified by three additional covenants: *Land* (the Land Covenant; Deut. 30:3–10), *Nation* (the Davidic Covenant; 2 Sam. 7:10–16), and *Blessings* (the New Covenant; Jer. 31:31–40).

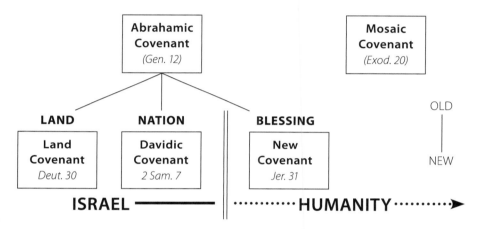

The land and nation aspects of the Abrahamic Covenant will find their ultimate fulfillment through Israel in the Kingdom Age, while the New Covenant blessings embrace all that Christ has done for the redemption of mankind. According to Hebrews 8, the New Covenant replaces the Mosaic Covenant (the Law; referred to as the Old Covenant) as the basis of eternal life.

As you can see, the covenants are the ubiquitous muscles of Scripture fleshing out God's active involvement in the affairs of mankind.

Two Types of Covenants

As we have seen, muscles of the human body exist in two basic types: striated (or voluntary) and smooth (or involuntary). As a point of interest, biblical covenants come in the same variety of types: voluntary and involuntary. Again, we are confronted by an amazing similarity in the body analogy of Scripture.

The fundamental contrast between covenants in the Bible can be seen in a comparison of the Mosaic Covenant with the New Covenant. In the Mosaic Covenant of law, God essentially said, "If you obey My commandments, you will be blessed; but if you disobey, you will be cursed." This covenant governs the moral actions of humanity in a conditional arrangement—that is, based upon the condition of compliance. It is a voluntary covenant. A person can voluntarily choose to obey or disobey.

The New Covenant, on the other hand, is unconditional. God said to Abraham, "I will" (Gen. 12:3), indicating His sovereign disposition to bless all the families of the earth through Abraham's seed. Jeremiah, when expressing God's thoughts in this regard, wrote, "I will make a new covenant" (Jer. 31:31). God was promising to provide eternal blessing without any complicity on man's part. This was accomplished when Jesus Christ (of the seed of Abraham) died on the cross for the sins of humanity (Matt. 26:27–28).

Participation in the blessings of the New Covenant is conditioned on a voluntary response to receive Christ as Savior, but the covenant itself is unconditional.

At the core of biblical truth, the smooth muscle of the New Covenant provides life for mankind. At the periphery of man's activity in the world and throughout Scripture, the striated muscle of the Mosaic Law sets the tone for success and failure. The two types of muscle are reflected in the two types of covenants. The muscular system does seem to have an analogous relationship to the biblical covenants of God with man.

THE CIRCULATORY SYSTEM

Blood flows through the veins to give life to the body. This is what the Bible means when it says, "The life of the flesh is in the blood" (Lev. 17:11). When considering the essence of life, God said that the blood is an essential ingredient.

Wherever the body is cut, it bleeds. Whether it be an abrasion on the scalp, a laceration of the arm, or a stubbed toe—blood will ooze forth as a result of the injury. The whole body pulsates with life-giving blood and every area of the body is dependent on an adequate supply.

Operating as a closed system, the heart and blood vessels service all the organs and limbs of the body. At the core of the system, the heart pumps the blood in a circulating flow, with arteries carrying the crimson fluid to every nook and cranny and veins returning the flow back to the heart. This is the cardiovascular aspect of the circulatory system.

Parallel to the veins, the lymphatic system adds another dimension. Lymph fluid is derived from blood and distributes immune cells called lymphocytes, which protect the body from foreign intruders like viruses and bacteria. Unlike the cardiovascular system, the lymphatic system is not closed and has no central pump. Together these two systems form the circulatory system.

Three Basic Functions

Under normal circumstances, one drop of blood has 5 million red blood cells (RBCs), ten thousand white blood cells (WBCs), and 250 thousand platelets. RBCs carry oxygen and nutrients to the cells through the arteries, arterioles (small arteries), and capillaries (minute arteries) like little UPS trucks. Then they return, picking up carbon dioxide and waste from the cells through the capillaries (minute veins), venules (small veins), and veins, like garbage trucks. It's an amazing process of delivery and cleanup. WBCs attack and destroy germs to help fight infection, while platelets help stop any bleeding.

In this way the circulatory system provides nourishment, cleansing, and protection for the body.

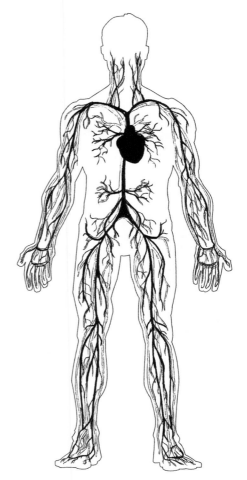

THE CIRCULATORY SYSTEM

Nourishment: Arterial pathways deliver life-sustaining elements to each and every cell of the body by means of the red blood cells.

Cleansing: These same RBCs cleanse the cells of detrimental waste by carrying the garbage to sites of elimination through the veins.

Protection: White blood cells in conjunction with lymphocytes police the system to eliminate intruders, while platelets clog the breaches to prevent serious leakage.

The circulatory system is the conduit for blood and lymph as they circulate throughout the body. Blood is indeed the life of the flesh.

Redemption by Blood

Critics of the Christian faith will sometimes characterize Christianity as a bloody religion, and to an extent they are right. As with the body, so with the Bible: wherever it is cut, it bleeds. The story of redemption from Genesis to Revelation pulsates with the blood of sacrificial substitutes dying in the place of sinful humanity. The last sacrifice — the one to whom all the others pointed — was Jesus Christ as He shed His blood for the remission of sins.

The Bible opens with the account of Adam and Eve's sin in the Garden of Eden. In that seminal story of sin, God covered the nakedness of the man and the woman with the skin of animals — implying the shedding of the animals' blood (Gen. 3:20). Their son Abel brought an offering to God out of his flock (Gen. 4:4), and the first thing Noah did after exiting the Ark was to sacrifice animals to God on an altar (Gen. 8:20). Israel had an elaborate sacrificial system where animal blood atoned for their sins (Leviticus 1–7), and for centuries the blood flowed at the brazen altar of the Tabernacle and Temple. The Old Testament is filled with references to sacrificial blood.

In the Gospels the Jewish priests were still practicing animal sacrifices in the Temple, which is why the selling of animals in the courtyard was a lucrative business (John 2:13–17). Finally, Jesus Christ, the Son of God, was sacrificed in a bloody spectacle of scourging and crucifixion for the ultimate atonement of the sins of mankind. The rest of the New Testament is a reflection on the atoning blood of the cross.

The four living creatures and twenty-four elders of the Revelation sing a new song extolling the blood of Christ (5:9). Thus, to the very end of the biblical record, atoning blood is the resounding theme. The Bible does have its own circulatory system of blood flow — a mirror image of the body.

THE BIBLICAL CIRCULATORY SYSTEM

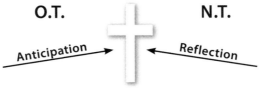

Redemption by Blood

Parallel Basic Functions

Like blood in the body, the biblical emphasis on the blood of Christ —

anticipated by animal sacrifices in the Old Testament and reflected on as the core of New Testament theology—has a threefold benefit. The blood of Jesus nourishes, cleanses, and protects.

Nourishment

Following the feeding of five thousand people by the miraculous multiplication of a little boy's lunch, Jesus taught that He was actually the bread of life (John 6). Speaking metaphorically (6:63), Jesus said, "Truly, truly, I say to you, unless you eat the flesh of the Son of Man and drink his blood, you have no life in you ... Whoever feeds on my flesh and drinks my blood abides in me, and I in him" (6:53, 56). Jesus was obviously not talking about cannibalism but about a figurative imbibing of His life. To receive Christ as Savior and to meditate upon Him as Lord of life is to eat His flesh and drink His blood. This is how a believer is nourished spiritually.

Cleansing

The purpose of blood sacrifice throughout the Bible, including the shed blood of Christ on the cross, is specifically said to be for the purification of life (i.e., the forgiveness of sin). "Indeed, under the law almost everything is purified with blood, and without the shedding of blood there is no forgiveness of sins" (Heb. 9:22).

Protection

In the Passover scenario, the death angel passed over the places where the sacrificial blood of the lamb had been placed on the door of the home (Exod. 12:7, 13). As Christ is the ultimate fulfillment of the Passover lamb (1 Cor. 5:7), so faith in His blood protects against eternal death and satanic aggression.

> Now the salvation and the power and the kingdom of our God and the authority of his Christ have come, for the accuser of our brothers has been thrown down ... And they have conquered him by the blood of the Lamb and by the word of their testimony. (Rev. 12:10–11)

The atoning blood of Jesus Christ, so poignantly pictured by Old Testament typology and so wonderfully exalted in New Testament fulfillment, accomplishes the same functions as the blood of the body. Like red blood cells, the blood of Christ both nourishes and cleanses the believer. Operating in the same fashion as white blood cells and lymphocytes, the blood of Christ protects the believer from eternal death. The circulatory system of the body and the Bible are indeed mirror images of each other.

THE NERVOUS SYSTEM

The right hand needs to know what the left hand is doing. This is a common way of expressing the body's need for effective communication. Coordinating all the bodily functions in any activity of life presents an enormous administrative challenge. To accomplish this complicated task, God has endowed the human body with an intricate system of communication called the nervous system.

Sitting on top of the human frame in its cranial capsule, the brain acts as the command center for all conscious and unconscious activities of the body. One hundred billion neurons in the brain energize to fulfill this herculean responsibility. Message impulses are carried to and from the body through the spinal cord where thirty-one pairs of spinal nerves gather and dispense the information. The brain and spinal column form the body's central nervous system.

Millions of nerve cells throughout the body form the network of communication spreading out from the central nervous system into the body. Called the peripheral nervous system, these neurons pass messages back and forth from every aspect of the body to the central nervous system for processing by the brain. The speed of transmission between the peripheral nervous system and central nervous system is so fast that it seems instantaneous. From head to toe the body is an amazing integrated system of communication.

Sensory Feedback

All five of the physical senses (sight, smell, taste, hearing, and touch) are plugged into the peripheral nervous system enabling the body to interact with its environment. Without these senses the human experience would be null and void. Failure of the senses to function in any area subjects the body to serious handicap. The connection of the senses to the brain through the nervous system provides the blessings of life.

Internal organs are also energized by the nervous system. From the beating of the heart to the digestive processes of the stomach and intestinal tract, neurons buzz with appropriate attention to every minute detail of bodily need. Usually all of this is taken for granted in the course of life, but the precise and accurate functioning of the nervous system is essential to who we are.

The Bible's Nervous System

If the body's nervous system specializes in communication, what is it that links the Bible together as God's revelation of divine truth? The answer is obvious: the Holy Spirit's inspiration of the entire biblical text. In the previous chapter we considered the fact that God is at the core of the Bible just as bones are central to the human body. Here the divine element of Scripture is expanded to include every word and thought of the Bible as an intricate network of communication from God to man. The Bible does indeed have a complete nervous system that operates in close conjunction with the skull and backbone of the skeletal system.

The Holy Spirit Himself is like the central nervous system. Emanating from an intimate association with Christ in the Gospels as the biblical Head, the Holy Spirit descended like a divine spinal cord to influence every human author. Inspirational tentacles, like the body's peripheral nervous system, spread out into the verbal expressions of each biblical book so that every word is from God. As Scrip-

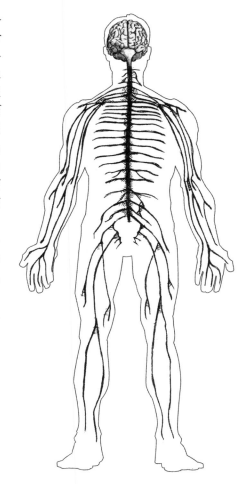

THE NERVOUS SYSTEM

ture declares, "holy men of God spoke as they were moved by the Holy Spirit" (2 Pet. 1:21 New Scofield). Therefore "all scripture is given by inspiration of God" (2 Tim. 3:16 KJV).

The apostle Paul gives an insightful look into the process of inspiration in 1 Corinthians 2:9–16. Speaking of the amazing things God has prepared for those who love Him (v. 9), he continues, "These things God has revealed to us through the Spirit" (v. 10). The reason for this, he says, is that only the Holy Spirit can reveal what God is thinking—"no one comprehends the thoughts of God except the Spirit of God" (v. 11). The words he is writing therefore are the words of God because they are inspired by the Spirit of God. "And we impart this in words not taught by human wisdom but taught by the Spirit, interpreting spiritual truths to those who are spiritual" (v. 13).

The product of the Holy Spirit's inspiration of the Bible is said by Paul to be the very mind of Christ: "we have the mind of Christ" (v. 16). In other words, the Bible is a revelation of divine thoughts flowing out of Christ's mind, which were transmitted to human authors by the Holy Spirit.

What a beautiful expression of the Bible's nervous system. The mind of Christ is the Bible's brain from which the Holy Spirit descends like a spinal cord into the body of Scripture. Together they form the Bible's central nervous system. Then the Holy Spirit sends inspirational pulses to the writers of each book in the same manner as the body's peripheral nervous system. All of this ties the Bible together as a single unit or body of truth.

The Bible's Sensory Feedback

The Holy Spirit not only inspired the text of Scripture, He also illuminates the inspired truth to the mind of the reader. In the verses we just considered, Paul adds this thought: "The natural person does not accept the things of the Spirit of God, for they are folly to him, and he is not able to understand them because they are spiritually discerned" (1 Cor. 2:14).

Jesus accused the religious elite of His day of being spiritually insensitive because they had eyes that couldn't see and ears that couldn't hear (Matt. 13:13–17). They had no sensory response to spiritual truth because there was no connection to the Holy Spirit's enlightenment. On the other hand, for the discerning person who is in touch with the Spirit, the Bible is like a CT-scan of the human soul. "For the word of God is living and active, sharper than any two-edged sword, piercing to the division of soul and of spirit, of joints and of marrow, and discerning the thoughts and intentions of the heart" (Heb. 4:12).

The Bible is a living body of truth that is intricately wired for intimate communication with God. Every word of Scripture pulsates with spiritual energy that touches the inner thoughts of the reader to elicit a response of faith. In this way spiritual impulses flow back and forth from the mind of Christ to the heart of the reader. The Bible is living and active because of the Holy Spirit, who acts as a spiritual nervous system to energize the text.

INTEGRATED SYSTEMS

Whether it be the *fundamental systems* of skin and bone, or the *functional systems* of muscle, circulation, and nerves, everything works together in harmonious fashion to produce a human person. The body may be filled with complicated networks, but it functions as a single unit.

The Bible is like that, too. The biblical systems integrate in exactly the same way as the bodily systems. A mirror image comparison between the body and the Bible extends to the very detailed interworking of the major systems.

Source and Function

Think about what we have observed. At the core of the human anatomy, bone provides the rigid structure that stabilizes the body, and skin is on the periphery to wrap the entire complex into a unified whole. In the same manner, God occupies the central place of rigid strength in the Scriptures, while the human element is the visible outer shell of the biblical text. Skin and bones seem to adequately represent the human and divine aspects of the Bible.

When we consider the other functional systems, each one depends on bone as the source of its effectiveness, and each one serves the flesh as the object of its function. This is also true of the functional systems of the Bible. God is always the source of vital effectiveness, and everything exists for the purpose of serving mankind.

First — Muscles and Covenants

For voluntary muscles to work, they must be anchored to bone. The original attachment of a muscle will be on one bone, and the insertion attachment of that same muscle will extend to another bone. As the muscle contracts and relaxes, the opposing bones will move. This gives the body both form and movement.

The Mosaic Covenant of moral law is the voluntary covenant of the Bible, and it is anchored in God while reaching out to govern the life of mankind. Obedience to God's moral laws, even for the Christian believer, provides form and movement for life in terms of divine blessings.

Smooth (or involuntary) muscles, on the other hand, are the muscles of the inner workings of the body. They too are dependent on bone to give them adequate room to operate; without a sternum, rib cage, backbone, and pelvic structure they would be unprotected and squashed together. Yet these organs and channels of bodily function exist between bone and skin as the essence of life.

Involuntary covenants — especially the New Covenant as an extension of the Abrahamic Covenant — are the essence of spiritual life and are dependent on God for their viability. These covenants benefit man, but man is not active in their operation.

So as muscles are dependent on bone to serve the flesh, the biblical covenants are dependent on God's provision as they serve the welfare of mankind.

Second — Blood and Redemption

Blood cells need to be replenished regularly. Where do blood cells come from? Bone marrow provides the manufacturing site for blood cells. The source of blood is bone, but the function of blood is to serve the flesh.

Biblically speaking, redemption by the blood of Christ originated with God. God is the one who conceived the plan of salvation, and the second member of the Godhead — the Son — came to shed His blood for the remission of sins. Mankind is the beneficiary of this act of redemption as individuals receive God's salvation by faith in Christ.

Again, as the source of blood is bone, so the source of redemption is God. In the same manner as blood serves the flesh, mankind is served by redemption.

Third — Nerves and Inspiration

The central nervous system of the human body is totally encased in bone. The brain fills the cranial cavity of the skull, and the spinal cord descends into the body surrounded by boney vertebrae in the backbone. Only then do the nerves reach forth their labyrinth maze of tentacles into the body to serve the flesh.

The mind of Christ is the Bible's brain. The Holy Spirit who descended like a spinal cord into each book of the Bible to inspire the writers is a member of the triune Godhead. God is clearly the source of inspiration. Then the Spirit of God controlled the pens of the human authors as the ink of divine truth poured forth into every word of Scripture for the benefit of humanity.

Here too, as with the body's nervous system, the source is God (bone) and the function is to serve mankind (flesh).

The Triune Godhead

Notice how every member of the Godhead participated in this process:

        The Father: Author of the covenants

        The Son: shed His blood for sinners

        The Holy Spirit: inspired the biblical text

UNIFYING SYSTEMS

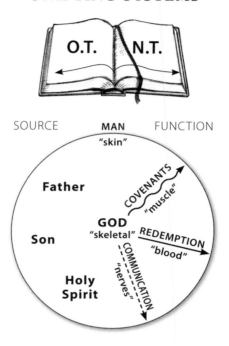

The body's holistic systems are paralleled by the systems that hold the Bible together. After considering all of the comparisons between the books of the Bible and body parts, it is somewhat climactic to observe the same mirror image in the systems that tie both the body and the Bible together.

The mosaic picture is complete. What binds all the books of the Bible together as a unit is a series of integrated systems similar to what existed in the body of Jesus Christ.

FINAL THOUGHTS

Well, that's it. I'm tempted to become assertive here and pronounce the body mosaic schema of the formation of Scripture a proven fact as a result of this study. But that would be foolish. *Crafted by God* is still a study in progress, and many of the areas touched upon in this book are in need of further analysis. In fact, I am hopeful that what I have written in this book will become an incentive for additional research.

In the final analysis, the *Written Word* of inspiration as a mirror image of the *Living Word* of incarnation is not a novel idea. Theologically it makes sense. I have simply pushed the edges of the theological envelope to see what it would look like if we pressed the analogy. Some of what I have suggested may seem questionable, but too many pieces fall into place to abandon the search.

As I have wrapped up the study with the integrated systems, my personal response is to worship the Creator for giving us *two words* of special revelation —the *Bible* and the *Son*. My personal conviction is that the form of each is indeed the mirror image of the other. Your response may be more hesitant or suspicious; but that's okay. The important thing for all of us as believers is to read the Bible and walk with Christ as the joy of our lives.

May God richly bless you as you continue to ponder the connection between the Written Word (the Bible) and the Living Word (Jesus Christ) —and to answer the question, why did God put the Bible together the way He did?

APPENDICES

EVERYTHING IS IN ORDER
OLD TESTAMENT

ORDER IS SIGNIFICANT

In important things, order is essential. The cosmos expresses order, which means that the movement of stars and planets is predictable. Living things —plants and animals—exhibit order in both their nature and behavior. In fact, the universe is so orderly that even secular scientists are forced to admit the concept of intelligent design. Everything fits, and random chance seems no longer to be a plausible option.

Humans also have a propensity for order, because we are created in the image of the Intelligent Designer. Every game and sport has boundaries, rules, and a goal. Whether medicine or music, athletics or engineering, space science, or archaeology—order is built into the fabric of our experience. Mankind is addicted to order and becomes irrational without it.

I begin in this way because the order of the books in the Bible is a formidable part of this study. Genesis is first and Revelation is last, with every book in between falling into its proper place. Order is significant. If the books of the Bible are where they are by random chance, this study is meaningless. But if they have been placed into a sequence by design, we can proceed with confidence.

I am often asked if I think that the order of biblical books is inspired by God. My quick answer is no! We tend to reserve the word *inspired* for the text of Scripture, and I have no desire to confuse the issue. On the other hand, I am personally convinced that the books of the Bible are providentially arranged. *Providence*, you see, is a better word than the word *inspired* to describe the order of biblical books.

In the final analysis, strong argument can be made that everything about the development of the Word of God was under the close supervision of the Spirit of God. As the divine Author, He was also the managing editor. The concepts of verbal inspiration (the very words) and plenary inspiration (the whole thing) suggest that everything about the Bible is exactly as God intended it should be. The apostle Paul summarized this observation by saying, "All Scripture is breathed out by God." (2 Tim. 3:16).

Then the Holy Spirit incubated the entire process so that it came together book by book in the precise manner that God intended. As He brooded over the waters in the days of creation (Gen. 1:2), and as He overshadowed Mary in the development of the divine fetus (Luke 1:35), so it would seem that the Holy Spirit also hovered over the progressive process that gave birth to the Written Word among men. Conceived in perfection, the Bible is a glorious tribute to the providential care of the Spirit of God.

Think of the alternative. God decided to write a book, but supposedly He didn't care how it went together. After inspiring each book, He exposed their collection and arrangement to random chance. Some of the books He liked were lost due to neglect; other books He had no interest in somehow got included in the finished product. Then the order in which they were arranged was left to sinful men, who undoubtedly got some of it wrong. So now God sits in heaven frustrated with the result and scratching His head in bewildering wonder. Is that what happened?

Not on your life! As I wrote this book, I cared very much about what came first and what followed. I am presenting a novel concept in biblical overview, and no one is going to be very impressed if I throw it together in random order. Sequence is everything and order is essential.

Is God any less concerned about His Book?

Everything about the Written Word of God is under the divine scrutiny of the Holy Spirit—including the order in which the books appear. The alternative is unthinkable. The Bible is God's Book. And, as with His meticulous oversight of the orderly development of the Living Word (Jesus Christ), intelligent design can be seen everywhere in the orderly arrangement of the Bible. Don't think for a moment that, although Scripture is inspired, the order of books is by random chance. Such a notion is unworthy of the biblical God and the working of divine providence.

Let's talk about order for a moment. Originally the Old Testament had a different order than our contemporary Bibles. So what's the deal with that?

THE SEQUENCE BEGINS

A woman strolled through a flower garden with the owner of an estate, admiring the spectacle around her and basking in the exotic scents. As they walked along together, the owner reached down, picked one of the flowers, and placed it affectionately in her hand. She held the exquisite flower to her nose and inhaled the fragrance. *Wonderful!* Examining again the flower's beauty, she expressed her thanks to the man as they continued their walk.

Soon the man added another blossom to complement the first. Then another. He continued to choose specific colors and various shapes to enhance the bouquet—the bundle growing in her hand until, in the judgment of the owner, the collection was complete. The look of delight and appreciation on the woman's face brought great satisfaction to him, for he knew that the bouquet had captured her heart.

This analogy is used by Rene Pache to demonstrate the process of gradual development in the collection of Holy Scripture.[1] Moses wrote the first books, after which God told him to put them in the safest place possible—in the ark of the covenant in the Tabernacle at the heart of Israel's camp (Deut. 31:24–26). As each "flower" of revelation was placed in the hand of God's beloved, its beauty and exquisite design immediately captured the nation's heart. The bouquet had begun.

Prophets then rose up to write the history of the monarchy (Samuel, see 1 Sam. 10:25; as well as Nathan and Gad, see 1 Chron. 29:29). Kings added their reflections on divine truth and their passionate thoughts toward God (David and Solomon), and then came more prophets. Finally complete in the days of Ezra and the restoration prophets, the bouquet of Old Testament Scripture adorned God's people, the nation of Israel (Rom. 3:2).

Initially the books of Moses stood apart as foundational, and they enjoyed an elite status in the collection. Later books were judged to be complementary to the books of the Law and were divided into Former Prophets and Latter Prophets, according to the time of their writing. This twofold division apparently emerged as the first attempt at organizing the books. Even when a threefold division appeared, the two-part organization still retained a historically significant status. We see this in Christ's famous statement: "Do not think that I have come to abolish *the Law or the Prophets*; I have not come to abolish them but to fulfill them" (Matt. 5:17, emphasis mine).

The organizing efforts continued. Several hundred years after Ezra and the Great Assembly organized and cataloged the collection of divine books into the Law and the Prophets, priests and scribes of the Hebrew tradition reasoned that a third category within the corpus of Scripture seemed justified. So they arranged the existing books to create a section called the Writings, which comprised three sections: poetry, the five rolls, and histories.

Merrill F. Unger, an eminent Hebrew scholar, succinctly explains the reasons for this reorganization to include a third division:

> The Writings ... are mixed in character, and are thus grouped because the writers had the prophetic gift, but *not* the prophetic office (e.g. David, Solomon, Daniel and Ezra). Among the poetical books, Psalms, standing first, probably gave the popular name, "The Psalms" (Luke 24:44), to the whole division ...
>
> The Rolls ... were grouped by themselves, and were so named because they were written each on a separate scroll to facilitate reading at the Hebrew feasts. The Song was read at Passover, Ruth was read at Pentecost, Ecclesiastes at Tabernacles, Esther at Purim and Lamentations on the Anniversary of the Destruction of Jerusalem.
>
> The third section of the third division is unclassified as to subject matter, but it is mostly historical. Daniel is partly history and partly prophecy. Ezra-Nehemiah is history. Chronicles ... is so named as though it supplemented the history recounted in Samuel and Kings.[2]

He notes that the classification and order of books depended on the status of the writer—not content or genre or historical continuity. The Pentateuch of Moses formed the foundation of the Hebrew collection, and always came first. The Prophets of the second division had both the prophetic gift and the prophetic office and were divided according to the time of their writing into a Former and Latter category. Finally, the third division included the books written by men who had the prophetic gift but not the prophetic office.

Although the standard Hebrew text and our modern English versions contain the same Old Testament books, the way they are counted is sometimes confusing. Today we count thirty-nine Old Testament books, but the Hebrew number was twenty-four. The Jews put the dual books of Samuel, Kings, and Chronicles together as one book each, as well as Ezra-Nehemiah. Then the twelve Minor Prophets were lumped together as one. In that way there are fifteen fewer books in the Hebrew Bible than in our Old Testament, but the actual collection of books has never changed since the days of Ezra in the fifth century BC.

Another interesting variation comes from Josephus, the renowned historian priest and Pharisee of the latter half of the first century AD. He indicated that there were twenty-two books in the Hebrew Scriptures, rather than twenty-four, because he connected Ruth to Judges and Lamentations to Jeremiah as single books. Some think that the twenty-two book arrangement was meant to correspond to the twenty-two letters of the Hebrew alphabet. Again, no matter how they were counted or arranged, the corpus has always remained the same.

So the original Hebrew order, in spite of an occasional variation, began with Genesis and ended with 2 Chronicles. For the Orthodox Jewish community, that's the way it has always been and continues to this day.

HEBREW DIVISION OF THE OLD TESTAMENT
Jewish Tradition: *24 Books 3 Divisions*

THE LAW	PROPHETS	WRITINGS
(5 Books)	(8 Books)	(11 Books)
Genesis	*Former*	*Poetical*
Exodus	Joshua, Judges	Psalms
Leviticus	Samuel, Kings	Proverbs, Job
Numbers		
Deuteronomy	*Latter-Major*	*Five Rolls*
	Isaiah, Jeremiah	Song, Ruth
	Ezekiel	Lamentations
		Ecclesiastes, Esther
	Latter-Minor	
	The Twelve	*Historical*
	(one book)	Daniel
		Ezra-Nehemiah
		Chronicles

CHANGING THE HEBREW ORDER

The Jews never arranged the books of the Old Testament in a strict, chronological order. Moses did write first, of course, but from then on the Prophets and the Writings sorted out independent of any historical sequence. Remember, the status of the author influenced the ordering process, not the historical setting of the books. Otherwise Job might have been the first book in the Bible.

Shortly after the development of the threefold classification, Ptolemy II (the Greek king of Egypt) requested a copy of the Hebrew Scriptures to be translated into the Greek language. In addition to wanting it for his famous library, Ptolemy had declared the city of Alexandria to be a safe haven for Jews, and he wanted the huge population of Jewish people living there to be reading their Scriptures in Greek rather than Hebrew. Furthermore, since the entire world spoke Greek in the late third century BC, with Jewish populations sprinkled all over Alexander's empire, it just made sense to translate the sacred books of the Jews into Greek.

Hebrew scholars of the Alexandrian tradition began the translation process and produced what became known as the Septuagint. Skilled in both Hebrew and Greek, these Jewish translators also brought a Greek sense of order to the collection. In spite of the strong traditional Hebrew order, these men felt constrained to rearrange the books into a combination of literary genre and chronological sequence. They are the ones who put the Old Testament into the order we have today.

So in approximately 200 BC, this is what they did: First they separated all of the double books into separate entities—Samuel, Kings, Chronicles, and Ezra-Nehemiah. Instead of four books, now there were eight. Then "the Twelve" was dissembled into twelve books rather than just one. The result of these separations was fifteen additional books, bringing the total to thirty-nine instead of the original twenty-four.

Next historical sequence emerged as a more effective way to tell the story of God's dealing with mankind; the historical books were arranged into a chronological order. The Chronicles were placed after the books of Samuel and the Kings, since they reviewed the same history, and Ezra, Nehemiah, and Esther concluded the historical section. Ruth also found itself nestled into its historical setting immediately after the book of Judges. Consequently the Books of the Law took on a historical perspective so that people could grasp a continuity of thought from creation to the time of the restoration when Israel was once again settled into the land of promise after the Babylonian captivity.

Recognizing a legitimate prophetic genre, the Septuagint translators retained the basic twofold distinction between *the Law* with its many ramifications on the history of Israel and *the Prophets* as the voice of God to the people. They then took the prophetic books and arranged them in a similar pattern to the books of history. Isaiah, Jeremiah, and Ezekiel were already in historical order, but two others were added to that sequence. Lamentations was inserted after Jeremiah, since he was the author of both books, and Daniel slid in at the end as a contemporary of Ezekiel. Instead of keeping Daniel as a third-category book because he didn't possess a prophetic office, they viewed him as a true prophet of the captivity period. Finally the twelve short Minor Prophets were left intact from Hosea to Malachi. This concluded the prophetic section.

One final task remained as the threefold classification retained its legitimate status. Instead of seeing a category of lesser prophets, the new arrangement emphasized a poetic genre as a distinct section of unique books. Here again chronology seemed important as Job came first, then the Psalms of King David and finally the Wisdom literature of King Solomon.

Furthermore, it apparently seemed more chronologically significant to place the entire section of poetic writings immediately after the Historical Books instead of the original placement after the Prophets. After all, Psalms, Proverbs, Ecclesiastes, and Song of Solomon were written mostly by two prominent kings of the united monarchy, and Job boasted an antiquity back to the age of the Patriarchs. That is why the Poetic Writings now come between the Historical Books of the Law and the Prophets.

So in the late third century BC, long before a Christian church emerged, Hebrew scholars prepared the Old Testament Scriptures for the Greek-speaking Jews around the Mediterranean world. As is true today, more Jews lived outside of than within the little nation of Israel. It seems that God was preparing His Word for the world so that the Scriptures would no longer be the sole possession of one small nation.

This is apparently why the status of the writer was no longer the crucial issue. Without minimizing the importance of the prophetic office, God directed the Septuagint translators to reorganize the books in a way that would speak more effectively to the people of the world. A twofold division of Law and Prophets remained intact, and a third category of Writings retained its integrity as well. Yet the new arrangement, reflecting a historical sense of chronology with sensitivity to genre, far surpassed the old order that was meaningful only to the Jewish culture.

It is important to note that a change in the order of Old Testament books occurred only once. It's not as though the order kept changing as different individuals and groups foisted their ideas upon the arrangement of Scripture. When the original Jewish concept was changed in 200 BC, Hebrew scholars representing the nation of Israel to the Hellenistic world made the change. That decision made by authoritative men at a crucial point in history has remained to this day. The order of the Old Testament books in the Septuagint is the *same order we* have in our modern Bibles.

ACCEPTING THE NEW ARRANGEMENT

How can we know that this arrangement was of God? Let me suggest a few thoughts that have convinced me to think this way.

The fact that Jesus and the apostles of the early church used the Septuagint as the authoritative Word of God is a strong argument for its legitimacy. In the first century AD Hebrew was the liturgical language of the synagogue, while most of the Jews in Israel spoke Aramaic. But because Greek was the universal language of the time, the Septuagint became the popular translation of the Scriptures. So while Jesus read from the Hebrew text in the synagogue, He did not hesitate to use the Septuagint in His ministry to the people.

The apostles also used the Septuagint with an obvious confidence in its reliability. They used it in ministry, and they often quoted from it in their writings. Many of the Old Testament quotes in the New Testament are from the Septuagint. There is no question about the fact that Jesus and the apostles held the Septuagint in high esteem. They seemed to have accepted the reordering of the books, never mentioning a concern.

Since Jesus influenced the apostles in His acceptance of the Septuagint, and the apostles in turn influenced the church, it is not surprising that the church readily accepted the Septuagint. Thus when Jerome translated the Old Testament into Latin (AD 383–405), he used the Hebrew text to make an accurate translation of the words but kept the Septuagint arrangement for the order of books. Obviously familiar with the Hebrew classification, he felt that what the Septuagint translators had done in rearranging the order was of God. A thousand years later, John Wycliffe translated the Bible from Latin into English and retained this same arrangement. Even when Luther and Tyndale went back to the original Greek and Hebrew for their translations into the vernacular German and English, they still perpetuated the Septuagint arrangement of Old Testament books.

Does anyone still follow the original Hebrew classification of Holy Writings? Yes—the Jewish community does. But then they do not accept Jesus as the Messiah-Savior, nor do they revere the New Testament writings of the apostles. They cloister the Hebrew Scriptures within the confines of their religious system and have little interest in sharing them with the world. Yet the Word of God was meant for the world, and it was through the Septuagint that God rescued it from Jewish hands and revealed it to the rest of humanity.

Speaking of the Septuagint, the Christian Hebrew scholar Merrill F. Unger offers this observation:

> Much more important in the history of redemption, it [the Septuagint] released the great revealed truths concerning creation, redemption, sin and salvation from the narrow isolation of the Hebrew tongue and people

and gave them to the world through the divinely prepared vehicle of the Greek language.[3]

When the Old Testament was translated into Greek in the late third century BC, it was as though God was preparing His Word for the addition of the Greek New Testament. Because of the universal acceptance of the Greek Septuagint, the Old Testament blended naturally with the new writings of the apostles to become the Christian Bible—the Bible that has reached the world.

> In a vital sense the Septuagint prepared the way for the coming of Christianity and the New Testament by releasing the Old Testament revelation in the same universal language in which the New Testament was destined to be written. The result was that the completed divine revelation became available to all in the *one* international language of the period.[4]

Changing the order of the Old Testament books seems to have been a strategic part of the divine process in establishing an arrangement of books that would be meaningful for all people. The Septuagint ordering became the universally accepted sequence of Old Testament books.

SEPTUAGINT DIVISION OF THE OLD TESTAMENT
Later (Third Century BC) — Christian Tradition: *39 Books / 3 Divisions*

HISTORICAL	POETICAL	PROPHETICAL
(17 books)	(5 books)	(17 books)
Pentateuch	Job	*Major*
Genesis, Exodus	Psalms	Isaiah, Jeremiah
Leviticus, Numbers	Proverbs	Lamentations
Deuteronomy	Ecclesiastes	Ezekiel, Daniel
	Song of Solomon	
Pre-exilic		*Minor: Pre-exilic*
Joshua, Judges, Ruth		Hosea, Joel, Amos
1 & 2 Samuel, 1 & 2 Kings		Obadiah, Jonah, Micah
1 & 2 Chronicles		Nahum, Habakkuk
		Zephaniah
Postexilic		*Postexilic*
Ezra, Nehemiah		Haggai, Zechariah, Malachi
Esther		

EVERYTHING IS IN ORDER
NEW TESTAMENT

APOSTOLIC WRITINGS BEGIN TO CIRCULATE

Although not as concentrated and precise as the formation of the Old Testament, the New Testament writings of the apostles also accumulated according to an observable pattern worthy of the designation *divine providence*. Two conditions however added a degree of difficulty to the collection of the new writings.

First, no single location emerged as a central repository for these documents. For the Jews, it had been the Tabernacle and then the Temple. Furthermore, a recognized priesthood and scribal tradition supervised the Old Testament collection from beginning to end.

But the church was different. Scattered throughout the Roman Empire, each local assembly cherished its own possession of manuscripts and shared them with other fellowships in the region. No central authority existed to provide a concentration for their efforts. To some extent large churches in great metropolitan areas succeeded in amassing significant collections, and their bishops became the authoritative voices in identifying legitimate Scripture. But these also were scattered throughout the empire. As a result, the process of determining a solidified body of New Testament literature was slow.

Second, the geographical distance between apostolic writers and the growing number of provincial churches often delayed the distribution of manuscripts. A given church, for instance, would obtain one or two of the Gospels, but not the others. The same was true of other writings. Yet over an extended period of time, all of the inspired writings of the apostles were eventually copied and recopied for distribution; formal statements by recognized church leaders began to appear with regard to the nature and extent of the official collection. The process was slow but steady, and in time all agreed that the New Testament was complete as a divinely intended collection of books.

Then around AD 200 Tertullian first used the term *New Testament* to refer to the accumulation of apostolic writings. A sufficient number of recognized books had come together to warrant the observation that a body of official writings was emerging to qualify as a new section of sacred Scripture. It would be a while before the total number of books, and the order in which they should be placed, would be determined.

SOME BOOKS WERE QUESTIONED

Note that most of the New Testament writings were readily accepted by the majority of churches. The four Gospels, the book of Acts, and the entire collection of Paul's writings enjoyed immediate recognition and began to circulate as official groupings of inspired Scripture.

The General Epistles were another matter, however. First Peter and 1 John were exceptions, as they were "universally and unquestionably recognized."[1] The book of Hebrews presented more of a challenge, because it was not signed and the author was unknown. Yet Clement of Rome, in AD 95, "declared the epistle canonical and apostolic, but did not say who wrote it."[2] Although Hebrews continued to be debated, especially in relation to authorship, the content was obviously consistent with apostolic authority, and most of the churches slowly began to accept it as genuine Scripture.

Another major writing to be questioned for a time was the book of Revelation. All the early church fathers (e.g., Justin, Irenaeus, Hippolytus, Tertullian, Origen) accepted the writing as authentic from John and valid as Scripture. But by the end of the third century, a problem had arisen. Jesus had promised to return again to set up His kingdom, but it had been more than two hundred years, and He had failed to come. Many began to wonder if they had misunderstood Him. That led to a spiritualizing of the idea of a millennial kingdom and cast a shadow of doubt over John's authorship. After all, how could John write a book with prophecies that didn't come true? This skepticism lasted only a short time, as the suspicion surrounding the Revelation "entirely disappeared by the end of the fourth century."[3]

Five small epistles—James, 2 Peter, 2 & 3 John, and Jude—"were the last to unanimously be admitted."[4] James and Jude were not apostles but were eventually accepted because of their kinship to Jesus. For a time, 2 & 3 John were thought to have been written by another John called "the elder" but finally entered the official list as genuine letters from the true apostle John. The most strongly contested of the small epistles was 2 Peter, and yet it too found recognition as a genuine writing from the hand of Peter.

We can readily see from this brief historical synopsis of the contested books that only the General Epistles suffered prolonged scrutiny. In the end all twenty-seven books that we now know as the New Testament were recognized as having divine sanction as sacred Scripture.

AN ORDER BEGINS TO EMERGE

Since the accumulation of New Testament books was slow and regionally diverse, establishing a significant order within the books proved difficult. How many gospels would there be, and in what order should they appear? Would Paul write another official letter ... and what about the other apostles? Would they also write inspired documents? How should all the writings be grouped—according to genre or author or date of writing or chronology of events? During the collection process, these questions challenged the various churches. It would be a while before all of the questions could be answered.

The Gospels seemed to fall together quickly as a group. By the end of the second century, the current ordering of the Gospel collection was widely recognized. The Western and Coptic traditions varied, putting Matthew and John first as apostles; but by the fourth century the Byzantine order of Matthew, Mark, Luke, and John prevailed. Eusebius (the historian), Athanasius, and Augustine all agreed on that sequence, and the ancient manuscripts at our disposal (Vaticanus, Sinaiticus, and Alexandrinus) confer. The order of the Gospels was established early and never seriously questioned.

Though readily accepted as a genuine writing of Luke, the book of Acts struggled to find its place in the canonical sequence. The fourth-century manuscript Sinaiticus placed it after the Pauline Epistles but before the General Epistles. Augustine, in the late fourth century, inserted it at the end, just before the Revelation. Apparently this uncertainty reflected a concern that Acts seemed to be a stand-alone book and not associated with any grouping (e.g., the Gospels, the Pauline Epistles). Eventually it was linked with the Gospels as a bridge to the Epistles because of its Lukan authorship and because it formed a natural "transition between the Gospels and the rest of the New Testament."[5]

Like the Gospels, the Pauline Epistles seemed to group naturally. Common authorship and the close geographical proximity of the letters' recipients led to an early recognition that the books belonged together. Furthermore, the current order of Romans–2 Thessalonians as well as that of the Pastorals (1 & 2 Timothy, Titus, and Philemon) were established early. Occasionally the book of Hebrews was inserted between Paul's church epistles and the Pastorals. And the Vaticanus (fourth century) and Alexandrinus (fifth century) manuscripts exemplify a temporary custom of putting the General Epistles before the Pauline Epistles. The point here however is that the Pauline order of books established itself early and was rarely questioned.

That brings us to the order of the General Epistles and their place in the sequence. Considerable variation existed in the early centuries with regard to Hebrews, James, 1 & 2 Peter, 1, 2, & 3 John, Jude, and Revelation in terms of their apostolic genuineness. By the end of the third century, many of the questions surrounding these books subsided; although the order of books was still debated, an accepted order began to emerge.

In AD 367, for instance, Athanasius (bishop of Alexandria) became "the first writer known to us who listed exactly the twenty-seven books which traditionally make up the New Testament ... without making any distinction in status among them."[6] Just twenty years later (about AD 386), Amphilochius of Iconium published his ordering of New Testament books in the precise sequence that would eventually become the common order. The concepts of a completed collection of inspired New Testament writings and a logical order of progression were finding acceptance among the churches. Ecumenical councils would merely ratify what the churches had come to accept as unalterable truth from God.

A COMMON ORDER PREVAILS

When did an official order of New Testament books establish itself for later generations?

The catalyst for a common order seems to have been Jerome and his Latin translation of the New Testament. This Bible became the recognized Bible of the Western church and most of the Roman Empire. The order in which the books were placed in the Latin Vulgate (as the Bible was called) thus became the official order that would be passed down through the ages.

Commissioned by Pope Damasus in the late fourth century (383–394) to make a common Latin translation of the apostolic Greek writings, Jerome included just those books that had been accepted by the churches with only a slight variation in order. As others had done, he placed Acts after the Pauline

Epistles and before the General Epistles. Yet that decision was soon revised, and the book of Acts found a permanent position between the Gospels and all of the Epistles where it remains today.

This does not mean that the order was not challenged from time to time. Augustine expressed a slightly different opinion than the Vulgate when he put James after Jude and also Acts at the end, just before Revelation. The Third Council of Carthage (AD 357), on the other hand, kept Acts with the Gospels but moved James before Jude right after the Johannine Epistles. In fact, only these two books (Acts and James) seemed troublesome with regard to order.

Nevertheless, as we have seen, the book of Acts found a resting place as an extension of the Gospels, and James eventually achieved a prominent status before the epistles of Peter and John. This prioritizing of the book of James reflected Paul's description of leadership of the Jerusalem church in Galatians 2:9 where James is mentioned first, then Peter (Cephas) and then John. Thus the General Epistles reflected that sequence, and were the last grouping of books to find an agreed-upon order.

Eventually the Reformation provided another glitch in the New Testament order of books. Martin Luther, having personal problems with four of the canonical books (Hebrews, James, Jude, and Revelation), included them as a quasiappendix at the end of his German translation.

> The Table of Contents suggested that he distinguished two levels of can-onicity in the New Testament: the names of the first twenty-three books (Matthew–3 John) are preceded by serial numbers 1–23; the remaining four books—Hebrews, James, Jude and Revelation—are separate from these by a space and are given no serial number.[7]

When William Tyndale translated the Bible into English in 1526, he was greatly influenced by Luther and followed his example, putting Hebrews, James, Jude, and Revelation in a category by themselves at the end. This variation from the Latin Vulgate Bible and the traditional church had more to do with Luther's suspicion of content and authorship than with any dis-satisfaction with the historically established order of the Vulgate. It was not long before the suspicions were resolved and the original order of books was restored.

> The Luther-Tyndale sequence of books was followed by Coverdale's Bible (1535) and Matthew's Bible (1537) and other English editions for the next few years, but the Great Bible of 1539 reverted to the now traditional

order with Hebrews and James coming between Philemon and 1 Peter, and this order has been followed by most editions of the English Bible since then.[8]

When discussing the order of New Testament books, therefore, it is important to recognize that the official common order began to solidify at the end of the fourth century with the capstone of Jerome's Latin Vulgate translation. You may remember that in Appendix 1, a similar story arose when contemplating the order of the Old Testament. There Jerome, acting in an official capacity for the church, recognized what God had been doing with regard to order in the Septuagint tradition of the Old Testament. Here too in the development of the New Testament order, Jerome and the Latin Vulgate Bible emerged as the key to finalizing the sequential ordering of books.

OFFICIAL ORDER OF THE NEW TESTAMENT BOOKS
Tradition of the Christian Church: *27 Books / 5 Divisions*

GOSPELS (4 Books)	PAULINE EPISTLES (9 Books)	PASTORAL EPISTLES (4 Books)	GENERAL EPISTLES (9 Books)
Matthew	Romans	1 Timothy	Hebrews
Mark	1 Corinthians	2 Timothy	James
Luke	2 Corinthians	Titus	1 Peter
John	Galatians	Philemon	2 Peter
	Ephesians		1 John
HISTORICAL (1 Book)	Philippians		2 John
	Colossians		3 John
	1 Thessalonians		Jude
Acts	2 Thessalonians		Revelation

A FINAL THOUGHT

As we have examined the concept of design in the overall construction of the Word of God, it has not been a foolish quest to base our study on the established order of biblical books. The Scriptures are inspired in their content, and they are providentially arranged in a specific order. Neil Lightfoot expresses this same conclusion with regard to the canonical order: "gradually each book on its own merit—not without, Christians believe, *a guiding Providence*—took its place in the accepted canon of New Testament Scripture"[9] (emphasis mine).

NOTES

CHAPTER ONE

1. J. Sidlow Baxter, *Explore the Book: Six Volumes in One* (Grand Rapids: Zondervan, 1966), p. 15.
2. Ibid.
3. See Appendices 1 and 2 for a historical perspective on the established order of biblical books.
4. A.B. Simpson, "Himself," at http://www.christianyou.net/pages/himselfabs.html.

CHAPTER TWO

1. Michael J. Behe, *Darwin's Black Box* (New York: The Free Press, 1996).

CHAPTER SEVEN

1. J. Sidlow Baxter, *Explore the Book: Six Volumes in One* (Grand Rapids: Zondervan, 1966), p. 83.
2. R.K. Harrison, *Introduction to the Old Testament* (Peabody, MA: Prince Press, 1999), p. 986.
3. Quoted in ibid., p. 1073.
4. Gleason L. Archer, Jr., *A Survey of Old Testament Introduction* (Chicago: Moody Press, 1974), p 467.
5. G. Campbell Morgan, as quoted in Baxter, *Explore the Book* (Grand Rapids: Zondervan, 1966), p. 142.
6. Raymond B. Dillard and Tremper Longman III, *An Introduction to the Old Testament* (Grand Rapids: Zondervan, 1994), p. 255.
7. Ibid., p. 264.
8. Baxter, *Explore the Book*, p. 172.
9. Archer, *A Survey of the Old Testament Introduction*, p. 488.
10. Baxter, *Explore the Book*, p. 181.
11. Gordon Jackson and Philip Whitfield, *Digestion: Fueling the System* (New York: Torstar Books, 1984) p. 78.

CHAPTER EIGHT

1. Quoted in Everett F. Harrison, *Introduction to the New Testament* (Grand Rapids: Eerdmans, 1964), p. 241.

2. Ibid., p. 242, quoting J. Weiss, *Das Urchristentum*, pp. 309–10 (*Earliest Christianity*, 2:408).

3. D. Edmond Hiebert, *An Introduction to the New Testament, Vol. 2: The Pauline Epistles* (Chicago: Moody Press, 1977), p. 14.

4. Ibid., p. 20.

5. Ibid.

6. J. Sidlow Baxter, *Explore the Book: Six Volumes in One* (Grand Rapids: Zondervan, 1966), p. 60.

7. J. Sidlow Baxter, *The Strategic Grasp of the Bible* (Grand Rapids: Zondervan, 1974), p. 383.

8. W. Graham Scroggie, *The Unfolding Drama of Redemption: The Bible as a Whole* (Grand Rapids: Zondervan, 1976), pp. 22–23.

9. Hiebert, *An Introduction to the New Testament,* 2:23.

10. Baxter, *Explore the Book*, p. 61.

11. D. Edmond Hiebert, *An Introduction to the New Testament, Vol. 3: The Non-Pauline Epistles and Revelation* (Chicago: Moody Press, 1978), p. 25.

CHAPTER NINE

1. D. A. Carson, Douglas J. Moo, and Leon Morris, *An Introduction to the New Testament* (Grand Rapids: Zondervan, 1992), p. 241.

2. Everett F. Harrison, *Introduction to the New Testament* (Grand Rapids: Zondervan, 1964), p. 345.

3. J. Sidlow Baxter, *Explore the Book: Six Volumes in One* (Grand Rapids: Zondervan, 1966), p. 275.

4. D. Edmond Hiebert, *An Introduction to the New Testament, Vol. 3: The Non-Pauline Epistles and Revelation* (Chicago: Moody Press, 1978), p. 79.

5. Carson, Moo, and Morris, *An Introduction to the New Testament,* p. 245.

6. Harrison, *Introduction to the New Testament,* p. 283.

7. Leon Morris, *The Expositor's Bible Commentary, Vol. 12, Hebrews–Revelation* (Grand Rapids: Zondervan, 1981), p. 5.

8. William Byron Forbush, ed., *Foxe's Book of Martyrs* (Grand Rapids: Zondervan, 1926), p. 6.

9. Orthogate for Patients, "Hand Anatomy," at http://www.orthogate.org/patient-education/hand/hand-anatomy.html.

10. Wikipedia, "Hand," at http://en.wikipedia.org/wiki/Hand.

CHAPTER TEN

1. Justification is being declared just (or sinless) by God and, according to the Bible, is received through simple faith in Christ's death on our behalf.

2. This summary of Galatians is taken from J. Sidlow Baxter's excellent analysis in *Explore the Book: Six Volumes in One* (Grand Rapids: Zondervan, 1966), p. 150.

3. Robert Gromachi, *New Testament Survey* (Grand Rapids: Baker Book House, 1974), p. 227.

4. Baxter, *Explore the Book,* p. 287.

5. Ibid., p. 124.

6. Gromachi, *New Testament Survey,* p. 219.

7. Baxter, *Explore the Book,* p. 121.

8. Gromachi, *New Testament Survey,* pp. 352–53.

9. Baxter, *Explore the Book,* p. 309.

10. Gromachi, *New Testament Survey,* pp. 363–64.

CHAPTER ELEVEN

1. Watchman Nee, *Sit, Walk, Stand* (London: Witness and Testimony, 1958).

CHAPTER TWELVE

1. D. Edmond Hiebert, *An Introduction to the New Testament, Vol. 3: The Non-Pauline Epistles and Revelation* (Chicago: Moody Press, 1978), p. 38.

2. Ibid., 3:172–73.

CHAPTER FOURTEEN

1. Wikipedia, "Reflexology," at http://en.wikipedia.org/wiki/Reflexology.

APPENDIX 1

1. Rene Pache, *The Inspiration and Authority of Scripture,* trans. Helen I. Needham (Chicago: Moody Press, 1969), p. 162.

2. Merrill F. Unger, *Introductory Guide to the Old Testament* (Grand Rapids: Zondervan, 1951), p. 56.

3. Ibid., p. 156.

4. Ibid.

APPENDIX 2

1. Rene Pache, *The Inspiration and Authority of Scripture*, trans. Helen I. Needham (Chicago: Moody Press, 1969), p. 176.

2. Ibid., p. 177.

3. Ibid.

4. Ibid., p. 178.

5. Paul D. Wegner, *The Journey from Texts to Translations* (Grand Rapids: Baker Academic, 1999), p. 61.

6. F. F. Bruce, *The Canon of Scripture* (Downers Grove, IL: InterVarsity Press, 1988), p. 209.

7. Ibid., p. 243.

8. Ibid., p. 246.

9. Neil R. Lightfoot, *How We Got the Bible*, 2nd ed. (Grand Rapids: Baker Book House, 1988), p. 109.

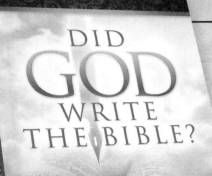
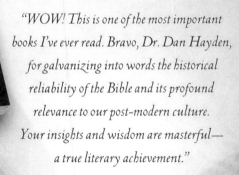